# MIND OVER MATTER

**THE DIAGRAM GROUP**

| | |
|---|---|
| **Editor** | Randal Gray |
| **Editorial assistant** | Katherine Rubidge |
| **Indexer** | David Harding |
| | |
| **Art director** | Richard Hummerstone |
| **Artists** | Elizabeth Benn |
| | Darren Bennett |
| | Brian Hewson |
| | Lee Lawrence |
| | Paul McCauley |
| | Kathleen McDougall |
| | Philip Patenall |
| | Micky Pledge |
| | Jane Robertson |
| | Graham Rosewarne |

Published in Great Britain by
George Weidenfeld & Nicolson Limited
91 Clapham High Street
London SW4 7TA

ISBN 0 297 79580 5

Typeset by Dorchester Typesetting Group, Dorchester

Printed in Great Britain by
Butler & Tanner Ltd, Frome and London

# MIND OVER MATTER

by J. Maya Pilkington
and the Diagram Group

WEIDENFELD & NICOLSON, LONDON

# Foreword

Maya Pilkington and the Diagram Group have, as always, diverted from the well-trod pathways and cut across disciplines and conventions to gather in these pages a fascinating wealth of detail, ideas and suggestions for your enjoyment. Nothing is left undisturbed; arguments are upturned and new ideas are stirred.

**Mind over matter** tests your nerve, challenges your thinking and presents you with exercises and techniques for you to try, in the incomparable Diagram style, **Who are you?** invited you to find yourself. **The Complete Book of Predictions** and **How to be a success** helped you to become who you are destined to be. And **Who were you?** explored your origins and your destiny. Now **Mind over matter** adds another rich dimension to your outlook.

**Mind over matter** takes you on a journey of exploration. In Chapter One you can contrast different states of mind. Chapter Two brings you examples of power minds and suggests techniques you can use to develop aspects of mind that interest you particularly. Chapter Three is devoted to the powers of prophecy and skills you can acquire to develop your own sensitivity to the unfolding future. Many various aspects of the will power of the mind are considered in detail by Chapter Four with examples of people who have applied their mind powers, often in difficult circumstances.

The final Chapter suggests ways of unlocking those parts of your mind that have become blocked. Some unusual ideas are explored and several simple practical exercises are suggested.

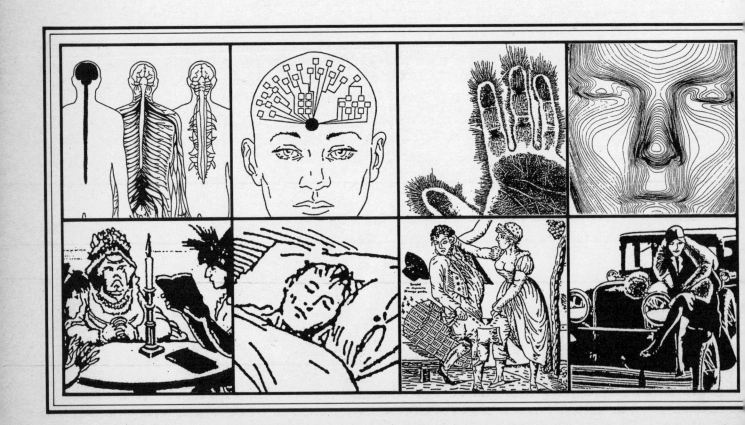

**Mind over matter** brings you a refreshing approach to the age-old principles of how to apply your mind powers to practical purposes.

There are adventures into the occult juxtaposed against the complexities of modern brain research. The many alternative states of mind are explored and expanded, while the veil of the mundane mind is lifted as you are invited to enter an exciting world where logic is the unopposed expert one moment and instinctive imagination reigns supreme the next.

This fully illustrated guide to the richly endowed realms of the mind is designed to add to your knowledge and increase your skills in the many arts of the mind.

**Mind over matter** will often leave your mind inspired to try new outlooks and indulge in unfamiliar pleasures. Throughout the book, the author reminds you that much in the world of brain and mind is open to possible misinterpretation or misunderstanding. She often leaves you, the reader, to make up your own mind on issues. She always makes it clear when there are opposing views and presents them both.

**Mind over matter** is a book you can pick up and open anywhere; every spread of two pages is a complete unit that can be read on its own or it can be read in sequence according to your preference.

The mind is not just an intellect; it is a world as big as life itself. As you read we hope you will enjoy expanding the powers of your mind over matter.

# Contents

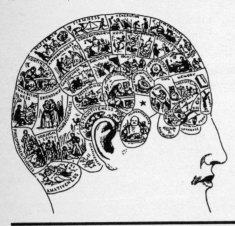
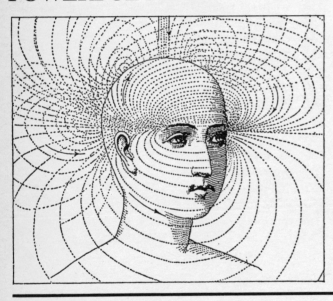

# CHAPTER FOUR
# THE WILL TO POWER

# CHAPTER FIVE
# UNLOCKING YOUR MIND

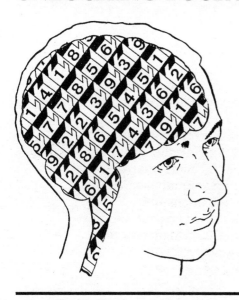

**Sun-Sign Table for 1936 to 1955**

| | Aq | Pi | Ar | Ta | Ge | Cn | Le | Vi | Li | Sc | Sg | Cp |
|---|---|---|---|---|---|---|---|---|---|---|---|---|
| | JA | FE | MR | AP | MY | JN | JL | AU | SE | OC | NO | DE |
| 1936 | 21 | 19 | 20 | 20 | 21 | 21 | 23 | 23 | 23 | 23 | 22 | 22 |
| 1937 | 20 | 19 | 21 | 20 | 21 | 21 | 23 | 23 | 23 | 23 | 22 | 22 |
| 1938 | 20 | 19 | 21 | 20 | 21 | 22 | 23 | 23 | 23 | 24 | 22 | 22 |
| 1939 | 20 | 19 | 21 | 20 | 21 | 22 | 23 | 24 | 23 | 24 | 23 | 22 |
| 1940 | 21 | 19 | 20 | 20 | 21 | 21 | 23 | 23 | 23 | 23 | 22 | 21 |
| 1941 | 20 | 19 | 21 | 20 | 21 | 21 | 23 | 23 | 23 | 23 | 22 | 22 |
| 1942 | 20 | 19 | 21 | 20 | 21 | 22 | 23 | 23 | 23 | 23 | 22 | 22 |
| 1943 | 20 | 19 | 21 | 20 | 21 | 22 | 23 | 23 | 23 | 24 | 23 | 22 |
| 1944 | 21 | 19 | 21 | 20 | 21 | 21 | 22 | 23 | 23 | 23 | 22 | 21 |
| 1945 | 20 | 19 | 20 | 20 | 22 | 21 | 23 | 23 | 23 | 23 | 22 | 22 |
| 1946 | 20 | 19 | 21 | 20 | 21 | 22 | 23 | 23 | 23 | 24 | 22 | 22 |
| 1947 | 20 | 19 | 21 | 20 | 21 | 22 | 23 | 24 | 23 | 24 | 23 | 22 |
| 1948 | 21 | 19 | 20 | 20 | 21 | 21 | 22 | 23 | 23 | 23 | 22 | 21 |
| 1949 | 20 | 18 | 20 | 20 | 21 | 21 | 23 | 23 | 23 | 23 | 22 | 22 |
| 1950 | 20 | 19 | 21 | 20 | 21 | 21 | 23 | 23 | 23 | 23 | 22 | 22 |
| 1951 | 20 | 19 | 21 | 20 | 21 | 22 | 23 | 23 | 23 | 23 | 23 | 22 |
| 1952 | 21 | 19 | 20 | 20 | 21 | 21 | 22 | 23 | 23 | 23 | 22 | 21 |
| 1953 | 20 | 18 | 20 | 20 | 21 | 21 | 23 | 23 | 23 | 23 | 22 | 22 |
| 1954 | 20 | 19 | 21 | 20 | 21 | 21 | 23 | 23 | 23 | 23 | 22 | 22 |
| 1955 | 20 | 19 | 21 | 20 | 21 | 22 | 23 | 23 | 23 | 23 | 23 | 22 |

# Chapter one

# STATE OF MIND

The powers we are able to use may depend on our state of mind. Often a person's state of mind is reflected in the face or by the attitude of the body. Although we may sometimes try to hide what we are thinking or feeling, another person may still sense our state of mind. But where is the mind, does each person have only one mind and what does the mind contain? Indeed, when we speak our mind, which mind is it that is speaking? These are the questions we explore in this chapter.

**1** A nineteenth century phrenological chart, entitled: *A Symbolical Head Illustrating the Natural Language of the Faculties*.
**2** We often try to hide our true thoughts and feelings behind a false mask.
**3** The brain has two hemispheres, said to be associated with different activities.
**4** We may be temporarily "out of our minds" for example when we are (**a**) very drunk or (**b**) in severe shock.
**5** These eight people are showing their states of mind by the way they are standing or sitting. Each person is also having an effect on the state of mind of their social partner.

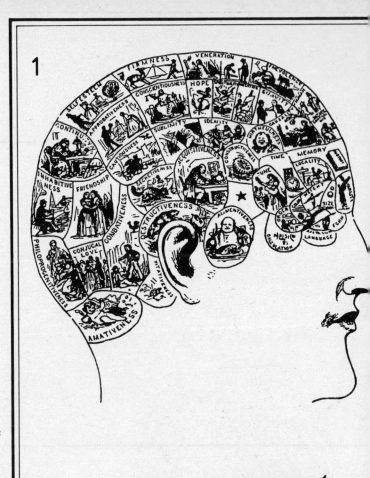

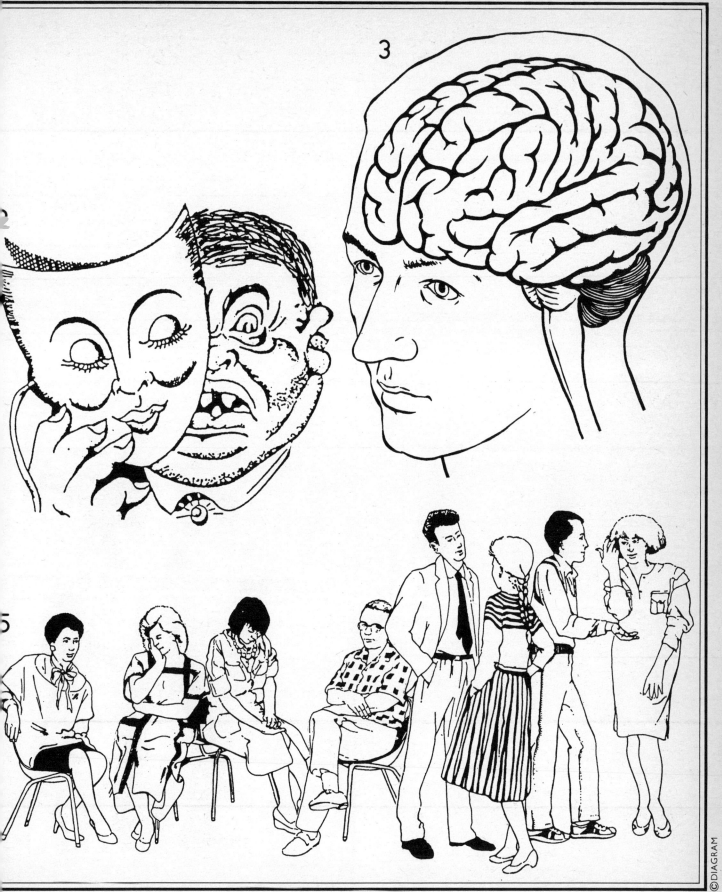

3

9

# How to make up your mind

Your mind is a wonderful facility. You can bring things to mind, keep something in mind and put it out of your mind again. You can be in two minds at the same time, change your mind and have a mind of your own. It is also possible to learn to read another person's mind or to go right out of your mind!

Some people tend to keep an open mind, while others close their minds against all other points of view.

The mind can be used to think but when asked "do you mind?" the enquirer is usually more interested in how you feel rather than in what you think.

Frequently choices have to be taken by making up your mind. How do you make up your mind: in a flash, after careful consideration or only with difficulty? Once your mind is made up do you stick to it, change it or tend to oscillate from one point of view to another?

---

**STEP BY STEP DECISIONS**

Making up your mind often involves defining your choices ever more finely. For example, when making up your mind what to eat. At stage one, you have a very wide choice of any kind of food. At stage two, you have limited your choice to only sweet foods. At stage three, from the choice of sweet foods, you have chosen fruit, and at stage four, from a wide choice of fruits you have finally chosen a peach.

**Make up your mind**

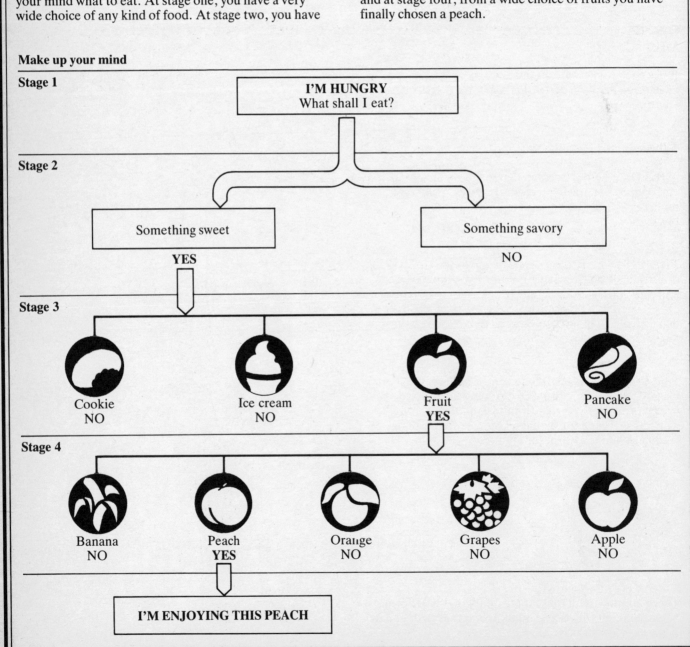

Stage 1

I'M HUNGRY
What shall I eat?

Stage 2

Something sweet
**YES**

Something savory
NO

Stage 3

Cookie
NO

Ice cream
NO

Fruit
**YES**

Pancake
NO

Stage 4

Banana
NO

Peach
**YES**

Orange
NO

Grapes
NO

Apple
NO

**I'M ENJOYING THIS PEACH**

**How to make up your mind**
1 Find out what you want.
2 Go out for it, keeping your options open in case exactly what you want isn't available.

When making a choice, you are automatically rejecting all other alternatives. Sometimes, this is how people make up their minds on many issues, by rejecting what they disagree with and accepting what remains. Do you ever do this? It often happens when what we really want isn't available. For example, if what you really fancied was an apricot, you might have settled for the peach as the next best.

The two-part formula for making up your mind is simple to state but depends on you knowing what you want, i.e. on knowing your own mind in the first place.

**In two minds**
You may feel like relaxing with a good book but want to finish a report for work. This situation puts you in a conflict and it appears there are two minds at work here. One that is responding to how you feel and the other responding to what you are thinking. While trying to make up your mind between the book and the report you may float off into a daydream about something entirely different! So are you now in three minds?

---

**WHICH MIND?**

It has been suggested by some individuals that we do have three minds: a body-mind, an intuitive mind; and an astral mind.

**A theory of three minds**

**THE BODY-MIND** is situated in the flesh and blood body and operates in practical, concrete terms. The body-mind says, "I'm tired, I want to relax and read a book."

**THE ASTRAL MIND** is a conscious part of ourselves that can detach itself from what is really happening here and now and operates in the abstract. The astral mind says, "There is a report in my briefcase that needs to be written. It will be better for me tomorrow if I have it completed when I arrive at work."

**THE INTUITIVE MIND** is an energy field pulsing both inside and for a little distance outside the body and operates instinctively. The intuitive mind says, "My instincts dream that I should be running freely along the beach under a warm sun."

Intuitive mind
Body-mind
Astral-mind

There is more about these three minds on the following pages: **Finding your astral mind; Using your body-mind; Knowing your intuitive mind.**

© DIAGRAM

# Finding your astral mind

## A WORKING DEFINITION OF THE ASTRAL MIND

The astral mind is the ability of the mind to step outside the body and view both the body, and everything around, in a totally objective, detached and emotionless way, as shown in the diagram opposite.

### What is the mind?
The mind is variously defined as: intellectual powers; remembrance; the desire to attain; a way of thinking and feeling; the seat of consciousness and volition; the soul as opposed to the material body and so on. Many of these ideas are conflicting and none clearly explain the mind. Nor do they suggest exactly where the mind might be situated.

The mind is a very complex function of the whole person. It is not an object, in the way that a leg or a heart can be regarded as a fairly distinct part.

In this, and the next five pages, three rather unusual ways of looking at the functioning mind are described. They have been distinguished as the astral mind, the body-mind and the intuitive mind, although there are many other descriptive names for them, as you will discover. Each of the three is part of the whole mind and cannot function separately.

### The astral body
In esoteric philosophies, the astral body is said to be the consciousness of the soul which can move out of the material body and have an independent existence after death.

Hence the term "out-of-body experience" is used to describe similar apparent separations of the conscious mind from the body, during life. This separating function of the mind is often called "abstraction" and could properly be called the astral mind.

### The astral mind
Out-of-body experiences or OBEs, have been well-documented in recent years. They generally occur under stress, in shock or under anesthetic, but they can also occur when our perception of what is happening does not match reality. When an OBE happens during a life or death situation, it may be called a "near-death experience" or NDE. Why they occur is not yet understood.

**Some examples of out-of-body experiences**

An OBE due to immobility of the body while travelling at great speeds.

An NDE due to physical shock during an accident.

An OBE due to culture shock in a totally unfamiliar situation.

# THE FUNCTIONING MIND IN DAILY LIFE

Theories of how our learning ability develops from childhood onwards have identified three major ways in which our minds function throughout adulthood.

### The spontaneous function of the mind
During gestation and later in babyhood we learn directly through our senses. We touch, suck, stare and listen without reference to memory, thought or commonsense. For example, we instantly like or dislike a piece of orange put before us, regardless of its food value. This intuitive function of our mind stays with us as we develop a more concrete view of life.

### The concrete function of the mind
During this phase of development we learn to use all our bodily abilities to distinguish between appearances and reality. For example, we learn to comprehend the constancy of volume by tipping the same amount of water from one jar into others and discover that the same volume of water only appears to be different in different containers. This concrete function of our minds remains with us as we learn to think in the abstract during adulthood.

### The abstract function of the mind
This is the ability to think about other things while doing something quite different. While mending the car we can think about a different part of the engine or about something quite unrelated, such as the football match we plan to see next week or the meeting we had at work last week. In other words, we can abstract ourselves from reality as it is now and and have our minds on something else.

   This abstract function of the mind, taken to extremes, allows us to go out of our bodies temporarily. Hence our astral mind is simply the abstract function taken to its limits.

REFERENCE: To learn more about your astral mind, turn to **Chapter Two: How to take an astral trip** (pp. 38-39).

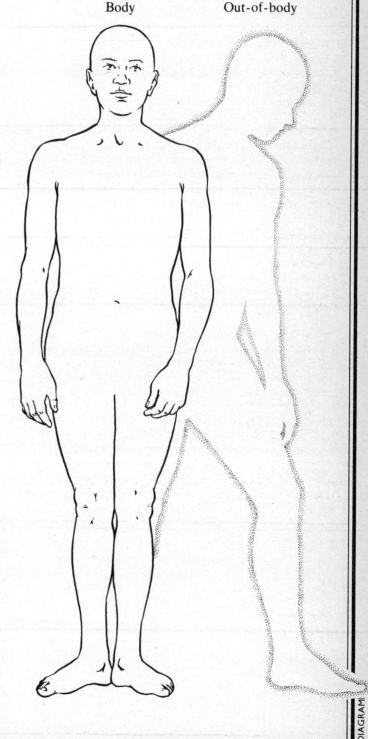

Body        Out-of-body

All three major functions usually operate together:

| Order of development | |
|---|---|
| ↑ | **THE ASTRAL MIND** abstract functions |
| ↑ | **THE BODY-MIND** concrete functions |
| ↑ | **THE INTUITIVE MIND** spontaneous functions |

©DIAGRAM

# Using your body-mind

## A WORKING DEFINITION OF THE BODY-MIND
The body-mind is all those functions connected with the central nervous system that control the physical, mental and emotional behavior of the body, as shown on the diagram opposite. The body-mind continues to function whether we are conscious or not.

## THE HUMAN BODY

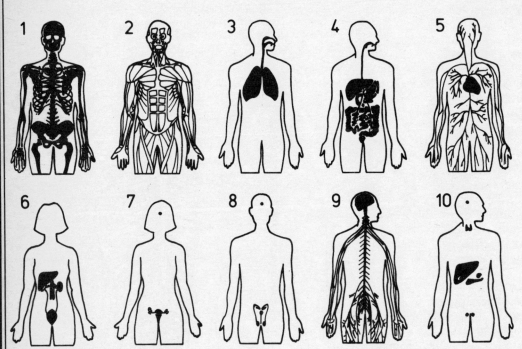

The body systems:
1 Skeleton – front and back
2 Muscles – front and back
3 Respiration
4 Digestion
5 Circulation
6 Liver and urinary
7 Reproduction – female
8 Reproduction – male
9 Nervous
10 Metabolism and endocrine

The physical, material structure of the body is fairly easy to study. The skeleton gives it a basic structure, the muscles enable that structure to move and the heart is merely a specialized muscle that pumps blood through the arteries and veins. As for the major organs, given the tragedy of an available donor, you can have a new heart, kidney or lung. Chunks of artery or colon can be removed and fitted with plastic tubes, and you can have damaged areas of skin patched up from a healthy area of your own body. A start has even been made to replace damaged brain cells.

Despite all this knowledge about the body, how it functions is largely still a mystery. The more we learn about the body-mind, the less we seem to know. One thing is certain, that when the brain dies, the body ceases to function.

## BRAIN DEATH AND CLINICAL DEATH
Clinical death occurs when the heart and lungs cease to function. Providing skill and facilities are instantly available, a person can sometimes be resuscitated if the brain is undamaged.

It is during this short period of apparent death that some people have experienced seeing themselves, as if from a little distance away, able to remember later the actions of doctors and nurses. Watching from outside is reported to be pleasant and painless.

Brain death occurs when the brain ceases to function and no trace is left on an electro-encephalograph, which measures electrical impulses from the brain.

Providing the body structure is not damaged, it has been possible in a few cases to keep some parts of the body functioning to some extent after the brain has died. For example, a pregnant woman who died in a coma within a few weeks of labor. The mother's body was kept alive on a life-support machine until delivery was due and an apparently normal, healthy baby was born. The mother's body-mind had ceased to function and the machine took over the very few basic physiological functions.

But what of the baby's mind? Was the baby's mind aware of the changes? It is also interesting to speculate that perhaps one function of the mother's mind remained close by, in the form of her astral mind. (See previous page for more details.)

# THE BODY-MIND AS THE MIND'S MASTER FUNCTION

It must be remembered, that while three minds have been named, i.e. the astral mind, the body-mind and the intuitive mind, it is the three major functions of the whole mind that are being described on these pages.

The body-mind is concrete, it consists of flesh, blood and millions of cells interacting electrically and bio-chemically with each other. It is this total interaction that is real. How we each interpret this personal reality shows in our attitudes, physically, mentally and emotionally.

It is a function of our minds to be able to separate from reality, to abstract from the total reality and sometimes by doing this we live in two minds.

Without the body-mind it is impossible to use the function of the abstract or astral mind. Or is it? If the body-mind is the master function, controlling all other functions of the mind, then nothing remains after death. But some people argue that the astral mind does continue after earthly life. Since there is no firm evidence either way, you must make up your own mind on this issue.

## The body-mind is the anchor

Your body-mind is sensible, logical and realistic. It is concerned with facts and keeps us grounded. It can test out situations empirically. It doesn't believe anything unless there is actual indisputable evidence and it isn't particularly creative either. It sends and receives messages and behaves accordingly. Without it we would be totally lost in a mess of conflicting abstractions. It can sort a myriad of impressions and intuitions and make some sense of them all. It can remember important things and dispose of what is superfluous. Without it, our excursions into the wonderfully creative world of abstract thought would lead us nowhere. The body-mind enables us to put that brilliant new idea into realistic action. The body-mind is the anchor that prevents us floating aimlessly around for ever.

## Where do you drop your anchor?

Alas, the body-mind isn't perfect. It can make mistakes due to that other function of the mind, the function with which we came into this world, the intuitive function of the mind. This will be explored over the page.

**Central nervous system**
There are three aspects to the nervous system:
**1** The brain and spinal cord central transmission.
**2** The somatic nervous system for conscious actions and reflexes.
**3** The automatic nervous system controlling heartbeat, breathing and other unconscious activities.

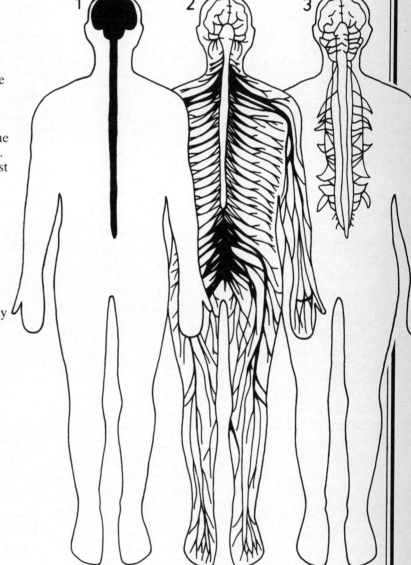

REFERENCE: To learn more about your body-mind, turn to **Chapter Two: Going beyond your mind barriers** (pp. 54-55).

© DIAGRAM

# Knowing your intuitive mind

**A WORKING DEFINITION OF THE INTUITIVE MIND**
Intuition is the ability of the mind to know something spontaneously without apparent thought or reason. The intuitive mind senses or picks up information from the outside world as if through the skin and similarly transmits information to the outside world as if through a radiation of energy, as shown in the diagram (*below*).

**THE INVISIBLE MIND**
As with all functions of the mind, intuition is a response of the mind to information coming from both inside and outside the body. However, while both abstract and concrete thoughts and feelings seem to have their source in the brain and nervous system, intuitions can be felt in different parts the body; for example, the general feeling that something is wrong or that the time is right.

It is thought by some people that the intuitive function of the mind can also both send and receive messages via an invisible radiation or energy force which is sometimes called the body aura. In esoteric philosophies the aura is a manifestation of the etheric body or total body energy without which the body would not be alive.

Architects and artists often relate their creations to human or animal proportions. Two examples (*right*) are the Sienese Francesco di Giorgio's 15th-century Italian church plan and the Swiss Le Corbusier's 20th century 'Modulor' system based on a 6ft ideal human figure.

**THE BODY AURA**
All living things give out energy. The constant pulsing and changing colors of this emanation are said to indicate the condition of life. Reichian therapists, such as Dr. John Pierrakos, Dr. Alexander Lowen, Stanley Keleman and others, have made use of this body aura for diagnostic and therapeutic purposes with great success. Close bonds have been discovered between their work and the philosophies of some oriental religions such as Buddhism.

The aura is invisible to the naked eye but can be perceived intuitively with practice and seen by those people who are particularly sensitive. Many healers and clairvoyants seem able to "tune-in" to the whole body energy via the aura. Kirlian photography is a method by which the emanations can be captured on a photographic plate, by exposing the hand or a leaf from a plant for several seconds.

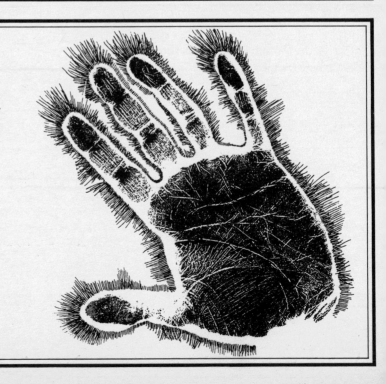

## THE PRIMITIVE FUNCTION OF THE MIND

Perhaps because the very first impressions received by our minds are spontaneous and unprocessed, intuition has a reputation for being primitive, especially as intuition is mixed with natural instincts which we have inherited.

Quite often intuitions are laughed at as irrational or immature, as indeed some of them are, since we need to use our concrete, body-minds to make sense of them.

On the other hand, intuition is a valuable function of the mind which remains with us all our lives and supplies us with those hunches that so often are absolutely correct.

Most of our beliefs are based on an intuitive feeling of rightness or wrongness. We may use our concrete and abstract minds to support our beliefs, but in the end they are largely intuitive.

### Knowing your intuitive mind

Few people spend much time sorting their intuitive gems from the surrounding mud of intuitive mistakes. For example, falling in love may be intuitive. Without any reason at all we can become passionately attached to a particular person. Over the years we may repeat the habit of falling for exactly the same kind of harbor in which to anchor our ship from the sea of life.

If it turns out to be a good choice, all is well. But if the same old problems recur, would it not be more sensible to be aware that our intuition is not to be trusted on this particular matter and make a different choice of partner next time? Anchoring in a different harbor does not mean there will not be any problems, but the facilities for solving those problems will be different.

The only way to educate your intuitive mind is to trust it, try out the hunch and use your body-mind and your abstract mind to check out the results. That way you will certainly clear away the mud and find some real gems among your intuitions that you might otherwise have missed.

REFERENCE: To learn more about how to use your intuitive mind, turn to **Chapter Two: How to use your healing powers** (pp. 60-61).

There are many examples of how the intuitive mind combines with the logical mind's accumulated store of knowledge and skills: predicting the outcome of a gambling game; painting a picture; and shooting an arrow.

©DIAGRAM

# Out of sight out of mind

In the days when computers were new, there was a story which illustrated how stupid this new breed of technology could be. It was said that a computer interpreted the phrase 'out of sight, out of mind' as invisible 'insanity'. This, of course, was a literal translation because the computer could not recognize meaning.

Recognition of meaning depends upon memory, although not necessarily the same kind of memories for one person as another. A sighted person will recognize the appearance of a chair and a blind person recognizes a chair by touch. A hearing person will recognize speech by sound but a deaf person understands the words by remembering their shapes, i.e. by lip-reading.

The eyes receive images and the ears receive vibrations but recognition and understanding are functions of the mind; both depend upon memory.

### Memory is vital to the mind

Without memory you would not recognize your own home. However, it would be burdensome to remember everything that happened in every moment of each day. Two processes ensure that we retain only what is important.

**Process 1**: Short term memory. During the first 30 minutes after an event, the memory of it is thought to be stored electrically. This is a temporary form of storage and more important events will leave a stronger trace than more trivial matters.

For example, lovers will remember tiny personal impressions and be totally unaware of even the most interesting events taking place around them.

On the other hand, a person receiving a severe bang on the head during an accident, is often unable to remember what happened in the half hour leading up to the accident.

**Process 2**: Long term memory. During, or after the first half hour, the electrical memory may fade or it may be transferred to long term store in a chemical form in the brain. The chemical store will further be impressed by repetition or the addition of further information.

For example, driving the same car daily along the same road may become second nature as sights, sounds, smells and movements become familiar and stored in the long term memory. The way to drive has been learnt and that includes any bad habits, such as driving too close to vehicles ahead.

---

### HOW GOOD IS YOUR SHORT TERM MEMORY?

Find a pencil and paper. Now read the following paragraph of information. Read it only once.

The Russian, Anton Pavlovich Chekov, was born in 1860 at Taganrog. Although a qualified medical practitioner, he preferred writing short stories. In 1896 he wrote his first play, *The Seagull*. He also wrote *Uncle Vanya* in 1899, *The Three Sisters* in 1901 and *The Cherry Orchard* in 1904, the year in which he died.

Now leave this book and take your pencil and paper some distance away. Then write down all the facts you can remember from the paragraph, in any order you like. When you have finished, return and check how many facts you remembered correctly.

Average would be 50% but do not despair if you could not recall very much. Interest plays a large part in memory and different people remember in different ways. Mozart had an auditory memory. Snooker players, dancers and footballers generally have excellent motor-tactile memories. Only visual-verbal memory was involved in this exercise. You may like to try the exercise again using a paragraph from a book or magazine on your favorite subject.

$\pi$ =3.14159265358979323846264338327950288419

Without a retentive memory quiz competitors, chess combatants, instrumentalists and actors would be unable to recall the information needed to display their skills.

In 1981 Rajan Srinivasen Mahadevan, a 23-year-old Indian, could remember the mathematical value of 'pi' to 31,811 decimal places. At the foot of these pages we print the sequence to over 80 places.

## EIDETIC MEMORY

Think about your favorite place or person. Close your eyes and try to remember the place or the person exactly in every detail. Most people will be able to conjure up a mental image, although some will only be able to recall part of an image. Others will not be able to create a mental visual image but may be able to remember the sound of a voice or the smell of a perfume.

Individuals who have an eidetic memory will be able to "see" the view or the person AS IF PRESENT IN REALITY. If you think you are the one in a billion who can do this, check by doing the following experiment.
1 Select any page in this book at random.
2 Look at it for 5 seconds.
3 Close the book.
4 Close your eyes.

Can you see the page of the book EXACTLY as if it was still open before you? If you can sit and read that page, you have an eidetic memory.

**A problem**

A person who remembers eidetically often confuses the eidetic image with reality and has to learn to drop a mental curtain over eidetic images.

Children are said to be able to perceive eidetically; the fantasy people children insist are sharing their lives or their meals are probably eidetic images. Fortunately, as we grow older and acquire language, the brain changes the way in which it stores information. This may also account for why we forget so many infantile memories.

## THE LOSS OF MEMORY

Alzheimer's disease, commonly called dementia, hits some elderly people causing short term memory to fail but leaving memories from long ago intact. A few people lose their ability to remember anything new due to a viral disease which can strike at any age.

Clive Waring, a British classical musician and conductor, had this disease at the height of his career in the mid-1980s. While his procedural skills, such as playing the organ, are unaffected, his short term memory does not function. He cannot remember the passing of each moment of the day, which is a frightening and disorienting experience. He often greets his wife as though he has just seen her for the first time, but forgets everyone else, even if he has just been introduced to them. He describes his life as a living death. His intelligence and the many non-verbal skills he acquired before his illness are the only part of his life that give him pleasure.

©DIAGRAM

**69399375105820974944592307816406286208998628034 8**

# What is the sixth sense?

Can we receive information from outside our bodies by means other than through the five sense organs? Clairvoyants are said to receive such extra-sensory perceptions, while telepathy is the transmission of messages between people without the use of any of the five senses. If we have a sixth sense, how do we operate this sensing? Is it done through our five sense organs or by some other means? Do we "tune-in" on someone else's wavelength, or are we resonating with our own inner lives? To find out what is meant by a sixth sense, we must first examine the better known senses.

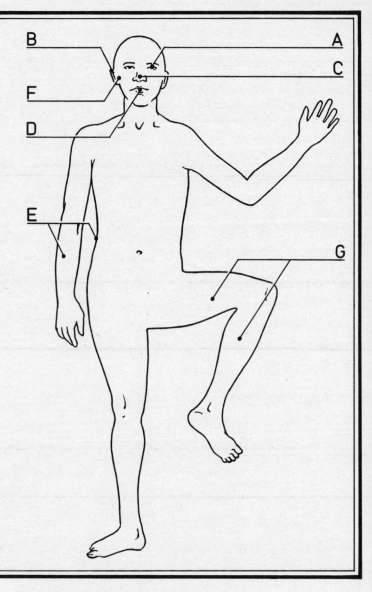

## THE FIVE SENSES

There are five senses which clearly receive stimuli from outside the body via receptors of the nervous system that are situated in the specially adapted sense organs **A** to **E**.

**A** The two eyes are the organs of SIGHT which receive light waves.

**B** The two ears are the organs of HEARING which receive sound waves.

**C** The nose is the organ of SMELL which receives chemical particles from substances carried through the air.

**D** The tongue is the organ of TASTE which receives chemical particles from solids or liquids.

**E** The whole skin is the organ of TOUCH which receives changes in pressure and temperature. We have many other senses that receive stimuli from inside the body. For example, a sense of balance and a kinesthetic sense, which are but two of the many other sensing devices in our bodies.

**F** The semi-circular canals in the two inner ears are the organs of BALANCE which receives signals from the movement of fluid within the canals.

**G** The proprioceptor cells in all joints, ligaments, tendons and muscles are the nerve receptors for our KINESTHETIC sense, which enables us to make smooth, coordinated movements.

**The sense organs**

| | |
|---|---|
| **A** Eyes | **E** Skin |
| **B** Ears | **F** Inner ears |
| **C** Nose | **G** Proprioceptor cells |
| **D** Tongue | |

All the sensing systems, **A** to **G** (*above*), depend on the receptor cells of the nervous system to receive the stimuli, which are then transmitted to the brain where they are interpreted. Is the sixth sense a sensing system that similarly relies upon nerve receptors?

### Four opinions about the sixth sense

OPINION ONE
All sixth sense knowledge consists of guesswork which sometimes happens, by chance, to be true.

OPINION TWO
The sixth sense is messages received by some or all other senses combined in a new way.

OPINION THREE
Information and messages can be received in some way that does not involve the use of the normal senses.

OPINION FOUR
Sixth sense information is impressions we received in the past and did not deal with but stored in memory. Are we picking up signals from outside ourselves directly into our brains or are we simply sensing something that we have already stored away, previously unknown to us? Examining how memory works may offer some further ideas on how a sixth sense might operate.

# THE MEMORY

Nobody has yet solved the mystery of how we remember things over a long period of time. Short-term memory is thought to be a reverberation in the neural pathways, rather like the vibration of a tuning fork or the waves from a stone thrown in a pool. The wave-form remains for a short time and then fades away. Long-term memory presents a more difficult problem to solve and there are several theories.

## The trace theory
Aristotle suggested that memories were preserved in the brain by some kind of mark, just as an impression can be preserved in wax. Modern ideas, although more sophisticated, are similar and assume that each memory leaves its mark in the brain that can be found and replayed, rather like a section from a tape.
Does the sixth sense leave traces in the brain?

## The code theory
During the late 1960s some researchers thought that long-term memories were stored in code form during the building of ribonucleic acid molecules, which are similar to the DNA molecules that store the genetic code.
Is the sixth sense an ability to interpret chemical codes?

## The synaptic modification theory
Nerve cells are connected at synapses. It is thought that the structure of synapses may be changed as new information enters the brain cells and that these modifications represent new memories.
Is the sixth sense a modification of the structure of some nerve cells?

## The morphogenic theory
It has been suggested that all organisms tune-in to a set of their own basic design elements, called morphic elements, and develop accordingly. Thus, to remember something from the past, we would only have to tune-in to these basic patterns by resonating with them.
Is the sixth sense an ability to tune-in to our own and other people's morphic elements?

## A map of how memory is thought to work
The memory system is thought to play a part in learning and creative processes. If extra-sensory signals can also be received from outside the body, as shown, could this also be a map of how the sixth sense works?

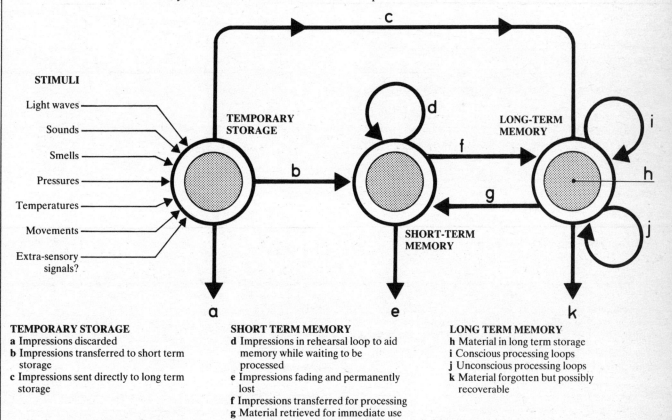

**STIMULI**

Light waves
Sounds
Smells
Pressures
Temperatures
Movements
Extra-sensory signals?

**TEMPORARY STORAGE**
**a** Impressions discarded
**b** Impressions transferred to short term storage
**c** Impressions sent directly to long term storage

**SHORT TERM MEMORY**
**d** Impressions in rehearsal loop to aid memory while waiting to be processed
**e** Impressions fading and permanently lost
**f** Impressions transferred for processing
**g** Material retrieved for immediate use

**LONG TERM MEMORY**
**h** Material in long term storage
**i** Conscious processing loops
**j** Unconscious processing loops
**k** Material forgotten but possibly recoverable

If we have a sixth sense that picks up extra-sensory signals and if those impressions are processed via the memory, then our sixth sense would sometimes be accurate and could also be prone to the same mistakes as are made by the memory. This could account for why clairvoyants and others who use extra-sensory perception are sometimes right and sometimes wrong.

# Are you tuned-in?

A consultant heart surgeon was once asked if he agreed with the traditional view that the heart was the seat of love. He replied that the heart was no more than a remarkably resilient mechanism for pumping blood and there were much better organs in the body for love. Presumably he was referring to the genitals.

The whole process of loving can be reduced to mechanistic terms and there are manuals describing fine techniques for stimulating each erotic zone of the body. If a robot was programmed to carry out the instructions, you would need to look no further for an ideal partner!

The brain, too, is often likened to a marvellous computing mechanism . . . so is this all we are? Just a fairly well designed chassis, put at our disposal for an average three score years and ten?

Or is there more to us than meets the eye of the mechanistic analyst? How do we differ from the computer and the robot we have built in our image? A comparison of the mechanistic view of the brain with more creative propositions will throw some light on the matter.

---

## A MECHANISTIC MODEL OF MEMORY IN THE BRAIN
Detailed descriptions of theories about how we remember are given on the previous pages. The trace theory, the code theory and the synaptic modification theory all take a mechanical view of the brain as a storage system. These storage units are shown as little boxes on the diagram (*right*).

This mechanistic model assumes that all learning, and other experiences, are stored away in the brain but do not fundamentally alter the whole person. Only a few mechanisms may be refined; for example, while learning to sing, the muscles of the throat and larynx may be developed, but the information about how to use them remains stored in the brain and not in the muscles themselves.

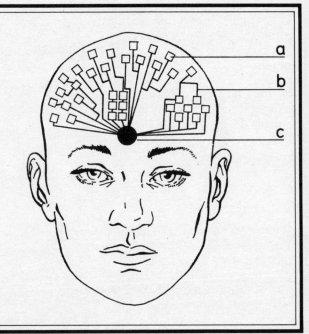

**The mechanical memory**
**a** Memories in storage units from which they can be retrieved and brought to a consciousness center
**b** Pathways along the nerves
**c** A consciousness center

---

## THE BRAIN AS A COMPLEX TUNER
If the brain acts as a tuner for memory, then it might seem reasonable to suppose that the whole nervous system of the body can become involved. Perhaps through this tuning capacity, we can tune-in to signals other than those received by our better known senses, such as our eyes and ears. And might it also be possible to transmit paranormal signals? A model of ourselves as tuning systems is presented for your speculation (*right*).

**Are you tuned-in?**
**a** Clairvoyant signals
I'm lost, please find me

**b** Telepathic signals
Why don't you phone?

**c** Precognitive signals
The tower will be struck by my powers

**d** Visions

**e** Signals from other worlds
UFO

**f** Mutual interest signals

**g** Music from deceased composers
Beethoven

**h** Understanding foreign languages
Bonjour

**i** Empathy
OUCH!

**j** Déjà vu
I have been here before

## A CREATIVE MODEL OF MEMORY

In this model, it is suggested that memory is one of the functions of the brain's ability to remember by tuning-in to morphic elements built into the design of the whole person at the time when the original stimulus was received.

For example, it is suggested that the brain remembers how to play the piano, not by retrieving units from storage, but by causing the whole body to tune-in; those parts that have acquired the piano-playing morphic elements are, themselves, part of the memory. These might include items built into the brain itself, such as sound patterns, sensitivity built into the ears, design elements built into the muscles of the hands and eyes and items built into the electro-chemical functioning of certain cells. Perhaps the energy patterns of the body also contain morphic elements, including the aura.

This creative model assumes that all learning, and other experiences, bring about changes in the whole person. In this example (*right*), the piano player changes his or her whole being many times as the skill is mastered and it is the whole person who remembers, stimulated by the tuning ability of the brain.

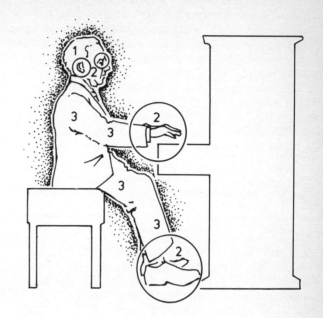

**The creative memory**
1 Brain as the tuner
2 Some morphic elements including the aura
3 The whole body is involved in the creative model

### Evidence for a creative model of memory

Researchers who assumed that memories are stored in the brain have been surprised to discover that the removal of different sections of the brain does not affect what is remembered. All kinds of memory diminish only when a very large quantity of brain is removed. Those who support the creative model claim this as evidence that the brain is an adaptable tuner rather than a storage device. Some people are also of the opinion that dreams are due to tuning activities during sleep.

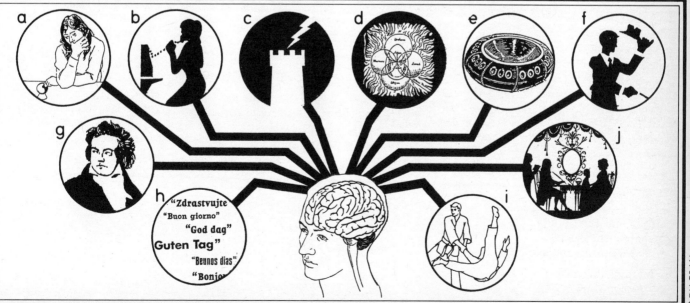

# Do you have physical ecstasy in mind?

It has been claimed by a psychologist that boys think about sex on average once every 12 seconds! Whether their thinking is always conscious is not stated, nor are any similar figures available for girls. However, it is true that the mind can fantasize wonderful experiences of physical ecstasy. Do you have physical ecstasy in mind?

Since you may have at least three minds, from which of the three do your sexual urges emanate? Are you the practical, committed type? Do you incline more to a lighthearted love life? Or are you at the mercy of cupid's wayward arrows?

## LOVESTYLES

While there is a wide range of lovestyles, it is said that we tend to gravitate towards a particular style in keeping with our predominant state of mind.

To find your predominant lovestyle, answer all the questions by circling the code letter of the answers that most nearly apply to you. Count the number of each code letters you have circled and enter them in the totals boxes. Your preferred love-style is the one with the highest score.

### How do you feel about "falling in love"?

**A** I'd like that very much.

**B** OK, but I'm not ready to settle down

**C** I prefer friendship to love

### Who do you start a relationship with?

**A** A stranger who arouses instant feelings in me

**B** A stranger who is attractive and acceptable

**C** A person I already know

### What kind of physical type attracts you?

**A** Usually the same physical types stir me

**B** I'm usually attracted to a variety of types

**C** Physical appearance is not of first importance

### How do you feel about a new relationship?

**A** I can't stop thinking about him/her

**B** It's great, but it doesn't change my life

**C** I like us to do more together

### How important is love?

**A** Without love, life isn't worth living

**B** Pleasant, but other things are more important

**C** It is part of friendship and life in general

### Are you monogamous?

**A** Yes, I can be very jealous of rivals

**B** No, several relationships are the spice of life

**C** I prefer faithfulness in both of us

### How do you prefer to express your feelings?

**A** We should always talk openly with each other

**B** Not too intensely

**C** Words are not always the best way to show feelings

### How do you feel about your life in general?

**A** With my partner at my side anything is possible

**B** I can achieve anything regardless of my partner

**C** I can rely on my partner to respect my achievements

**Totals boxes**

### How do you view relationship problems?

A  Love will keep us together no matter what

B  We don't get close enough to have many problems

C  We will find an amicable solution in the end

### How important is sexual compatibility?

A  People deeply in love are bound to be compatible

B  Sex should always be satisfying and fun

C  There are many ways of showing we care

### How would you see the end of your relationship?

A  I'll never give up trying to make it work

B  Everything has to end, but we would stay friends

C  We'd get professional help to resolve the situation

## THE SPONTANEOUS LOVER

You feel a powerful and immediate attraction to a complete stranger. You fall in love deeply and think about him/her all the time. Sex is a very active part of your relationship. You become quite possessive and may fight a lot over quite trivial things and imagined slights. Your deep emotional involvement often blinds you to how our partner really feels. You tend to assume that because you feel passionate, so must he/she. If the relationship ends, it takes you a long time to recover from the sense of loss.

You tend to make relationships intuitively and although your intuitive mind may sometimes be right you may fail to take into account practical, day-to-day issues. Subjectively you are always sure this is the right person when you are in love. Because you are charged up and you fail to recognize objectively that there are many other people who can excite you.

## THE DETACHED LOVER

You treat each of your relationships as special, for as long as it lasts. You enjoy sex and talking about sex but deep emotional involvement does rather frighten you, for you don't like things to become too serious. You sincerely care for your partners and try not to cause pain ending a relationship. Commitment is not your forte. You tend to be fairly self-sufficient and rarely make any real changes in your life to accommodate your partners. If sexual problems occur, you prefer to find a new partner.

You tend to enjoy flirtatious, lighthearted relationships and may even have more than one at once. Your abstract-mind knows what you like when you see it but your heart is rarely involved. Every love affair is like taking a beautiful astral trip, but when you come down to earth again, you are disappointed with reality.

## THE COMMITTED LOVER

You treat your relationship as an important part of your life. You are unsentimental, though not necessarily unromantic, and you are not looking for love or a brief affair but for a long-term partner. You expect both yourself and your partner will have to make an effort and especially in sexual matters. You enjoy the sexual part of your relationship but warmth, affection, understanding and companionship are equally important to you. You expect a relationship to be lasting and an important part of your life.

You tend to build a relationship from a basis of friendship and like to find common interests. Your body-mind can certainly keep your feet on the ground and let you to listen to your heart. However, you may get bogged down in reality and forget to let yourself dream sometimes, losing the sense of joy that two people can have who are also very good friends.

# Chase the shadows from your mind

Are you happy? Do you enjoy your life, no matter what is happening? When everything is fine, are you full of joy or are you pessimistic that it won't last?

When things aren't going too well or when a tragedy has struck, do you throw yourself wholeheartedly into doing something about it, such as grieving, or do you try to push unpleasant experiences aside and hope that they will go away?

Happiness is partaking fully in all the experiences life has to offer and enjoying them. Yes, even grief can be enjoyed, that's how it passes in time.

Happiness is a state of mind and its opposite state of mind is misery. Joys and sadnesses that you haven't enjoyed cast a shadow on your mind and lead to chronic misery, depression and dissatisfaction. So how happy or miserable are you? Where would you place yourself on the scale of happiness?

## HOW TO RATE YOURSELF ON THE SCALE OF HAPPINESS
It is not the cards you were dealt in life that count, it's how you play them that leads to happiness. If you play your cards well, you will display some of the symptoms of happiness. If you play them badly or not at all, then you will have many of the symptoms of misery.

### Noticing the symptoms
Several hundred people were asked to say how they could tell if they were happy or unhappy. From the replies, these two lists of symptoms were compiled. Look down each list and tick the symptoms you know you have most of the time.

| | Twelve symptoms of happiness | |
|---|---|---|
| 1 | I am making the most of what I've got | |
| 2 | I feel perpetually young at heart | |
| 3 | I have at least one new project on the go | |
| 4 | Today is a wonderful day | |
| 5 | I like most of the people I know | |
| 6 | When alone, I enjoy my own company | |
| 7 | I don't worry if things aren't exactly right | |
| 8 | Almost everything in life has a funny side | |
| 9 | I enjoy doing things that please others | |
| 10 | My days are full but I always have time to relax | |
| 11 | I am never bored | |
| 12 | I have a good life | |
| | Total | |

| | Twelve symptoms of misery | |
|---|---|---|
| 1 | Opportunities don't seem to come my way | |
| 2 | I am afraid of growing old | |
| 3 | There is not much that interests me | |
| 4 | Things will be alright when . . . | |
| 5 | I only like a few of the people I know | |
| 6 | I mostly dislike doing things on my own | |
| 7 | If something isn't perfect it's not worth doing | |
| 8 | There isn't much to laugh at in this life | |
| 9 | Nothing I do seems to please anyone | |
| 10 | I'm too busy to have any time to relax | |
| 11 | I'm often bored or too tired to do anything | |
| 12 | Sometimes life doesn't seem worth living | |
| | Total | |

After adding the ticks in each column, deduct your misery score from your happiness score; this will give you a number of points. If your happiness total is smaller than your misery total, the result will be a minus number of points. If your final score is a plus, you are more often happy than miserable. If you have minus points you are more often miserable than happy.

Misery score ...........................................

Happiness score ....................................

FINAL SCORE ....................................

## How to increase your score

If you want to be happier, you must decide to be happy. Happiness is not something that comes to you out of the blue. Nor does it depend on only good things happening to you. Once you have decided to be happier, look at your symptoms of misery and go to work on them. The corresponding happiness symptom will give you a clue and here are some tips for dispelling the shadows of misery from your mind.

### 1 Opportunities

Learn to recognize opportunities; they are always around just waiting to be taken. Go to confidence-building classes to learn how to create opportunities. Search for information and keep in touch with what is happening in the world. Many opportunities are missed because you just don't know they exist. Watch how other people find opportunities.

### 2 Age

Scrap all your youthful idols and start collecting pictures and information about successful, attractive people who are much older than you are. There are thousands who are fine examples of how to turn age into an advantage. Keep in touch with current ideas and learn to recognize what is redundant about your own attitudes.

### 3 Interests

Investigate new sports, hobbies, social clubs, magazines, voluntary organizations, jobs, fashions, food, wines, places, people, languages etc. Go out and try things you have never done before, even if you think you won't like them. Set yourself a goal to find at least three new interests and follow them through. Stimulation is often the key to finding new interests.

### 4 Live now

Keep a short diary of each day, writing down only the things which you enjoyed. Make it a habit to find at least one thing in each day that was enjoyable. Then increase your aim to two and then more. Look for pleasure in each day and you will find it. Start with simple things such as food, clothes, a smile from someone, a flower or a piece of music.

### 5 People

Some psychologists estimate that we spend 96% of our time thinking about ourselves. Pick one person you know and spend time thinking about him or her; what do you notice that upsets him or makes him happy? Try to see things from his/her point of view. Look for his/her good points. Then repeat the exercise with other people, including those you don't like.

### 6 Yourself

When you look in the mirror, greet yourself and listen carefully to yourself. Agree to stop criticizing yourself and learn to like who you are. If you already think of yourself as a great gift to mankind, allow yourself to be weak and needy too. You are neither a giant nor a dwarf, just one among millions of human beings. So make friends with yourself.

### 7 Perfection

A photographer once put together the perfect features from the faces of several well-known beautiful women and handsome men. The resulting pictures were utterly boring and totally lacked character. So when you are urging towards perfection, remember, it is the oddity, the imperfection or the curiosity that adds interest.

### 8 Humor

If you rarely find life funny, listen to those born comedians who can laugh at themselves. Collect jokes and don't let your life be dominated by too much seriousness. There is a time and place for genuine concern about the evils of this world. When you can do something to help a situation do it, otherwise leave it and refuse to let it get you down.

### 9 Pleasing others

Doing something that helps to make someone else happy is one of the best ways to experience happiness. Learn to distinguish between insincere flattery and genuine pleasure-giving. Find out what others really like and do it. Often it's the smallest things that count most.

### 10 Time

Many people fill every moment because they are afraid to stop and do nothing. If you are such a person, take a break of a few minutes at a time to daydream; you will find the world won't fall apart. Later have a whole day without plans and see what happens. If the shadow creeps into your mind when you are inactive, at least you can meet it head-on and learn to dispel it.

### 11 Boredom

Chronic boredom is usually a form of depression. Activity will stir all manner of fears. The only way is to start slowly and meet those fears one by one. Nothing terrible will happen and you may find that they are only anxieties about being a success!

### 12 Life

You only have one life; it is up to you to use it and enjoy it. Nobody owes you anything. You can decide to enjoy what you've got and play your cards to advantage or you can choose to let things get you down so low that you feel nothing is worthwhile. Innumerable people have discovered that as one door closes, another opens . . . providing you look for it.

# Chapter two

# POWERFUL MINDS

Nobody has yet clearly defined what is a mind yet we all recognize a powerful mind when we meet one. A person who uses their mind to succeed in creating a new concept, a piece of research or a great composition is generally accepted as having a good mind. There are others who have powerful minds which produce quite different results; minds that pass through madness to reach sanity, minds that can control the actions of other people and minds that are superior to the normal.

The realm of psychic phenomena such as telepathy and clairvoyance is still a mystery that is little understood. We are equally at a loss to understand the minds of those who succeed despite severe handicaps and of those who can perform feats of mental arithmetic and photographic memory.

Then there is the question of other minds than our own such as disembodied minds both from our planet and from other galaxies. Ideas about the mind are also linked with the development of computers; indeed some people believe that computers can think and may overtake the abilities of human minds.

In this chapter are examples of some functions of the mind to show the variety and power of human minds.

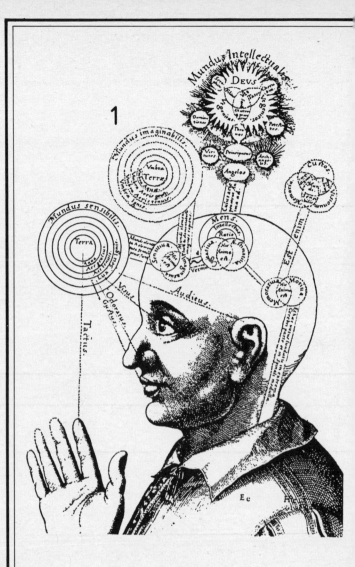

**1** Metaphysicists and philosophers have long searched the areas of the Brain for evidence of an independent mind, or soul. 'The Spiritual Brain', a 1620 chart by the English physician Robert Fludd.
**2** Perhaps the mind can emit force lines which, by psychomagnetic powers travel great distances to influence others. Illustration from Babbitte. *Principles of Light and Colour.*
**3** Artists have constantly used their inner mental conditions to invent fantasies and illusions of unknown worlds as in *The demon* by the German illustrator Heinrich Kley (1863–1945).
**4** Practitioners of hypnosis are often thought to possess super-extending powers of mind control. A 19th-century illustration of Dr. Mesmer.
**5** Authors have used their inner mind pictures to create fictional characters which appear to readers as real as the physical world. A 19th-century illustration of Charles Dickens at his desk.
**6** Perhaps our minds are controlled by disembodied minds from our planet or from other galaxies. Science Fiction writers use these possibilities to describe cosmic forces.

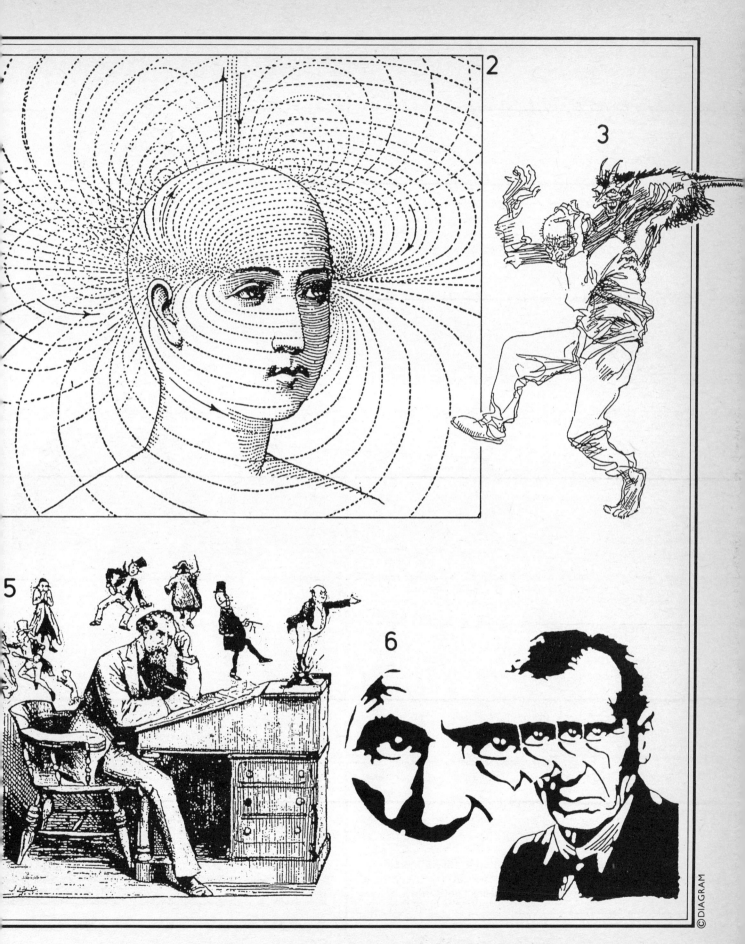

29

# Developing a super-mind

Like Superman, the super-mind is a fictional mind that represents the heights of human hopes and ambitions. The super-mind can perform beyond the limitations of normal human minds; it can retrieve accurate memories on demand; perform several complex thinking processes at once; control events; heal disease; create ideas; communicate across great distances without mechanical aids; and perform miracles and magic tricks to order.

The super-mind has looks that can kill and a third eye that can heal. It can interpret all languages, including that of animals and plants. So how could we develop at least some of the characteristics of a super-mind?

Let us assume that the mind is usually located inside the body and that it is a manifestation of the brain at work in all its complexity. This normal, human mind is capable of learning and acquiring facts, knowledge and ideas. Perhaps the superior mind is one who "knows" without bias, predjudice, ignorance or doubt. So let us examine the problems of knowing and consider if we can upgrade our own minds by clearing away bias that impedes our progress.

## WAYS OF KNOWING

What is todays' date? How do you know it is the date? There are five main ways of knowing. Which did you use? Which was the most appropriate method for knowing today's date?

**1**

**Reasoned thought**
Did you remember yesterday's date and reasoned that today's date is the next in sequence?

**2**

**By direct experiment**
Did you make several guesses and chose the one that looked right?

**3**

**By reflecting on observations**
Did you collect evidence which you could then reflect upon and discover the date, for example by asking several other people, listening to the radio, watching events and looking at the season outdoors?

**By personal experience**
Have you already studied the passage of time and made measurements so that today you are able to use all that personal experience to discover today's date?

**By accepting expert authority**
Did you look at the date printed on today's newspaper, consult your diary or ask some other authority?

For much of the time we only use one or two of these ways of knowing, since each method is appropriate to different situations. For example, methods 2, 3 and 4 would not be helpful in finding out today's date. They would be more appropriate if you wanted to find a better route from your home to work. Method 1 would be a useful way of knowing today's date but it involves some personal effort. The easiest way of finding out the date is to consult an authority.

**Knowledge by authority**
This is a very common method of acquiring knowledge because it is impossible for us all to learn about everything. However, by accepting knowledge from authority we may be tempted to allow other minds to determine the course of our lives, instead of thinking for ourselves.

We can develop one aspect of our minds to super-mind standard by understanding and improving the way we select and use knowledge by authority.

## The process of knowing by authority

Here is an example of how we may learn of a new discovery from an authority on the subject.

**Step 1** Professor X has studied the universe for many years, using all five methods of knowing. One day he announces: "I have discovered a new planet in our solar system."

**Step 2** Other people who have studied the universe test out his claims and say: "We agree with you . . . there is a new planet."

**Step 3** The information is published, for example in a research paper, a newspaper and on television.

**Step 4** The new planet is named and included in textbooks and encyclopedias. Professor X is now an acknowledged authority on the subject and is often invited to speak at conferences and on television and radio. His book on the new planet is published and his reputation established.

If he announces further discoveries or makes statements on any other aspect of his subject, he is likely to be believed by the public and by many of his colleagues.

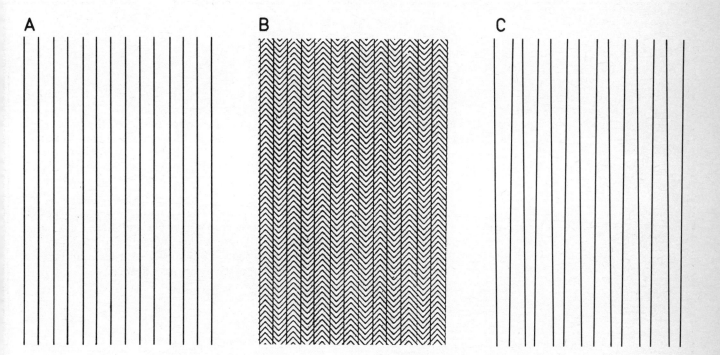

A    B    C

## Don't believe everything you read

Because some of what is reported in newspapers is true, there is a tendency to regard all media as authorities in themselves. This is a dangerous mistake and can lead to misunderstandings and prejudices.

Newspapers cannot print everything, so they have to be selective and present one angle on the news. They are also there to make money, so headlines are chosen because they sell the paper, not because they are entirely accurate.

The opinions and bias of editors and producers inevitably color the reporting and the choice of people to present television news and documentary programs themselves add another dimension to the message. Be aware too that commercial channels also know how to present information authoritatively . . . their incomes depend on it.

Finally, the contents of this book should, like any other book you read, be subjected to some thought. A super-mind does not accept information just because it comes packaged in a printed book, nor does the super-mind reject unfamiliar ideas without first giving thought to them. And in the end, be aware that you, too have beliefs. A belief is something you have faith in . . . something you accept as truth which you do not have the resources or opportunity to discover or prove for yourself.

The authority of seeing for yourself is not always reliable either. Without measuring the distances between the lines in the above three diagrams, is **A** or **C** a correct illustration of the center drawing **B**?

Answer: **A** and **B** are parallel lines. The apparent bends in **B** are due to visual illusions. The lines in **C** are alternately converging and diverging.

31

# Animal magnetism

Until his death in 1815, Dr.F.A.Mesmer, an Austrian physician, was using a mind power called animal magnetism for both diagnostic and curative purposes. It was not until later that his method became known as mesmerism and is now acknowledged to be akin to hypnosis.

It was not until the 1880s, when the American and the British Societies for Psychical Research began to investigate such phenomena, that any careful analysis was made of the process and its effect. Consequently there remain only Dr. Mesmer's own notes and some reports from his patients and other people who had been involved.

**The magnetizing process**

The operator

The subject

The trance which is believed to be a quasi-electrical magnetic fluid from the mind of the operator directed to selected parts of the subject's nervous system by the operator's will.

To induce a trance, the operator used various methods such as a firm, monotonous and rather soporific voice giving clear, simple instructions to "go to sleep" and, later, to "wake up." Sometimes the patient would be instructed to stare at a light or a swinging object. In general the vocal instructions were sufficient as the subjects stared into Mesmer's "hypnotic" eyes.

Much of his later work was with women who were known to be psychic mediums. In this work, the operator was regarded as the activator or male medium and the female medium was the message carrier.

**Magnetic fluid**
Mesmer's description of the transference of a potent fluid from the operator to the patient has a close parallel with sexual seduction and insemination, while male strength and potency has always been linked with seminal fluid.

**The power of hypnosis**
If mesmerism was simply the practice of hypnosis, and, since the process is similar, it should be remembered that a person cannot be hypnotized if he or she is unwilling. In practice in the majority of cases some level of hypnosis can be achieved, although the subject cannot be induced to behave in a way that is against the

unconscious mind. If it occurred to Mesmer, he never appeared to consider seriously that wilful cooperation was necessary to the success of his efforts.

**The experiences of female mediums**
Stimulated by the animal magnetism of Mesmer, the subjects were not manipulated to perform tricks but appeared to be possessed (by Mesmer?). These women had clairvoyant vision, i.e. they could "see" diseases in other people and locate objects lost or hidden in boxes. They claimed to taste whatever Mesmer ate, feel things he felt, such as a pin prick, and read his thoughts. They were also said to be in contact with the angels and those who were dead.

## WHAT IS A MEDIUM?

In general a medium, male or female, is a person who is able to become a channel for information, messages and other expressions which are said to come from other people or spirits by extra-sensory means.

Involuntary mediums are naturals who discover their skills; voluntary mediums are those ordinarily unskilled people who choose to pass through great mental upheavals to acquire their skills of mediumship. If you are a natural medium, all you will need is the help of an experienced medium to develop your skills. If you aren't a natural medium and still want to go ahead, the support of an experienced involuntary medium is essential. Mental chaos can lead to great wisdom or permanent neuroticism, if not insanity.

### SOME TYPES OF MEDIUMS

| Involuntary mediums | Voluntary mediums |
|---|---|
| **Healers** | **Witchdoctors** |
| These use the natural healing properties of their hands, which are transferred to a patient through touch. | These learn from other witchdoctors how to administer spells and potions to control evil spirits. |
| **Clairvoyants** | **Shamans** |
| These naturally see or hear, extra-sensorily, things that exist in the present that cannot be perceived normally. | These learn, as a consequence of mental upheaval, to heal and prevent sicknesses of mind and body. |
| **Prophets** | **Seers** |
| These naturally see or hear, extra-sensorily, things that are in the chronological future. | These learn from others and from experience, to foretell immediate and future circumstances. |

**How is the medium's message expressed?**
The medium is a channel for a message which may be expressed through the normal channels of speech, drawing, movement or writing. Sometimes the message is said to take the form of bangs, raps or the moving of objects, the energy for which comes from the medium.

**Whose mind is in control?**
Was Mesmer using his mind to control his patients or were they using their own minds to reveal or control their own diseases? When he magnetized mediums, the question becomes even more pertinent, since a genuine medium does not require stimulation from an operator.

Animal magnetism is a term used today to describe a form of instant and powerful attraction that is usually sexual... and nobody who has ever come under its spell can deny its existence. What, then, was Mesmer doing? Was he using hypnotic induction, sexual seduction or was it really a case of his mind over his subjects?

Finally, the power of the subject must not be forgotten. Were his female subjects compliant to the powers of his mind or did they actively cooperate? Did they, too, use their animal magnetism in return and was Mesmer himself under the power of their minds?

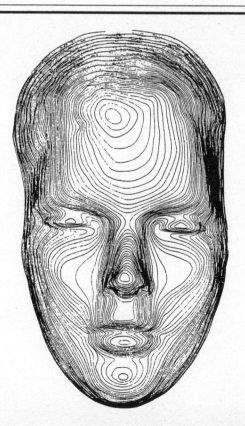

# Using telepathy

Four main types of paranormal activity are telepathy, clairvoyance, precognition and psychokinesis. They can be defined as follows.

**Telepathy:** communication between two minds at a distance without any technological means.

**Clairvoyance:** the ability of the mind to see things which are out of sight.

**Precognition:** foreknowledge.

**Psychokinesis:** the ability of the mind to cause objects to move without any physical contact.

More people tend to believe in telepathy than in the other three; perhaps this is because many people have had an experience that has led them to believe in its possibility. Also, telepathy is more believable.

If you turn on your radio, the sounds heard are signalled from a transmitter to a receiver, the aerial in your radio. There are no visible means by which the message travels between the two. Is it feasible, then, that human minds can send and receive messages through the air waves ?

---

### A STRANGE STORY

All four types of paranormal activity happened when Jean and Kevin Davidson went house-hunting in Brighton on the south coast of England in June 1964.

#### Jean Davidson's dreams

Kevin's company wanted him to move into Brighton so they took a trip there to collect details of available houses. From the beginning Jean was quite sure what kind of house she wanted. She had seen it in a dream on five or six occasions.

Neither Jean nor Kevin had ever visited Brighton before, but they did know it was a seaside town with a large number of three-storied terraced houses, so it was not surprising that Jean's dream-house had a view of the sea from a third storey window . . . a description that could apply to hundreds of similar houses.

However, Jean's specification of the interior was difficult to explain. The wallpaper of the ground floor room that overlooked the street was a pattern of pink roses and faded green velvet curtains hung at the windows. There was a black piano along the wall behind the door on top of which was a white figure of a bird.

In the back room, which overlooked a garden, she described a walnut dining table and chairs in detail, even making a sketch of the feather motif worked on the seats of the chairs. Jean felt as if she had visited the house many times. She was convinced the house was numbered 64 and had a street lamp immediately outside the front door, so they looked for any such houses that came on the market.

#### Mrs. Martin's strange experience

In May 1964 Mrs. Martin, a widow, decided to sell her home in Brighton and retire permanently to Corsica, where she had been invited to join friends. Two days after the sale board was erected, Mrs. Martin had the first of three strange experiences. Hearing the doorbell ring, she walked towards the front door. Before she reached the door, she saw a tall, slender, dark-haired young woman move silently and effortlessly along the hallway and turn into the front room. Alarmed and intrigued, Mrs. Martin followed the apparition who was smiling and lightly touching the white glass figurine of a pelican that her husband had made at his nightschool class. Then the apparition vanished and Mrs. Martin was left wondering.

The second appearance occurred a few days later, when the woman visited the back room and this time ran her finger around the featherly leaf pattern on the tapestry seat of a dining chair. The third took place early in June, when the apparition returned to the front room. Mrs. Martin kept a very detailed record of these visitations and took them to the meeting of the spiritualist circle to which she belonged, where they were lodged. Unfortunately, Jean Davidson did not write down the details of her dream before they began house-hunting, so her side of the experience was difficult to verify.

---

#### Was it mutual telepathy?

It transpired that Mrs. Martin's house was number 46 (the reverse of Jean's precognitive dream) but in all other details the house matched the one Jean had visited in her dreams.

Had Jean really visited the house during an out-of-body experience, or was the information transmitted to her by telepathy? Were Mrs. Martin's experiences precognitive, clairvoyant or telepathic messages received from Jean Davidson?

When the Davidsons finally came to look at Mrs. Martin's house (and subsequently buy it) an independent witness was present and agreed that the first thing Jean did was to touch the pelican figure on the piano. She also asked to see the walnut dining suite and the feather motif tapestry before she had been into the back room.

Jean and Kevin were very surprised to find that a dream could apparently come true. Mrs. Martin took the episode in her stride, as she was familiar with paranormal activities, but even she was surprised how clearly the real Jean Davidson matched the appearance of the apparition she had seen.

If telepathic ability exists, then the other three paranormal activities are feasible and any combination of the four types of activity could be possible.

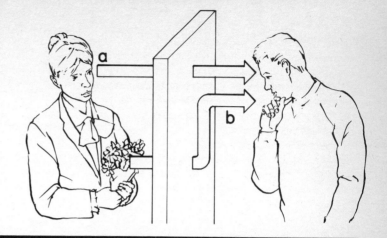

**The difference between telepathy and clairvoyance**
**a** Telepathic message between two minds
**b** Clairvoyant vision through solid screen

## TESTING YOUR TELEPATHIC POWERS

This can be done by using a pack of Zener cards which contains five each of cards printed with a star, wavy lines, a cross, square and circle; in total 25 cards.

While sitting in adjoining rooms, one shuffles the cards and runs through them in order, trying to communicate by telepathy the sign to the other person who draws or writes down which sign he thinks has been communicated to him. A buzzer or bell should be rung by the sender to warn the receiver that he is starting to transmit the next card. An equal amount of time should be given to each attempted transmission; 30 seconds is sufficient time.

Zener cards can be obtained from the Society for Psychical Research in London, or you could make a set of cards of your own with any five different signs on them or use five different colors.

After one run of trying to guess all 25 cards, the receiver has a 50-50 chance of getting five correct; there is a only a 1 in 20 chance of scoring 9 in any one run of 25 cards.

This test can be quite boring, so do not make too many runs at one sitting, or boredom will interfere with the results.

**Which scores are significant**
The odds are 20 to 1 against the significant scores being due to chance.

| Runs of 25 guesses | Chance score | Significant scores |
|---|---|---|
| 1 | 5 | 9 |
| 2 | 10 | 16 |
| 3 | 15 | 22 |
| 4 | 20 | 28 |
| 5 | 25 | 34 |
| 10 | 50 | 63 |

Even if you obtain significant scores, you cannot be certain you are using telepathic powers. Your results may be obtained by clairvoyance, so further tests should be done. Refer to **Writing to order** (pp 40-41) for a further example of thought transference.

A home-made pack of cards for testing telepathy

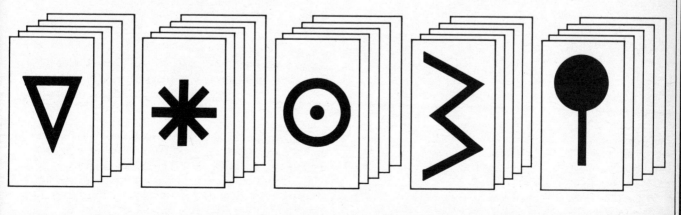

# Clearing the air

The conscious brain is always busy. Thousands of signals are being received, sorted and stored all day long. Just as there can be interference during radio transmissions, it is thought by some researchers that other signals stimulating the brain may interfere with paranormal signals. A technique to clear the air of interference during thought transference (or telepathy) experiments is called the Ganzfield technique. In a Ganzfield experiment there is a sender who tries to transmit thoughts and a receiver who attempts to visualize them. Ganz is a German word meaning "the whole of" and the aim of the technique is to present the receiver with an even surrounding field of diminished signals against which the telepathic signals can be more clearly detected.

### How the Ganzfield is created
The person acting as the receiver will sit or lie alone in a room. A ping-pong ball is cut in half and the pieces are placed gently over the closed eyes, the cut edge padded with a little cotton wool. The half balls are taped in place with medical tape. A low wattage red lamp is shone on the ping-pong balls.

A tape recording of white noise is played through large, earphones at a level that the receiver finds comfortable. White noise is a soft mixture of all sound frequencies and sounds rather like a muffled waterfall. If you want to try the experiment at home, make a tape recording of the static noises that come from your radio when it isn't tuned to any station; then play the recording through the headphones.

When all is in place, the receiver has neither aural nor visual images to distract him or occupy the brain.

The whole test room is then surrounded by a wire mesh which is earthed, to shield the person from radio and television signals. It is not essential to do this for a home experiment but it is wise to turn off and unplug all unnecessary electrical equipment. Also close windows and ensure there are no interruptions.

**A Ganzfield experiment**

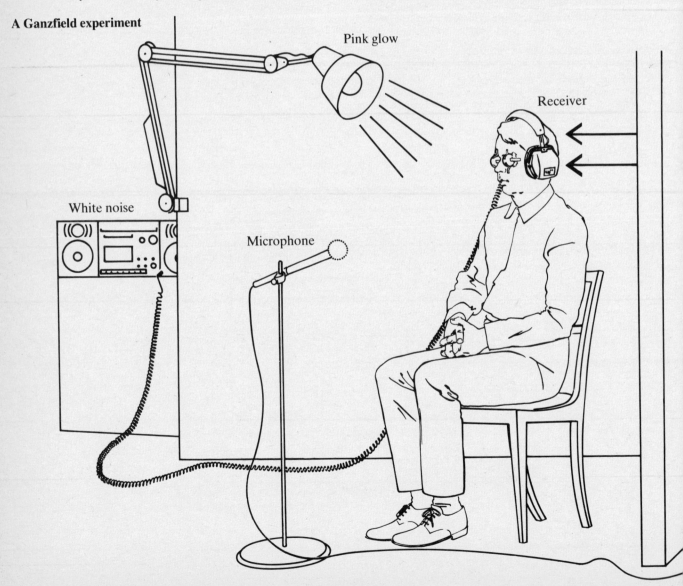

Pink glow

Receiver

White noise

Microphone

## Recording the results

A microphone is placed near the receiver so he or she can say what images are received during the attempt to transmit thoughts. The microphone should be connected to a tape recording machine in an adjoining room.

There an independent judge keeps a record of the timing and of the items the sender attempts to transmit. The judge also listens to the tape recording later and decides which descriptions can be counted as hits, because they can be recognized as the items the sender was trying to transmit.

## The sender

The person acting as the sender should be in the room with the independent judge and indicate, on paper only, which thought he or she is trying to transmit. The best results are obtained when the sender is alert and wide awake. Usually four words, preferably nouns, are randomly selected. The sender is asked to choose the first item and make a thought picture, concentrating on trying to transmit it for a few seconds. The receiver tries to visualize this thought picture.

## Measuring the relaxation level of the sender

It has been discovered that better results are obtained when the person acting as the receiver is relaxed. To find the level, a small electrode is fixed to the receiver's finger to measure the galvanic skin response. This is done by detecting the level of sweat on the skin which relates to the level of relaxation. It is not necessary to have this apparatus if you want to try the experiment at home.

## Understanding your results

Do not jump to conclusions if results from one or two experiments seem to be positive, some results will be perfect "hits" by chance. The experiment must be repeated many times to gain enough results to give a proper indication that thought transference is actually taking place. However, results from 11 studies done in research institutions in the USA show positive results of 100 billion to one over chance.

The odds against positive results being by chance have been calculated by mathematicians. In a run of 25 attempts at thought transference, five positive results could be due to chance. So a greater number of positive results than five out of 25 would become significant.

REFERENCE: For further details about statistical significance, see the table on the previous page, **Using telepathy**.

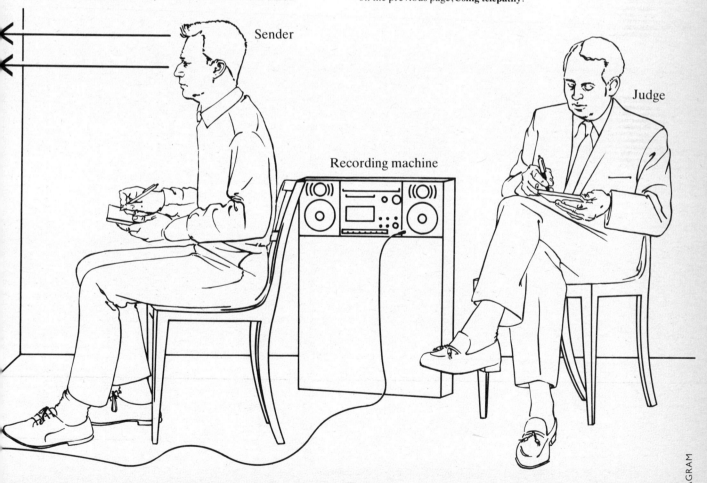

Sender

Recording machine

Judge

©DIAGRAM

37

# How to take an astral trip

Astral travel is one of the four out-of-body phenomena. All the other three occur spontaneously. Astral travel is consciously determined and can be achieved with practice. Astral trips could be regarded as voluntary out-of-body experiences.

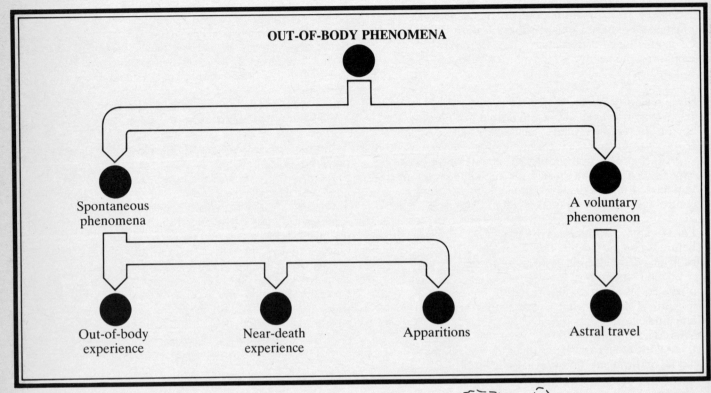

OUT-OF-BODY PHENOMENA

Spontaneous phenomena

A voluntary phenomenon

Out-of-body experience

Near-death experience

Apparitions

Astral travel

**Examples of spontaneous out-of-body phenomena**

**An out-of-body experience due to physical restriction**
When the body experiences continuous stress due to either physical position, as when driving, or to psychological anxiety, as when in a totally unfamiliar or apparently threatening situation, the person may find himself "beside himself" consciously watching his body perform from a distance of two or three feet.

He may describe the experience as "being on a high". The experience will only last as long as nothing interferes that requires a change of his position. Unfortunately, at high speeds he may not have time to return to his body and react sufficiently quickly to avoid an accident.

**A near-death experience due to clinical death**
When the body's vital functions cease, as may occur during illness, operation or as a result of an accident, the person's consciousness float above, watching the resuscitation process.

During this experience, she may float about, moving more than t or three feet away from herself but will be aware of having to turn back and re-enter her body.

Sometimes, a person in a near-death experience may have a vision related to religious beliefs. Some people who have reported seeing their loved ones also say they have no fear of dying and actually loo forward to the pleasure of the experience.

# HOW TO BECOME AN ASTRAL TRAVELER
## Preparations
Serious yogis have undertaken years of meditative practice before taking astral journeys. Certainly their warnings that astral travel is not for the impatient or the unclean should be taken into account.

Some western practitioners claim that a lifetime's practice is not necessary and short astral trips can be taken after a little practice. They, too, will emphasize the need to work toward a quiet mind and a clean body.

## What is a quiet mind?
It is a mind free from desires, neuroticisms, upsets, angers, prejudices, worries, anxieties, sadnesses, fears, ecstasies and other common human states.

A quiet mind is free because these states have been experienced and gone through. A free mind is not one that has learnt how to avoid human feelings or how to control them. Fine examples of people with quiet minds are some of the saints from different religions. For example, St. Francis of Assisi (1182-1226), who, before becoming a calm, loving person, spent his time rollicking through a life of utter debauchery!

Like the saints, people with truly quiet minds are often serious about taking life lightly and do others no harm. They are strong people with realistic views and kind hearts.

## What is a clean body?
It is a body of any age that is functioning well, even if it is handicapped. This is usually achieved by exercise to improve strength, suppleness and stamina. A clean body is washed on the outside and well-balanced on the inside. This implies eating sensibly and not taking in substances that upset the balance, such as alcohol, tobacco etc. Some people would exclude all meat, fish and dairy products, while others would exclude only products which are from dead animals.

## How to take an astral trip
Before attempting the exercise, clear your mind of any unfinished business that needs your attention.
**1** Choose a time that is at least 12 hours since the last meal and 48 hours since last eating meat if you are a meat eater.
**2** Take some gentle exercise to help relax tensions. Have a shower or bath and dress in warm, loose clothes.
**3** Choose a time when you will be undisturbed for about two hours. Lie on a comfortable bed or couch in a room that is pleasantly warm, has low lighting and with no noisy activity going on outside.
**4** Relax totally, even falling asleep, while mentally repeating that you are going to float away to the other side of the room. If, after trying several times, nothing happens, try again another day.

It may take several weeks to reach a state when astral travel is possible. For some people it never happens. Once you have experienced your first astral trip to the other side of the room, you can be more adventurous and try going outside the room a little distance. With confidence you can then take longer trips. Astral travel can happen while awake or asleep.

REFERENCE: For details about your astral mind, see **Chapter One: Finding your astral mind** (pp. 12-13).

©DIAGRAM

**The apparition of Hamlet's father**
When an absent or dead person is seen by others, it may be an apparition. An apparition can be seen and/or heard but is transparent. If it is of a deceased person, it is often called a ghost.

It is claimed by some researchers that a person taking an astral trip can appear as an apparition to someone who is receptive to that person but this is thought to be a very rare occurrence.

Most regular, ghostly apparitions are said to be either unaware they are deceased, because death was untimely, or people who had unfinished business on earth. Some apparitions are limited for a special purpose, for example, religious visitations.

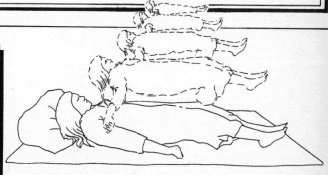

**An astral journey across miles**
The traveler leaves the physical body on a couch and passes through walls and across distances to a chosen destination. It is said to take hardly any time at all. The traveler is invisible and can see and hear what is happening wherever he stops but cannot participate in events.

Although some practiced yogis can take astral trips over great distances for up to two hours, most people find it extremely difficult to travel more than a few yards or for longer than a few minutes. Any disturbance, or potential disturbance of the vacated body breaks the concentration required and brings the traveler back into the physical body.

# Writing to order

William T. Stead (1849-1912) was an accomplished journalist and editor who lived in England in the late 19th century. In those days all communications across a distance were by letter. However, William Stead saved his friends much time and trouble by using his skill in automatic writing to write the letters himself that they would have sent to him.

He first developed this uncanny knack of writing letters from other people when, by chance, he found himself automatically writing in the style of a journalist friend who had died. The opinions, too, were those of his dead friend and not of William himself.

The automatic writing of messages from the dead is very difficult to prove and easier to explain as a hidden ability or an outstanding memory on the part of the writer. However, William Stead's ability to tune in to messages from other people extended to the living.

## A letter from a friend

One Monday afternoon, after a weekend away, a lady friend of William's was due to travel the 30 miles from Hazlemere to London. William wanted confirmation that she had arrived safely.

He sat down at his writing desk with pen and paper and mentally asked his friend what kind of journey she'd had. This is a brief outline of what he claims his hand wrote automatically:

"I am sorry to say I have had an unpleasant experience . . . I left Hazlemere at 2.27pm in a second class compartment in the company of two women and a man . . . At one of the stops, the women got out and I was left with the man. He came and sat by me and I was alarmed . . . he tried to kiss me…there was a struggle and I seized his umbrella and hit him with it until it broke . . . fortunately the train stopped some way before Guildford and the man jumped out and ran away . . . I kept the umbrella."

When the automatic writing ceased, Stead immediately sent a messenger with a note to the lady's house, offering his sympathy and asking her to bring the umbrella to their next meeting. The lady replied that she was sorry he'd learnt what had happened as she had decided to keep the whole episode a secret . . . he was right about the experience but wrong about the umbrella . . . it was her's and not the attacker's.

## Psychic abilities

Thought to be possessed by all human beings, psychic abilities are forms of mental communication that can transcend time, place and the material world.

The psychic skill of automatic writing consists of words or symbols written without conscious intention on the part of the writer. A person who regularly writes automatically may be regarded as a medium for the passing of messages. In order to receive messages, a medium uses extra-sensory perception (ESP). There are many manifestations of psychic abilities and in order to develop a particular one, others may need to be practiced first.

## SOME PSYCHIC ABILITIES

Of all these psychic activities, psychometry is the one most useful to the beginner who has no knowledge of his or her potential in this field.

If you wish to try your hand at automatic writing, first explore your ESP potential through psychometry.

**Telepathy**
Mental communication over a distance.

**Clairvoyance**
Knowledge of the living by sight.

**Precognition**
Knowledge of the future.

**Spiritual mediumship**
Knowledge of the dead.

**Automatic writing**
Involuntary writing of messages from the dead or the living.

**Dowsing**
Locating things hidden underground.

**Psychometry**
Using an object to tune-in to information.

### Learning to use extra-sensory perception

Psychometry is the art of selecting an object that becomes the vehicle to stimulate extra-sensory perception. Typical objects may be a ring or another piece of jewelry, a scarf, a photograph or something more solid such as a box or pot.

It was thought for a long time that images that come to mind while holding the object came from energy vibrations within the object. In fact, it is still thought by many that the owner of the object leaves some kind of message within it that can be picked up by the investigator.

Research has shown that in many, many cases information can be gained while focusing on objects the person has never touched, including photographs. In general, the object chosen is a focus, not a carrier of the message.

In general, a psychometrist is asked about the past, present or future of a person. The enquirer gives the psychometrist a small, personal object to hold.

When you begin, try with a ring and then with other small objects. Hold them and be aware of what images, thoughts, sounds, odors or ideas come to mind. Some people have a flood of images, while nothing will happen for others.

When you have found the type of object that best suits you, then you can get into practice and try out your psychic skills on your friends. Be most careful to ask your friends to check your readings of their affairs. In general, you are unlikely to ever be more than 65% correct . . . unless, of course, you have outstanding psychic ability. In this case, contact a reputable psychic society and learn to use the skill.

---

## A MODERN PSYCHOMETRIST

Born in the Netherlands, Peter Hurkos is internationally famous for his work with the police in the search for lost people and for the solutions to some crimes. He uses psychometry, tuning-in to the location of a person or an object by holding something that is strongly associated, such as a piece of clothing. He has had a very high number of successes in the search for missing persons, the victims of crimes and even of the whereabouts of the criminal. Often he has desribed the location of a crime in detail and sometimes had a vision of the crime as it was committed.

He also worked successfully with the police on well-known cases such as the 1969 Manson murders in California and the recovery of the Coronation Stone following its theft from London's Westminster Abbey in 1950.

### Testing the psychic detective

Tests of Peter Hurkos' psychic skills were carried out at a parapsychology laboratory in Maine during 1958. Professor Ducasse of Brown University sent Peter Hurkos a sealed package. Only Ducasse knew its contents. Here are some extracts from the description Peter Hurkos gave of the contents:

"This object blew up . . . there was an explosion . . . a long time ago. I can hear a strange language. It is very old. It is connected with water. I don't know what it is . . . a dark color, cylindrical, jagged with sharp points, it has been repaired. It had three owners, all dead. Dr. Ducasse has been given it, he did not buy it!"

The parcel contained a small pottery jar which a friend, now dead, had purchased and given to Dr. Ducasse. The jar was one of the remains of the volcanic eruption at Pompeii in AD 79, which had been pieced together and mended. It was bought by Dr. Ducasse's friend in 1922.

The description given by Peter Hurkos was extremely accurate but related only to what Dr. Ducasse knew about the jar and its history. It is thought that psychometrists are actually using telepathy and clairvoyance to acquire their information, the object, in this case the parcel, serving as a tuning device.

---

### Have you any skill in automatic writing?

After developing your psychic sensitivity and awareness with some pschometry exercises, you may like to try automatic writing.

Simply sit quietly with a pen or pencil and some clear paper at the ready and let your hand move as it will. You may like to ask your hand if it has any messages to write.

There are no known ways in which automatic writing can be learnt; most practitioners suddenly found it happening to them spontaneously. For example,

Rosemary Brown, an English medium, who has been writing music since the age of seven, claims she is dictated to by the past great masters, including Beethoven, Mozart and Bach. Certainly her music is in the style of many different composers.

Some people believe she is a medium in touch with the spirits of dead composers while others are of the opinion that she is a highly creative individual who simply does not recognize her own talents.

© DIAGRAM

# Using both sides of your brain

The human brain has two hemispheres, each of which is associated with different approaches to thinking. They are known as left brain and right brain activities; there are, of course, other parts of the brain that are independent of the two halves.

The left brain is more concerned with logical thinking and the right brain with intuitive thoughts. The hemispheres can work together, each contributing a point of view; they can work separately when problems require their particular mode of thinking or they can work against each other… this is often the case when you find yourself "in two minds" about things.

Although everyone uses both hemispheres of the brain, most people tend to use one side more than the other. Once we get accustomed to one kind of thinking we tend to stick to it and ignore the other. This leaves us

## WHICH SIDE OF YOUR BRAIN PREDOMINATES?

Check the statement from each pair that is most typical of you. Then total the columns. A greater score on one side indicates that side predominates, so you should make more use of the other side. If your scores are roughly equal, then you already use both hemispheres and could concentrate on increasing the cooperation between them.

**Left brain** 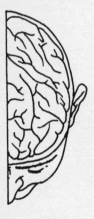     **Right brain**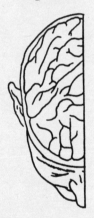

### Actions to increase use of your left hemisphere
Select the left hemisphere questions which you feel are definitely not how you normally operate. Then, using one at a time, practice applying the principles. For example, punctuality or logical order are two areas you could try out in daily life. You may prefer to take part in a course that demands left brain skills, such as science, technology, computer programming, carpentry or dress-making.

### Actions to increase use of your right hemisphere
The best way to stimulate your right brain is to take a course in something that demands spontaneity and intuition, which you would normally never have chosen. For example, dance-drama, jazz, art and design, creative fashion, flower-arranging or silver work.

**Left brain dominance**

I usually analyze, looking for the sequence of causes and effects which led to a situation

When asked to describe an acquaintance, I would give details of name, age, occupation, clothes, etc

In conversation I move from one idea to another

When talking, I keep my hands still or put them in my pockets

I am punctual and can estimate time

I am very good at explaining how things work, how to do things or giving directions

I am good at crossword puzzles and word games

I enjoy making plans and carrying them out

I prefer maths and sciences to the arts and drama

I tend to keep my feelings hidden but I can put them into words

I rarely dream and cannot remember them

I usually look for the reasons behind the behavior of other people

I keep files, papers and tools in logical order

I prefer representational art to any other kind

When dancing, I prefer a formal dance where the steps are known

I would find it very difficult to walk about my house with my eyes closed

**Total**

sadly lacking when it comes to solving problems that need the skills of our neglected hemisphere.

Consequently, an excellent way to improve your mind-power is to use both hemispheres as fully as possible. To do this, you must find out which is the under-used hemisphere and then concentrate on using it more often.

## Great work requires the use of both hemispheres

Inventions, creations and discoveries all involve periods of insight and periods when careful, logical organization takes precedence. The same applies to all research projects. Everyone has heard of scientists who had a flash of insight, few of us realize the years of painstaking experimentation that has to be done to ensure a new concept or a new drug is viable and safe.

The Scottish-born American inventor Alexander Graham Bell (1847-1922) combined right brain inspiration with painstaking left brain logic. Above the portrait is his May 1875 sketch for signal transmission without a battery in which touching B produced a musical note from A; and below Bell's schematic diagram of his first 1876 telephone.

### Right brain dominance

- [ ] I usually synthesize. Each piece of information I find is part of the whole picture
- [ ] When asked to describe an acquaintance, I would give a summary of moods, beliefs, inclinations, etc
- [ ] In conversation, I link ideas to each other
- [ ] When talking, I gesture a lot with my hands
- [ ] I am not a punctual person and cannot easily estimate time
- [ ] I am not good at explaining things even when I can do them well myself
- [ ] I find crossword puzzles and word games difficult
- [ ] I dislike planning ahead and enjoy doing things spontaneously
- [ ] I prefer the arts and drama to maths and sciences
- [ ] My feelings show easily but I find it hard to express them in words
- [ ] I often dream and can remember them
- [ ] I don't usually look for motivations behind other people's behavior
- [ ] Although I can usually find what I need I don't keep things in any particular order
- [ ] I can respond to all kinds of visual images
- [ ] When dancing, I prefer free movement in which there is opportunity to use my intuition
- [ ] I would find it quite easy to walk around my house with my eyes closed

- [ ] **Total**

# How to keep your mind on charge

Communication is the best way of keeping your mind on charge. Without communication we tend to become depressed and disinterested and our minds only continue to operate at a low level. As with the rest of your body, the best way to keep your mind active, fit and on charge is to use it.

Good communicators are exciting and stimulate our minds. In drama and entertainment, they make us want to laugh or cry and in schools, colleges and training courses good communicators inspire our enthusiasm to learn. Similarly, medical, legal and spiritual counsellors and consultants make us feel important and eager to proceed.

All these people who are good communicators have their minds on charge all the time and they fire our enthusiasm and interest.

## What is communication?
Communication is the sending and receiving of verbal and non-verbal messages. All living things communicate and it has been estimated by researchers that most human beings spend about three quarters of their waking life communicating verbally.

## Some ways of communicating

| | |
|---|---|
| Listening | Painting |
| Reading | Displaying |
| Talking | Gesturing |
| Shouting | Signalling |
| Singing | Dancing |
| Whistling | Touching |
| Writing | Kissing |
| Drawing | Hugging |
| Scribbling | Fighting |

## LEVELS OF LISTENING

Dr. Anthony Alessandra, an American researcher, has observed that we have three levels of listening.

### 1 Active listening
The listener is attentive and interested in the speaker and in the background, motivations and meaning of what is being said. This is very positive listening and there are several types that can be practiced to improve the power of your mind.

**Diagnostic listening**: Questions are asked to encourage the speaker to give more information or explanation.

Never make criticisms, judgements, or suggestions, nor be upset by silences. Attend with your eyes and body language as well as your ears but do not put pressure on the person. This kind of listening is used by the best counsellors and the most caring friends when a person has something important or difficult to say or a problem to work out.

**Empathic listening**: The listener shares the speaker's feelings. Distinguish this from sympathetic listening in which the listener imagines that the speaker must feel the same way as he does.

This kind of listening needs little response, just a word or two to show you are still listening carefully.

**Attentive listening**: The listener gives the speaker full attention and remembers the important points being made. It is often some time later you can show how attentive you have been. Attentive listening is essential in relationships. . . for example, you notice in passing that your friend does not like onions.

Later you make sure he or she is not offered onions during a meal.

### 2 Neutral listening
Listening is done with attention but no attempt to find motivations or react to the speaker. This kind of listening is best used for facts, information and the exchange of ideas and techniques. However, neutral listening is not as easy as it might seem to be. Many people forget the name of a person within minutes of being introduced to them.

To improve: Pause and repeat what the speaker has said to check if you have the details correct. To learn names, link the person and the name in some way that you find easy to remember. . . usually an illogical connection works best.

### 3 Negative listening
Listening is not objective but occurs through a series of mental, intellectual, emotional or social filters that change what we hear. There are eight types of filter. Negative listening often occurs when the language, customs or idioms are misunderstood.

Consider each of the eight types of negative listening and check those you are aware you do quite frequently. Then put yourself in a listening situation and concentrate on trying to eliminate the types of negative listening you have checked, using the suggestions for change.

## The components of verbal communication

It has been estimated by researchers that most people use listening and talking more than any other kind of verbal communication. The percentage of time spent communicating verbally in a waking day is as shown in the circle.

Watching is combined with reading, since the two activities are similar: both involve concentrating on looking at something and interpreting what is seen.

For example, reading a book or a set of symbols and watching television or people in the street.

Clearly listening is the most important part of communicating and it is in this area that the most outstanding improvements can be made. It was the way you learnt most things, including your language, when you were a baby. To keep your mind charged up and active, you must learn how to improve your listening.

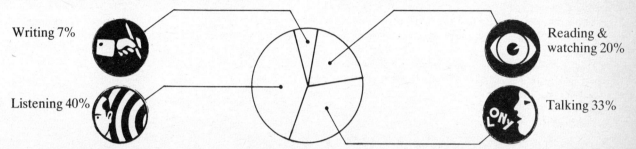

Writing 7%

Reading & watching 20%

Listening 40%

Talking 33%

## Eight types of negative listening

☐ **Emotional listening**: The speaker's powerful emotion rouses an opposite emotion in you and blinds you to what is actually being said.
To change: If too upset, stop the conversation or go away from the speaker for a cooling-off period. Try diagnostic or empathic listening.

☐ **Dismissive listening**: The listener quickly decides that what the speaker has to say will not be worth listening to. Dismissive listening is common when someone who is being given bad news respond with, "Oh no, it can't be true!"
To change: Explore your true feelings; what is it about the speaker or the words that worries you? Do you doubt your confidence or ability to produce an effective counter-argument?

☐ **Destructive listening**: Similar to dismissive listening but the listener is only intent on putting-down the speaker in the most crushing way in a game of destructive powerplay. Politicians frequently do this to each other; so do ordinary people who have prejudices against different cultures. The listener usually attempts to prove the speaker is inferior.
To change: Acknowledge that there is a clash of styles, beliefs or customs. Learn more about your differences.

☐ **Judgemental listening**: Jumping to incorrect conclusions.
To change: Try to improve your range of thinking styles.

☐ **Distracted listening**: This results from trying to do two or more things at once and not giving any one of them your full attention.
To change: Give attention to one thing at once, especially when someone wants to say something to you.

☐ **Submissive listening**: The listener thinks of the speaker as powerful, wonderful, god-like or aloof. Pop stars and sports heroes are often given this kind of adoring attention. It is more dangerous if you put your boss, your parents, your spouse or a colleague in this position (or if they try to take it).
To change: Try regarding people, including yourself, as equals and yourself as neither the giant of your dreams nor the dwarf of your fears. Acknowledge that some people are cleverer at some things and that other points of view are interesting but not absolute.

☐ **Anxious listening**: This happens when you are so awe-struck that you submit completely and hear little of what is being said. Often important information from medical consultants or lawyers can be missed due to anxiety. Sometimes you may feel bored, apathetic or even contemptuous. Usually there is a deep-seated fear behind apathy.
To change: Teach yourself to be less submissive without becoming aggressive. Assertion training may help you to face your fears in a level-headed way and a friend could be a great help when attending difficult interviews with lawyers etc.

☐ **Impulsive listening**: This happens when you are too eager to get going and don't listen properly to instructions or have brilliant ideas of your own stimulated by the speaker.
To change: Use neutral listening techniques.

## Memory

Improving your listening abilities will also improve your capacity to remember important things. Memory is discussed next.

# Acquiring an expert memory

Some people are able to remember detailed facts and figures and recall them at will, rarely making a mistake. Quiz show champions, antique dealers, sports enthusiasts, doctors, actors, garden lovers and dozens of other people who have expert knowledge in a particular field can remember a mass of information about their chosen subject. Able to add to their store of information indefinitely, they can also delete and adjust the stored facts in the light of new research.

Many musicians can remember a tune after hearing it only once and some, like Mozart and Beethoven, carry lengthy new compositions in their heads before they write them down on paper.

A college professor from Berkeley, California, claims that within a week he is able to identify 1000 new students by name and an 11 year old schoolgirl in Bradford, England is known to have memorized the names, addresses and telephone numbers of 100 people selected at random from a telephone directory and recited them correctly one month later.

The length of time between learning a set of facts and recalling them, does not seem to make any difference to people who have an expert memory. Those of us who haven't a good memory know how easy it is to forget, even if we manage to remember a fact for more than a few seconds.

### How to improve your memory
Memory is a function of the brain, just as movement is a function of the muscles; the ability to remember varies. However, improving your memory depends on interest and intention. If you have neither, your ability to remember is unlikely to improve.

In the beginning, practice memory exercises on subjects that interest you. Remembering names is a good way to begin and details are given in Chapter Five: Finding the key and Who do you have in mind?

Other ways to improve your memory all involve an intentional focusing on what you want to remember and the elimination of details you do not need.

### Method 1: Write it down
Times, dates, shopping lists and lists of jobs can all be written down. For example; organizer book, electronic diary, month by month calendar, year planner, tear-off shopping list, magnetic notepad in the car, ideas book by your bed, a message-book with a pencil tied to it placed next to the telephone is very useful for all the family,

### Method 2: Develop your own mnemonics
A mnemonic is an aid to memory, first used by the Greeks and consists of associating what is to be remembered with a key or code and is a very efficient way of improving immediate and long-term memory. Some Universities and colleges are now teaching their students how to use mnemonics.

A mnemonic consists of linking two factors which superficially resemble one another. The familiar is used to recall the unfamiliar. For example, words which sound the same such as two-shoe, seven-heaven, and five-hive. The method can also be used where the subjects look similar, so we remember a simple shape like a boot to draw a simple map of Italy. Remembering sequences by mnemonics is achieved by replacing the elements which have no direct link with a series that does. For instance, the musical scale EGBDAF can be remembered by the sentence Every Good Boy Deserves A Favor.

To make your own mnemonic it should be something you find easy to remember. You can then use it over and over again to remember all kinds of things.

---

## WHAT CAN YOU REMEMBER?

Try questions **A** and **B** to test your personal and general memory. Take what time you need.

**A** From memory, and without looking at your diary or personal records, write down 10 dates that are important to you or your family and say why, in the top box (*opposite*).

**B** From memory write down the date when each of the listed historic events happened, in the bottom box (*opposite*).

### How to score
Consult your diary or personal records for answers to **A**, and then check the list (*below*) for answers to **B**. From a starting score of 20, delete one point for every mistake or omission.

If you have 16-20 you already have an excellent memory; between 8 and 16 points you have an average memory and probably could improve on your performance. A score of less than 8 is not very good . . . but you will already know you find remembering facts difficult. Your memory probably works better with different kinds of material connected with things that interest you.

**Answers B**

| | |
|---|---|
| 1 August 1945 | 6 July 1969 |
| 2 June 1953 | 7 July 1981 |
| 3 April 1961 | 8 November 1985 |
| 4 November 1963 | 9 April 1986 |
| 5 December 1967 | 10 July 1988 |

## How to make imaginative links

The link should be as visual as you can make it. Images that are easiest to remember are suggested here, but keep each image pure by only using one method at a time. A clear, single image without too many extras will be the most effective.

- Exaggerate – make the image huge, loud, monstrous.
- Laugh – make the image absurd or ridiculous.
- Be naughty – make the image sexual or even vulgar.
- Animate – make the image move, smell or make a noise.
- Add color – use bright, even gaudy colors.
- Use your experience – use very personal images.

Astronomers have learnt to memorize the star positions (*below*) by linking the constellations to easily identifiable and remembered forms.

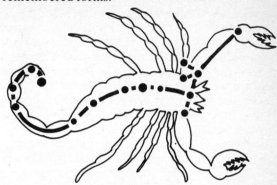

**A**

| Date | Reason for importance |
|------|----------------------|
|      |                      |
|      |                      |
|      |                      |
|      |                      |
|      |                      |
|      |                      |
|      |                      |
|      |                      |
|      |                      |
|      |                      |
|      |                      |

**B**

| | Event | Month and year |
|---|-------|----------------|
| 1 | The dropping of the first atomic bomb, on Hiroshima | |
| 2 | The conquest of Mt Everest by Sir Edmund Hillary | |
| 3 | The first manned space flight by Yuri Gagarin | |
| 4 | The assassination of John F. Kennedy in Dallas | |
| 5 | The first heart transplant by Christiaan Barnard | |
| 6 | The first step on the moon by Neil Armstrong | |
| 7 | The wedding of HRH Prince Charles and Princess Diana | |
| 8 | The volcanic eruption at Armero in Columbia | |
| 9 | The fire at the Chernobyl nuclear power station | |
| 10 | The Seoul Olympic Games | |

# Taking control over your phobias

The powers of the mind are rich and varied, although not always desirable. Anyone who suffers from a strong phobia will know how debilitating it can be and how very difficult it is to control.

A phobia is an aversion to or morbid fear of something or someone. Normally there is obvious cause or reason for this psychological problem. The fear is great and the person suffering from the phobia is likely to believe their very survival is threatened.

Phobias should be clearly distinguished from realistic fears and mild anxieties which can be controlled more easily by awareness and logical steps.

A phobia is often irrational and some major phobias can cause reactions such as panic, fainting or vomiting. Others are very specific aversions that can easily be avoided.

**Some examples of phobias**
- Agoraphobia – a dread of open or public spaces
- Ailurophobia – strong aversion to cats
- Arachnaphobia – fear of spiders
- Claustrophobia – a terror of being enclosed
- Haemophobia – a horror of blood
- Hydrophobia – a dread of water
- Xenophobia – a morbid dislike of foreigners

A -phobe is the person suffering from the fear, for example an Anglophobe is a person who has an irrational fear of the English. A phobia is often the opposite of a passion for something. This is indicated by adding -phile to the end of the word, for example a Russophile has a passion for everything Russian and a gynotikolobomassophile is a person who loves stroking a woman's ear-lobe.

## FEEDBACK

Giving and receiving feedback are useful ways of clearing the mind and reducing the anxiety level caused by a phobia. Feedback can be internal (from yourself) or external (from other people). Both kinds should be used to get a balanced point of view.

### Feedback methods
1 Asking others for opinions and observations of your reactions both while you are in action and in retrospect.
2 Asking others how they see you are likely to react. Other people can often tell you more about your own usual mode of behavior than you realize.
3 Responding internally to your immediate felt experiences and learning by trial and error.
4 Reflecting at leisure on what you hear and see, and using some thinking skills to consider the ideas carefully. This can be done alone or could be a discussion with other people who will offer different points of view.
5 Giving other people feedback.
Two-way feedback can give your experiences some perspective.

### Using a self-help group
Sharing experiences in a small group with others who have phobiasis always helpful.

Each person is invited to talk openly about their phobia. It should be described in detail: when it occurs, how it feels and the ways in which it affects daily life.

Listening to others talk about their phobias can release many of the feelings people have in common that are associated with phobias.

As people talk about their phobias, familiarity takes away the fears and lessens the effect of the phobia. Making friends with a phobia is the best way to control it. Laughing with it (not at it) reduces its impact.

After that, a risk can be taken, with help in the beginning, to face the phobia. These steps should be taken slowly, there is no necessity to force the issue. The aim is to be able to handle situations in which a phobia was interfering with daily life.

### Fear of madness: a classic story
When the British writer Patrick Hamilton had his play *Gaslight* produced on the London stage in 1938, little did he realize that it was a classic story, to be repeated many times and made into movies. They have been variously titled *Gaslight*, *Angel Street* and *The Murder in Thornton Square*.

The play is a psychological thriller, set in 1880s London, the action takes place in the ancestral home of the wealthy heiress, Bella, who has recently married the charming but calculating Paul Mallen.

Mallen wants the family fortune, especially the jewels that have never been found since the death of Bella's aunt, who used to be a famous actress. He sets out to control Bella's life completely by convincing her that she is crazy. He does this by accusing his wife of forgetting names, missing appointments and misplacing various objects. . . all of which he has arranged himself. He also uses Nancy, the maid, encouraging her to treat her mistress with contempt.

**Phobias**
They can be classified into four main types: animal phobias (**A**) tending to begin around age 4; social phobias (**B**) such as fear of crowds begin at an average age of 19; other specific phobias (**C**) such as fear of water or of heights start at 23 on average; and agoraphobia (**D**), fear of the outdoor world, in the region of 24.

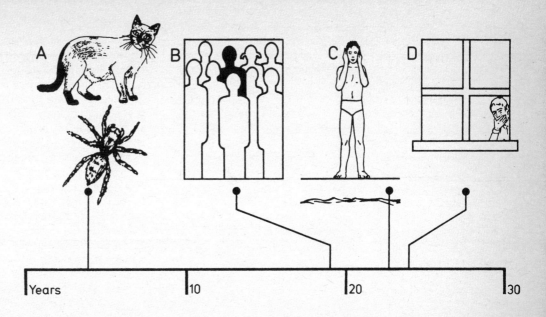

Years   10   20   30

Bella wants to be the perfect wife and sees herself first as a failure and then as a sick woman in danger of completely losing her mind. Almost everything becomes a phobia to her: she is terrified of going out, of meeting other people, of speaking to any of the servants and of displeasing her husband any further.

Her madness seems complete when she apparently hallucinates, seeing the gaslights in the house dim and brighten by themselves.

Positive feedback for Bella comes in the form of Inspector Rough, who is investigating Mullen's nightly activities. Rough takes an interest in Bella and eventually convinces her that Mallen has been playing tricks on her. The brightness of the gaslights changed every night as Mallen explored the attics of the house, turning the lights up there as he searched, thus altering the gas pressure in the rest of the house.

Finally Inspector Rough shows Bella how her husband has been searching the attics for her aunt's lost jewels. It becomes apparent that Mallen only married Bella to be able to carry out the search. . . but how did he know they were hidden? Mallen had been in that house before. He was there on the night he killed Bella's aunt as he tried to force her to tell him where her jewels were hidden.

In the first movie version, Anton Wallbrook and Diana Wynyard played Paul and Bella Mallen and many people will remember the performances of Charles Boyer and Ingrid Bergman in a later version.

**The source of a phobia**
In the story, *Gaslight*, the source of all Bella's fears is the relationship between her and her husband.

In the 1880s women were very much under the control of their husbands, which made it easier for Paul Mallen to convince his wife. Fear of not being a good wife, turned to fear of displeasing him and fear of her own madness. It is a classic situation of dominance and submission; a story all too common even more than 100 years later. . .the story of a battered wife.

Battering can be physical or psychological and the situation can be reversed or can occur between two people of the same sex, as in bullying of a smaller person by a bigger person.

Quite often, feedback and discussion with others can resolve the situation. Final action to move away from the situation is not easy to take because there are often two reasons holding a person in the submissive position. First the dominent character's physical power and second the submissive person's lack of a personal sense of worth. Fears often do temporarily affect our self-confidence.

Further understanding of phobias can be gained by reading **Chapter Two: Can you spot the mind-snatchers?** (pp. 52-53).

# How to unknot your thoughts

Confused or conflicting thoughts are like pieces of knotted string; it is not easy to distinguish one piece of strong from another nor to test the length and strength of each string. Knotted thoughts, like tangled string, must be untied and separated before they can be of much use.

To unknot string, each piece must be followed through carefully and extracted from its neighbors by understanding how they got knotted in the first place. The same approach is effective with tangled thoughts.

**Some causes of knotted thoughts**
1 Inadequate information
2 Jumping to conclusions
3 Blind emotions
4 Lack of thinking skills

Tangled strings: a symbol for confused thinking

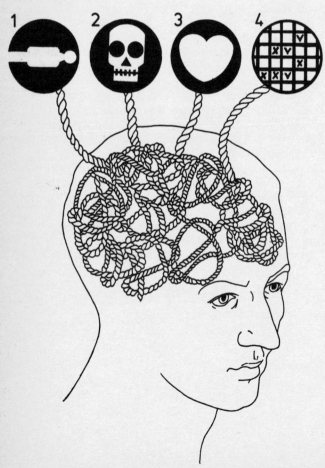

Four ways to untie your thinking.

# 1

**Increase information**
1 Consult sources of information
eg diary, directory, encyclopedia
2 Ask direct questions
eg "Where were you at 9pm last night?"
3 Ask searching questions
eg "What did you do last night?"
4 Check accuracy of existing information
eg "Is your name George Amadeus Consiglio?"
or "What is your full name?"

# 2

**Challenge assumptions**
Walking along a road you see ahead a woman lying on the ground with a man bending over her. Using only this inadequate information, try jumping to conclusions and write down what you might assume is happening.
To challenge your assumption, generate some alternative explanations and list them. Here is a list of alternatives, which may include your original assumption.

**List of alternatives**
- he is helping her
- he is attacking her
- they are lovers
- they are arguing
- she is play-acting to get attention
- they are lying in wait for you
- they are actively protesting about something
- they are making a TV advert or movie
- they are actors rehearsing a play
- they are the bait for a "candid camera" scene
- they aren't real; they are sculptures
- any other ideas . . .?

Having challenged your original assumption, the next step is to collect more information, by observation in this instance, and decide which of the alternatives are possible. Only then can you take sensible action.

Assumptions and beliefs are built on past experiences, so it may be difficult to remember to challenge them, as they are often deeply ingrained.

# 3

## Understand emotions

Emotions are an essential part of human thinking processes. In any response to a situation, emotion can be used at different points.

**1** Blind emotion is an immediate, automatic response that immediately stops thought.

Any emotion can be hot or cold. In blind rage, or in blind love, for example, some people are hotly demonstrative, while others seem to freeze up. Reading their emotions is more difficult, for example, the only clues to blind rage may be fists clenched tightly and increased sweating.

**2** Conditioned emotion enters our thoughts whenever we recognize a familiar pattern. From then on our thoughts are narrowed. For example, two people may be swapping information about their new neighbors, who are about to move in. As the amount of information increases, their feelings towards the new people will change. What are the triggers that condition your thinking? Watch out for them.

**3** Delayed emotion occurs after we have explored the situation fully.

During the pause for thought, the emotional response is adjusted, though not necessarily changed. For example, instead of blind rage, there may still be anger but tempered by a degree of understanding that will alter the final decision and the action taken. Value systems are the link between events and emotion. When a "blind" or conditioned emotional response is made, it is generally due to one of these values predominating regardless of others.

Pausing long enough to think first, does not change our values, but will alter our selection of which value we allow to influence our decision. There are four general groups of values.

**Personal values**: ego-image; security; pleasure; self-importance; sexuality; self-respect; privacy etc.
**Group values**: sharing; loyalty; belonging; contracts; membership; parenthood; etc.
**Moral values**; social customs; ethnic culture; the law; religious customs; rightness and wrongness etc.
**Human values** (relatively new): human rights; ecology; pollution; nuclear power; weaponry; health etc.

Look around your house in it you will find some simple indications of your own values. You might like to check them out. It is also interesting to discover which of the values you claim to hold dear, are not represented in the living space you see as most important to you.

# 4

## Improve thinking skills

Here are a few basic approaches to clear thinking:
**1 Pause to think**
For example, giving a friend bad news. Think carefully about the way you are going to present this information and anticipate what the reaction might be.

Pausing to think puts your friend in focus and helps you to clarify your own feelings.
**2 Collect the facts**
For example, before interviewing someone for a job. Collecting the facts and putting them in order puts the focus on the job in hand and what you want to achieve.
**3 Use thinking tools**
There are many tools available and you can invent your own. Here are a few examples.
**a** Sorting by using your own categories
For example, when deciding what is needed, such as how much income, you might use three categories: essential, desirable or nice if it happens.
**b** Getting a balanced view
For example, when trying to assess the relative values of several new ideas, you might check each feature of each idea as positive, negative or interesting.
**c** Tabling
It is useful to draw a table with a list of features and columns for each model when selecting an appliance. In this way, different models can be compared efficiently.
**d** Checking
For tasks that you have to undertake frequently, a check list is helpful. Checklists are best remembered if they make a rhyme or the initials of the words on the list make sense. A lecturer can utilize checklists to help remember the items to be included, similarly recipes, concepts, processes can be checklisted.

There are more thinking techniques in **Chapters Four** and **Five.**

# Can you spot the mind-snatchers?

Mind-snatchers come in all shapes and sizes, often when we are least wary. Some are within ourselves, others come from outside and dominate our thinking.

Sometimes, mind-snatching is temporary and soon a sense of reality is regained. On other occasions only a small part of your mind is stolen.

Mind snatching is not always unpleasant or dangerous; getting high may snatch your mind for a while and gives you a rest from more weighty mundane matters and falling in love is a wonderful experience.

**Have you a mind of your own**?
Mind-snatching occurs because we allow it to happen, usually because we want to belong somewhere. Then our minds become transfixed by the norms of our particular group and we come to believe in them with such fervor that we also believe we are always right. that, for instance, we are always the "good" side in wars.

Alternatively, we can change our minds to suit the company we keep. In this way we can still belong to a social group and be on the "right" side in any dispute. When a new fad, fashion or philosophy arises we can change our minds again and follow the new guru.
Once more we have allowed our minds to be snatched and we are no longer in charge of our own thoughts.

**How to handle the mind-snatchers**
**1 Live alone in the wild**
There are still a few places left on this earth where a person could be a hermit. Living entirely alone we could avoid the mind-snatchers. . . except, perhaps, inner irrational thoughts.
**2 Drop out and start another group**
Dropping out was popular in the 1960s, when new gurus and new ideas abounded. Those who sought freedom by dropping out of society realized they could not exist in a vacuum and had to create new rules.
**3 Stay put and drop into yourself**
Dropping in, means going inside yourself to discover freedom. People who drop in have compassion for themselves and other human beings. They have humor, open minds and accept total responsibility for how they respond to the world around them.

## SOME POTENTIAL MIND-SNATCHERS

There are many more that could be added to this list. Not all potential mind-snatchers are "bad", many are neutral but it depends how the message is put across and how discriminating you are.

| | |
|---|---|
| Alcohol | Logic |
| Advertising | Magazines |
| Authority figures | Mass hysteria |
| Current "bandwagons" | Movies |
| Books | Phobias |
| Comics | Popular beliefs |
| Cult figures | Prejudices |
| Deep resentments | Psychic phenomenon |
| Desperate needs | Radio |
| Dominating people | Television |
| Drugs and medicines | Tobacco |
| Emotional blackmailers | Sense of inferiority |
| Fashions | Sense of superiority |
| Food additives | Superstitions |
| Indoctrinations | Sympathy |
| Inner fears | Videos |
| Knotted thinking | |

## Responsibility

Responsibility is an attitude of mind, not an obligation, illustrated by the story of the three sisters.

Three sisters were looking forward to going to a party at the weekend. Unfortunately they all three fell ill and couldn't go.

The sister with a sense of superiority complained bitterly and was thoroughly grumpy and bad-tempered all weekend; she wasn't going to let a little sickness get a hold on her. By Monday, her fever was worse and she was angry with everyone.

The second sister, who usually felt inferior, moaned, sighed and hid herself in her room, analyzing her problems; she believed that her sickness was her own fault. By Monday she was pale, weak and needed urgent medical attention.

The third sister took responsibility for how she responded to the sickness and spent the weekend quietly resting, giving her body the best opportunity to fight the infection. She also soothed herself by listening to music, laughing at a book of cartoons and dreaming the day away. She enjoyed the experience and by Monday was fit and well again.

See **Chapter Two: Taking control over your phobias** (pp. 48-49) for further ideas on how to use feedback.

---

## SOME MIND-SNATCHERS AT WORK

### The president superstition

It has been a popular belief among some people that American presidents who took office at 20 year intervals since 1841 would all die in office.

Here is a list of such presidents

- 1841 William H. Harrison – died in office
- 1861 Abraham Lincoln – assassinated 1865
- 1881 William McKinley – assassinated 1881
- 1901 James A. Garfield – assassinated 1901
  Followed by Theodore Roosevelt
- 1921 Warren G. Harding – died 1923
- 1941 Franklin D. Roosevelt – died 1945
- 1961 John F. Kennedy – assassinated 1963
- 1981 Ronald Reagan – resigned to retirement Jan. 1989

Is the pattern predetermined, coincidence, part of a natural cycle of events, a symptom of political life or what? Make up your own mind. Ronald Reagan couldn't have allowed the mind-snatchers of popular belief to worry him, even though he was nearly murdered himself in 1981.

### The Indian rope trick

In the 13th century Marco Polo reported seeing the trick done in the court of Kubla Khan. The fakir, or magician, throws a rope up into the air which his boy assistant climbs. The boy disappears into a cloud and is heard to scream; shortly his severed head falls to the ground. The fakir puts the head into a basket and after a short while during which magic pipe music is played, the boy emerges complete from the basket.

The fakir is said to be able to levitate and cause others to levitate to order, using the power of his mind only. A true fakir claims also to be a master mind and can make people see visual hallucinations. Perhaps the fakir could be called a master mind-snatcher.

### The moving madonnas

Visions, apparitions and religious miracles are all very profound experiences, difficult to either prove or disprove. Personal experience of such phenomena is very convincing even to a non-believer.

The story of the moving madonnas began in February, 1985 when a party of school children saw the statues of Jesus and Mary move in the church at Asdee in Co Kerry, Ireland.

By September of that year, there were reports of 40 sightings of moving statues in shrines all over Ireland, the most famous being that of the Virgin Mary at Ballinspittle, Co Cork, which is said to have smiled, winked and swayed.

Such stories are called miracles by believers and mass hysteria (emotional suggestion) by disbelievers. Sceptics may consider both views to be mind-snatching and leave their minds open to future understanding.

### The Esso tiger

Advertisements affect us profoundly. A modern art form, they are proof that what we see on television affects us. Babies of barely two years of age have been heard reading words written in big, bright letters displayed on the screen and we all remember a jingle associated with some advert or other. Some people even use adverts for party games.

The tiger used for the Esso advertisements is known internationally and has been continuously effective for more years than virtually any other symbol used for a single product. It is the consistent use of the same basic image that has the profoundest effect. The Esso tiger has been seen in all kinds of situations and, although his color and shape have varied a little since the 1960s, he remains to this day, the Esso tiger and a supreme example of the most effective way to snatch minds. . . repetition in a variety of stimulating situations.

# Going beyond your mind barriers

Your mind has abstract, concrete and intuitive functions, the last of which includes those natural instincts with which you were born. During childhood you test out your intuitions and acquire many facts with which to operate in the real world; hence your concrete mind.

The concrete part of your mind is the Doubting Thomas and is your true body-mind. This mind knows what it sees, hears, touches or smells. This is your sensible mind, the one that does not play clever games.

This part of your mind does not put up barriers, it is the innocent mind you had as a growing child, that stays with you all your life. It is neither good nor bad; it is the lifeline that keeps you in touch with reality.

During the teenage years, most people begin to think in the abstract, i.e. to think about one thing when something else is happening. The concrete mind can only think about things as they are happening but the abstract mind can think about things past, present or future.

The abstract mind can do wonderful things, such as think up solutions to problems, think about other people, plan ahead and discuss memories. Because we can think in the abstract, we can also say one thing and do quite the opposite.

Abstract thinking enables us to erect barriers of inappropriate beliefs that make us unhappy, resentful or prejudiced or prevent us from fulfilling our dreams. These are the barriers that we have free will to remove on our way through life.

Our abstract minds can also dream up impossible ambitions and push our sensible, concrete thoughts aside. These, too, are barriers we can remove if we choose.

### What are the barriers in your mind?
Check the ones you put in your own way:
1 Because I fail at something I am a failure.
2 I just can't live without a lot of love; status; power; money; sex; admiration; a fast car; a fur coat; a pretty, young woman; a rich sugar daddy; my daily "fix" of . . . etc. Fill in your own words.
3 One day I'll show them, then they will . . .
4 I don't know how to . . . so I can't possibly do it.
5 I ought to keep my problems hidden.
6 I shouldn't have to work hard.
7 No matter what I do, I'll never make it.
8 It's all right for him/her/them . . . but me, I've really suffered.
9 If only she/he would change, then I'll be all right.
10 I ought to be good.
Think of each one you have checked as a wall you have built yourself through your mind and which your mind can just as easily demolish.

Write the opposite of the statements you have checked. In this way you begin to demolish your own barriers. For example, the opposite of 9 is: He/she doesn't have to change. I can accept them as they are and work from that point. Use your own wording; it will be more effective.

### Spotting removable barriers
Dr Jane Spence was newly qualified at 26 and she had ambitions to become a consultant surgeon. She also wanted to marry and raise a family.

Here we show her life as a pathway stretching into the future. There were several obstacles on the way. Some of these were barriers of Jane's own making which she removed by altering her thinking. Others were not of her making and she had to adjust her approach and her ambitions.

### How to proceed
Jane's fulfilled hopes and ambitions are shown in capitals and the obstacles are shown in lower case words. Each obstacle has a code letter. Check the code letters of the obstacles that you think were barriers in her thinking that Jane had to remove before she could proceed. There are also some alternative pathways open at varying points in her life; one or two are shown as examples.

### Which choice did you make?
The obstacles due to inaccurate abstract thinking, which could have been barriers to Jane's progress were:
**B** Going out to work does not make a woman a bad mother. Neglect is a mark of bad motherhood. Jane confused the two. She realized that she was in danger of using her maternal "guilt" to avoid being a success as both a doctor and a mother.
**E** Because a person fails a set of exams does not make the person a failure. Failure in any activity is an opportunity to learn how to improve. Nobody is ever a success who hasn't learnt from mistakes made on the way.
**G** Because a couple have problems does not make the woman a bad wife, nor the man a bad husband. Problems arise from differences in expectations. Discussion will show if the expectations can be modified to suit both partners, or if a separation would be better.
**J** The fear of not begin good enough eats away at most people from time to time. Doing what you can, the best way you know how and doing it with pleasure, is always more than good enough and recognizing differences in levels of talent is realistic.
**L** If you aren't getting what you want, it is easy to find an excuse such as discrimination. On the other hand, discrimination is a fact of life, so behaving as if it didn't exist might help other people forget about it too.
**N** Perhaps Jane was still fighting those abstract beliefs that a woman should be the one to look after an aging parent . . . fortunately she had a sensible partner who saw the advantage of taking early retirement to care for Jane's father himself.

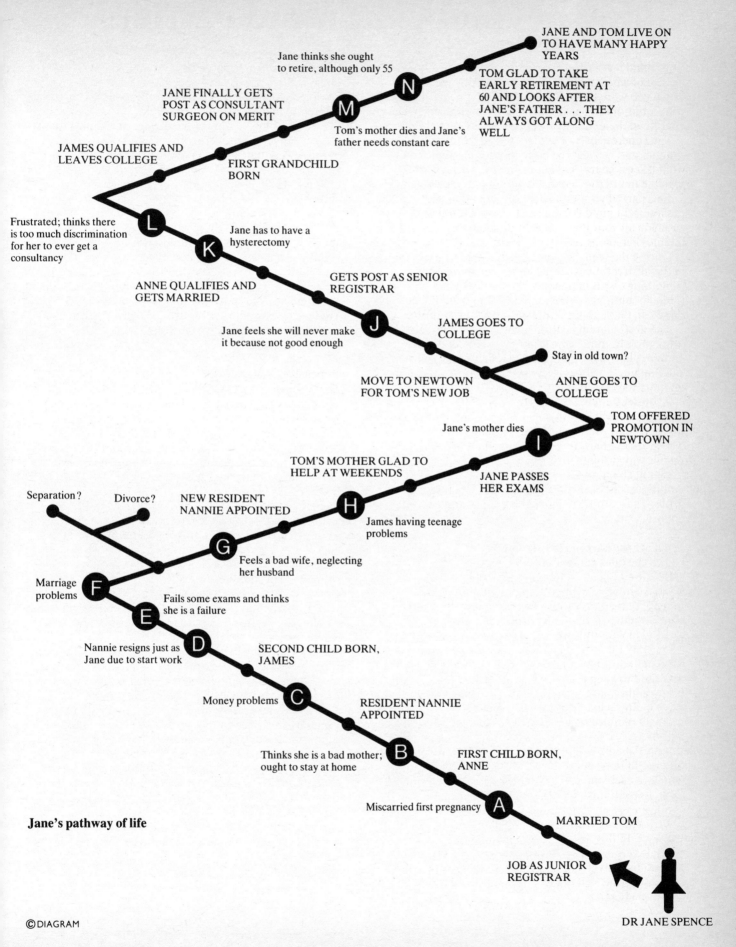

JANE AND TOM LIVE ON
TO HAVE MANY HAPPY
YEARS

Jane thinks she ought
to retire, although only 55

TOM GLAD TO TAKE
EARLY RETIREMENT AT
60 AND LOOKS AFTER
JANE'S FATHER . . . THEY
ALWAYS GOT ALONG
WELL

JANE FINALLY GETS
POST AS CONSULTANT
SURGEON ON MERIT

**N**

**M**

Tom's mother dies and Jane's
father needs constant care

JAMES QUALIFIES AND
LEAVES COLLEGE

FIRST GRANDCHILD
BORN

Frustrated; thinks there
is too much discrimination
for her to ever get a
consultancy

**L**

Jane has to have a
hysterectomy

**K**

ANNE QUALIFIES AND
GETS MARRIED

GETS POST AS SENIOR
REGISTRAR

Jane feels she will never make
it because not good enough

**J**

JAMES GOES TO
COLLEGE

Stay in old town?

MOVE TO NEWTOWN
FOR TOM'S NEW JOB

ANNE GOES TO
COLLEGE

TOM OFFERED
PROMOTION IN
NEWTOWN

Jane's mother dies

**I**

TOM'S MOTHER GLAD TO
HELP AT WEEKENDS

JANE PASSES
HER EXAMS

Separation?

Divorce?

NEW RESIDENT
NANNIE APPOINTED

**H**

James having teenage
problems

**G**

Feels a bad wife, neglecting
her husband

Marriage
problems

**F**

Fails some exams and thinks
she is a failure

**E**

Nannie resigns just as
Jane due to start work

**D**

SECOND CHILD BORN,
JAMES

Money problems

**C**

RESIDENT NANNIE
APPOINTED

**B**

Thinks she is a bad mother;
ought to stay at home

FIRST CHILD BORN,
ANNE

**A**

Miscarried first pregnancy

MARRIED TOM

**Jane's pathway of life**

JOB AS JUNIOR
REGISTRAR

©DIAGRAM

DR JANE SPENCE

55

# You can do the impossible

Sudden acts of courage always bring admiration. The person who dives into freezing water to save a drowning child; the one who breaks into a burning house to save a trapped family and those who stay cool and keep their heads while under threat…. These are people we all recognize as brave in the face of frightening, impossible situations.

Often such people do not recognize their acts as courageous. They would not call themselves heroes and heroines and nor do those amazing people whose daily lives are a series of less spectacular courageous acts. You may know one of them… people whose lives are productive and fulfilling despite situations that would overcome the faint-hearted.

If a person with many handicaps can overcome obstacles, how much easier it must be for those with fewer problems. Unfortunately this is not always true. The high level of concentration required to express even a moderate talent is difficult for anyone to sustain because life is full of distractions. A few people have become great achievers despite both a daunting handicap and these normal distractions; Christy Nolan and his mother are two such people.

BADER (LEGLESS PILOT) IS FRE[E]

The World War II British RAF fighter ace Sir Douglas Bader (1910-1982) overcame the loss of both legs before shooting down 22 German aircraft.

---

## MUTE, SPASTIC AND A WINNER

In 1987, the prestigious British Whitbread Prize for biography was awarded to Christy (Christopher) Nolan for his autobiographical book *Under the Eye of the Clock*. An extract from the work illustrates his talent, his literary wit and the difficulties under which he wrote it.

The book is written in the third person, about a character called Glee, who ". . . struggled to find and tip the required keys. Glee was gambolling but he had to be sure… Perhaps it won't happen to me today, he teased himself but he was wrong, desperately, delightfully wrong. Yes, he could type."

Christy Nolan is profoundly spastic and unable to speak. He lives in a wheelchair, his head supported and his arms awkwardly rigid. He is dependent on others for help in all the normal daily routines that most people take for granted.

He was born in 1967 to Bernadette and Joseph Nolan, who were farmers in the Irish midlands. Bernadette

almost died during the same Caesarean operation that is thought to have damaged her son at birth. His first three weeks were spent in intensive hospital care and when he went home there was no certain evidence of the seriousness of his physical handicaps, although doctors thought he would be retarded.

Bernadette disagreed, she knew instinctively that her disabled son was a bright lad and treated him accordingly. She tells how, when Christy was 18 months old, she decided to try toilet training. She said to him, "Look, you're getting to be a big boy. I'm not going to put your nappy on, and if you want the bathroom, you nod towards it and I'll take you. It doesn't matter if you wet yourself." Christy grasped the idea very quickly.

As he grew up, Christy devised a code of glances and jerky nods with which he communicated to his family. His parents and his sister, Yvonne, treated him as normal. They never answered questions for him and spoke with him as they did with each other. Strangers who ignored him and asked about him, for example,

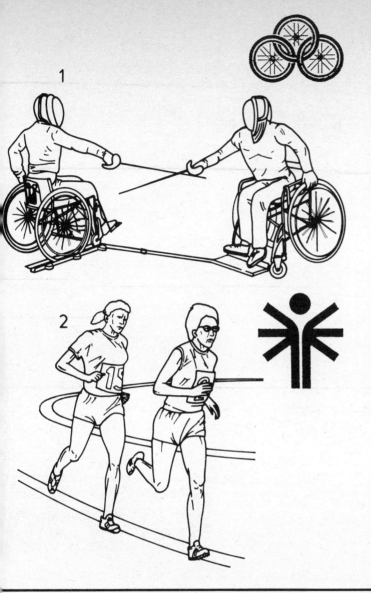

The remarkable achievements of handicapped athletes are an inspiration to us all:

**1** The Olympics of the Paralysed were founded in 1948 and are held annually at Stoke Mandeville, England. Now over 1000 paralyzed competitors from 45 countries participate.

**2** The Special Olympic Games first held in the USA in 1968 cater for mentally-retarded participants over the age of eight and with a maximum IQ of 80.

## Achieving the impossible: how is it done?

Once something has been achieved, it can no longer be regarded by anyone as impossible. Achievers never regard their achievements as impossible and get on with what they have to do without worrying about failure. They accept the consequences of their actions, learn from their mistakes and never waste time, resources or opportunity. Driven from within by a need to get something done, they do it, often inspiring others who work with them.

"does he take sugar?" were told to ask Christy himself. Another member of the family only intervened to translate Christy's side of the conversation when necessary.

Educational psychologists assessed Christy's intelligence as above average for his age and the family moved to a Dublin suburb so Christy could attend a special school. The greatest frustration Christy felt was not life in a wheelchair but his inability to communicate normally. Once he tried to suffocate himself with a pillow and by the age of nine he was crying himself to sleep at nights. Later he told his family this was because he could not tell anyone what he was thinking.

A wonderful breakthrough occurred for Christy when he was eleven. A new drug had been developed that enabled him to relax his muscles enough to bow his head at will. This small movement opened a whole new world of communication. At school, Christy had access to a typewriter suitable for use with a unicorn. Christy began very slowly to learn how to type using the probe strapped to his head. At first his teacher held his chin as he jerkily tapped each letter.

His first short sentences were about a family visit to see caves with stalagtites and stalagmites. Christy wrote about them in detail, even spelling the words correctly. Although unable to speak, he had been using his eyes and ears and could write and talk in his head. More writing followed, including some very witty poems.

Christy opted to go to a normal secondary school and attended Mount Temple Comprehensive School in Dublin, where he made many friends who often visited the Nolan household. At the age of 15 he completed his first book: *Dam-Burst of Dreams*. With this he won The Spastics Society literary prize and even then was being recognized as a major literary talent.

At home, his mother now works with him, helping to support his head as he works on his third book, a novel. It can take him several hours to write only one sentence. Such work requires enormous patience from both Christy and Bernadette.

# Casting the evils from your mind

There are at least three kinds of evil. That which you personally believe is evil, that which some other person believes is evil and things considered to be evil by the majority of people, such as the intention to do harm. The unknown can be frightening, so quite often we perceive as evil, things that we do not understand and are different from us.

What do you believe is evil? Are things intrinsically evil or only evil under certain conditions? Some of the things you consider evil will be universal beliefs and some will be personal.

## WHAT IS EVIL?

Here is an alphabetical list of occurences and activities that have been called undesirable, bad, wrong or evil by someone at some point in history. Clarify your own ideas about what is evil by checking which of these you believe are intrinsically evil. Cross out any that you consider should not even be included in this list.

There are no correct answers but you may like to discuss your choices with family or friends in order to clarify your ideas.

| | | | |
|---|---|---|---|
| ☐ Abortion | ☐ Contraception | ☐ Murder | ☐ Sexual desire |
| ☐ Adultery | ☐ Devil worship | ☐ Negligence | ☐ Smoking |
| ☐ Alcohol | ☐ Euthanasia | ☐ Nerve gas | ☐ Stealing |
| ☐ Ambition | ☐ Genetic engineering | ☐ Nuclear weapons | ☐ Swearing |
| ☐ Anal sex | ☐ Group sex | ☐ Occultism | ☐ Tax avoidance |
| ☐ Apartheid | ☐ Hatred | ☐ Oral sex | ☐ Torture |
| ☐ Bigamy | ☐ Hijacking | ☐ Organ transplantation | ☐ Vandalism |
| ☐ Blackmail | ☐ Incest | ☐ Pornography | ☐ Vivisection |
| ☐ Blasphemy | ☐ Indoctrination | ☐ Profit motivation | ☐ Witchcraft |
| ☐ Bullying | ☐ Kidnapping | ☐ Propaganda | ☐ Any others? |
| ☐ Capitalism | ☐ Masturbation | ☐ Prostitution | |
| ☐ Communism | ☐ Mugging | ☐ Rape | |

Caricatures (*left*) carried to extreme can be cruel and even mildly evil or at least thought to be so. This 1832 transformation of King Louis-Philippe of France into a pear by Honoré Daumier for the magazine *La Caricature* cost the artist six months in prison.

## Lycanthropy

In the mythologies of many countries, the transformation of a man or woman into an animal is commonplace. Most usually, the process that takes place is lycanthropy: transformation from man to wolf by the power of the imagination.

It is said that a man needs only to imagine himself to be a wolf and he will immediately begin to behave like one; his eyes will turn red, he will growl, grow hair and fangs and have a taste for fresh blood. A person able to transform himself in such a way was known as a werewolf.

Such transformations were considered to be the work of evil forces that included the devil. Vampires are transformations: a dead body re-animated by the power of imagination and with a helping hand from the devil.

## METHODS FOR CASTING EVILS FROM YOUR MIND

### Imagination

One of the most effective ways to cast out evil thoughts is by the use of the same imaginative powers that can generate evil.

After a hard day's work or a brisk walk, lie down quietly where you will be undisturbed. Make sure you will not become chilled. Then bring the evil thoughts to mind and turn them into a monster with which you do battle; you may fight hand to hand or with weapons, but whichever method you use, in the end you stand victorious and the monster is dead.

Another way is to imagine yourself carrying out the opposite of evil act. For example, if murder is the evil, then imagine yourself personally bringing the intended victim to life instead. As you do this, you will notice that something inside yourself comes to life too.

### Burning thoughts

This is an old and tried method that concentrates the mind, brings the evil thought to light and disposes of it as the ashes rise and disperse in the air.

Write your evil thoughts on a piece of paper; allow yourself to put them down in full detail. When complete, take a fire-proof dish, crumple the paper and place it in the dish with a few dried herbs or dry pine needles. Incense can be used instead of herbs.

Take the dish outside and light the paper. As it burns it will heat the herbs and pine needles; they will give off their perfume and help to release the thoughts from the paper and clean your mind.

### Laughing

Evil, depressing or sad thoughts can be transformed by humor. Try sitting in front of a mirror and laughing . . . you will find the reflection laughs too! If laughter is difficult, try taking several deep breaths, opening your mouth very wide and breathing out make the sounds: HA HA HA HA! Repeat this several times; soon you will be laughing spontaneously.

Even if you are too uptight to let loose of yourself, the breathing exercise itself will help you to relax.

When you have finished, lie down quietly for a while and let your mind dwell on pleasant thoughts. Having a new interest can help to displace negative thoughts and you can enjoy thinking about the new ideas as you relax.

NOTE: Do not confuse clinical conditions of the mind with evil. If someone has a depression or a mental illness they need medical or psychiatric help.

# How to use your healing powers

Healing by the intuitive laying on of hands has been common in many cultures throughout history. Warmth and stimulation through touch and massage reduce pain and accelerate the natural healing processes.

**Natural healing**
Whenever you are cured of a disease, it is your body's own processes that have fought infections; put you in temporary shock; made you rest; clotted your blood and provided the raw materials with which to knit broken bones; make new tissues and compensate for losses.

## HAND POWER

Faith healing laying on of hands

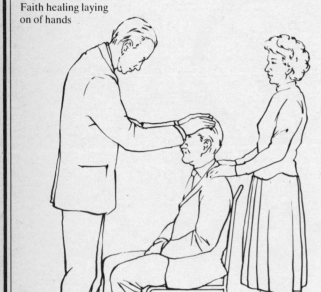

Masseur easing muscular tensions.

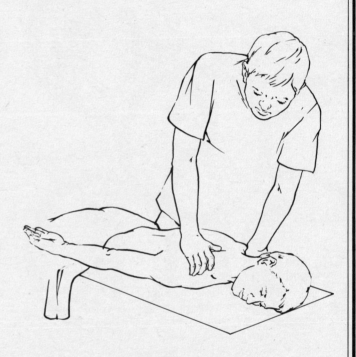

**Humanistic and paranormal healing powers** Many religious denominations believe that certain of their members have "devine" powers which they can transmit to a patient and produce healing effects.
**Metamorphic masseurs** use hand massage to rewaken prenatal energies.
**Faith healers**: Protestant and spiritualist healers use the laying on of hands to transmit healing forces.
**Therapeutic healers** use touch and the laying on of hands to transmit energy forces.

**Manipulative healing powers**
There are many different manipulative therapies, which are now established as alternative medical solutions to our mental and physical complaints.
**Aromatherapists** rub oils and aromatic essences into your skin.
**Osteopaths** manipulate your joints.
**Masseurs** rub and press your muscles.

**Rolfers**, (or Structural Integrators) use deep massage techniques on your body.
**Alexander principle practictioners** concentrate their massage techniques on re-adjusting the alignment of your spine.
**Feldenkrais technique practictioners** use manipulative body massage on areas of the body other than that effected.
**Relexologists** manipulate the soles of your feet to influence zones of life force in your body.
**Kinesiologists** use touch and stroking to relax tense muscular situations.
**Shiatsu masseurs** use a Japanese technique of applying pressure on your body with their fingers, fists, knuckles and elbows.
**Physiotherapists** use manipulative massage to increase your body's mobilty.

**Use your intuition**

Let your intuitive mind direct you. Do whatever self-massage makes you feel good. If you are giving massage, do whatever the person asks and only put on as much pressure as they find acceptable and pleasant. Remember, that your intuition works best for your own needs, not those of other people.

**Sports injuries**

Physiotherapists who have specialized in rendering first aid to sportspeople use manipulative massage to get the person mobile. They also know which areas may need extra support until further treatment is possible.

## MASSAGE POWER

Stroking stimulates the nerve endings in the skin. These in turn stimulate the brain and affect other areas of the body, relaxing and stimulating natural processes.

   Both the person being stroked and the one who is stroking will be positively affected, so gentle massage can be used in every day life for general good health. There are many ways of stroking and being stroked, in addition to formal massage methods. Here are some of the ways in which you can use your healing powers for yourself and others.

**Lying on a sheepskin rug** keeps the circulation moving and induces restful sleep.

**A hot and cold shower or a sauna** is stimulating and helps the general circulation.

**A jaccuzzi or other water massage,** such as rhythmic swimming, is a marvellously health-giving activity.

**A warm bath** is most relaxing and induces sleep… so don't stay in too long.

**Regular, steady walking** massages the muscles of the legs and keeps circulatory problems at bay.

**A morning stretch** gives you an internal massage to help keep you supple.

**Stroking a furry animal** reduces stress and the chances of heart trouble. A teddy bear is the next best thing!

**Foreplay** that includes a lot of gentle, loving strokes relaxes both partners, making sex more enjoyable.

**Clothes** that feel good against your skin gives you an all-day massage.

**A back massage** helps you to unwind after a day of tension. If you have no partner, try rolling gently on a rough towel or thick sheepskin.

©DIAGRAM

# Living in three worlds

Throughout history many cultures have recognized the existence of different worlds. One world that is different from the earthbound world of everyday life is often called heaven in a religious context and may be known as the spirit world in a secular context.

Some people believe that these two worlds co-exist and when we die, we leave the earthly world and take up full residence in the other world.

The third world is a dimension we can experience while on earth but is perceived as an out-of-this- world type of existence. It could be called a twin world, ie while you experience yourself as a bodily person, you can also experience yourself as a separate consciousness: a twin being.

To some people the dimension where the two worlds overlap is a place where we seem to hover between the earthly and the spiritual. To modern physicists it is the wondrous world of new physics, where particles of matter and particles of energy are one and the same.

In this strange, unseen world new experiences are available to us. Many different names are given to this world and to the twin-experience of being in it. Each name is special to the way a particular culture interprets these experiences.

## Some names given to the third, twin-like world
The psychic world of extra-sensory perception. The ka domain of the soul in ancient Egypt. The chi universe of subtle energy in ancient China. The ethereal world of celestial matter.

## Features of the twin world
This third dimension is not physical, nor is it subjective. It has space and time, although the rate of time changes. It is independent of the ordinary world and interacts with it.

## Some examples of experiences of the twin world
These can occur spontaneously but most need some preparation such as a course of meditation, diet, psychological catharsis or rituals of sound and movement.

1 Lightness of body and the physical body hovering above the ground with no physical support.
2 A movement away from the physical body which can be watched from a few feet away.
3 Seeing through solid things and through time and space.
4 Hearing sounds and music with no physical source.
5 A shift into another space where things appear clearer and sharper and reaction time is speeded up.
6 Suddenly the face of someone at rest appears changing, mobile and translucent.
7 Awareness of other worlds immediately on waking, before rememberance of the ordinary, everyday world flows back into consciousness.
8 A slip into a vortex spiralling upward and seeing the world across mountains and seas. A similar experience can be of being sucked through a tunnel to a place of great light and peace.
9 Seeing or sensing presences which are protective without being possessive or threatening.
10 Being completely at one with a part of the living world and recognizing the life force at work.

## Getting to the truth of the matter
Many other-world experiences are ambiguous; they may be explained as twin-world activities and they can also be explained as illusions, psychological conditions, deceptions and misunderstanding of ordinary experiences etc. People who frequently have twin-world experiences often acquire a clear awareness of the distinction between what is of this world and what is of another dimension.

For most people there will be a tendency either to accept all strange experiences as those of another world or to dismiss all such ideas as nonsense. The best way to examine what seems to be a twin-world experience is to examine it as it is happening.

Other world experiences cannot yet be proved; that does not mean they do not exist.

1 When having an other world experience, accept it, enjoy it and attempt to let it expand.
2 While it is happening, assume it could be another world or this world.
3 Be a witness to what is happening.
4 Afterward, record what happened but try not to interpret it. Be as specific as possible, for example, if there was a bright light, call it a bright light but don't assume you know its source. Speculate on the possible sources if you wish. In doing this, include ordinary world sources of light.
5 Remember that nobody "knows" there are other dimensions; they are a matter of belief, not provable fact.
6 Don't claim any superior powers. If you think you may, for example be clairvoyant, approach a reputable society for guidance.
7 Don't assume you are crazy, sick or evil. If you are worried, go to a reputable psychiatrist, doctor or religious counsellor and get a check up.

# METAPHORS OF THE THREE WORLDS

Many people have attempted to make art, music and objects that encompass the essence of the three worlds. For example, the three worlds are often combined in the design of handmade carpets, rugs, blankets and wallhangings.

## Carpets with which to fly

The magnificent Persian carpets, that were woven in the sixteenth and seventeenth centuries for palace walls or the floors of large houses, were called khali and were metaphorical pictures in miniature of the universe as it was thought to be.

The central design was often an eight-petalled flower or medallion (**a**) marking the center of the universe, the eight petals being the eight main compass directions. At the center of the center is a motif called the Skygate (**b**); this is a hole in the sky which is the gateway from earth to heaven.

The body of the carpet illustrates life on earth and life in heaven as concurrent (**c**). Sometimes the sun (**d**) and the moon (**e**) are shown as lanterns. Dark and light borders (**f**) represent both the succession of night and day and the existence in the same time band of two dimensions, which were called heaven and earth. The corner motifs (**g**) are the apertures in the sky through which the sun sets and rises at different seasons. Trellis work (**h**) on carpets is the lattice through which souls can pass to and fro from one dimension to another.

Carpets were always powerful metaphors and are revered as prayer mats especially in the Islamic religion. The weaving and knotting processes used to make carpets are themselves metaphors for the intertwined dimensions of life.

The making of carpets involved many people and was a meditative activity because the work required lengthy concentration and repeated movements. In this meditative state, the minds of the people doing this work may have wandered into the other dimension. It is not surprising, therefore, that carpets became a route to the other world and entered the storyteller's mythology as flying carpets. Flying has always been one of the great dreams of mankind, how better to fly than on the carpet that was itself a metaphor for the whole universe, both earthly and divine?

A Persian carpet design

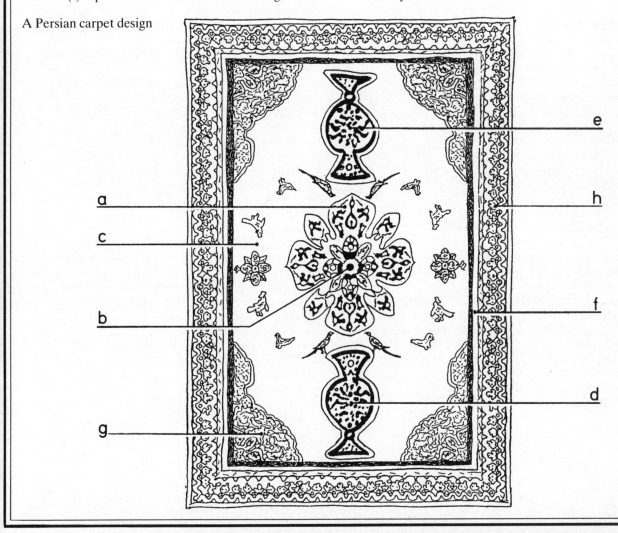

# Using blind power

Our sensory information about the world outside us comes via sets of specialized reception areas located in different parts of our bodies, such as the eyes, ears and nose. Each area is organized to receive a particular type of stimulus and send what is seen, heard or felt to the brain. The skin receives touches, the inner ear receives information about our position in space and helps us to keep a balance.

### Sensual perception

In any one person, some senses may be keener than others and some reception areas may need a little assistance. For example, a person might have excellent hearing but need spectacles for reading, while another person may have a poor sense of position in space and have a very sensitive and accurate sense of smell.

Sometimes the brain links certain kinds of sensory input, for example, there are people who can taste a shape, hear a touch or smell a color. This production of mental sensory impressions by the stimulation of another sense is known as synesthesia and is most commonly found as a link between sight and sound or sight and touch.

These synesthetic links are thought to be formed in the brain at an early age and may be genetically determined. Some people claim to have trained themselves to link colors and sounds; it may be that they have simply developed a latent ability or they are conditioning themselves to see a given color when they hear a given sound.

If you can see instantaneously certain colors when you hear particular sounds, or if you can identify colors by touch only, with your eyes properly blindfolded, then you are probably experiencing a synesthetic link. The perception of colors and shapes through the skin is called dermo-optical perception and may be a latent ability in many people.

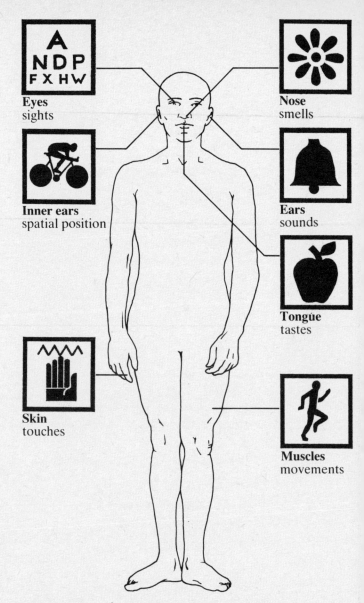

Eyes
sights

Inner ears
spatial position

Skin
touches

Nose
smells

Ears
sounds

Tongue
tastes

Muscles
movements

### Dermo-optical perception

Reading words or colors and shapes through the skin is quite common and would appear possible to learn.

Early this century the psychiatrist Cesare Lombrosco claimed that one of his female patients could see with the tip of her nose and the lobe of her left ear.

In the 1960s a Russian school teacher, Rosa Kuleshova, was being treated for epilepsy by a Dr. I. M. Goldberg. She told him she could read through her skin and he tested her, discovering she could read words and newspaper headlines through plates of metal.

Although she became discredited because of much pressure and the demands of the researchers and the media, it was due to her case that the Russians set up research centers and discovered other individuals who could read through their skins. Because Rosa could do it even without touch, it may be that dermo-optical perception is a form of extra-sensory perception, such as clairvoyance.

### How to teach yourself dermo-optical perception

Begin with colors, giving yourself regular sessions during which you try to read the colors from their feel. You will need a friend to help and a set of colored cards all the same size. Cover your eyes with a blindfold and ask your friend to select a color for you to touch. Remember that if you have, say, 10 colors, you have a 1 in 10 chance of being right by chance.

Another way to learn, is by collecting together a set of wooden blocks small enough to be held in the hand and painted in a variety of colors. In this way you can have several of each color and reduce the odds of being right by chance.

People who can read colors through their skin say that different colors feel different: red is said to be "warm, rough and sticky" while blue is "cold, smooth and slippery"

## Another view of sight perception

In 1945 two American psychologists, Viktor Lowenfeld and W. Lambert Brittain, published some research findings which indicated that there were two types of sight perception: visual and haptic. Their researches also suggested that about two thirds of the population used mostly visual perception and only about one third used haptic perception.

## Visual perception

A person using mostly visual perception will see an object proportionately and in its natural colors. The visual artist sees things logically, from one point of view in perspective and is concerned with the details. Anatomical accuracy is of paramount importance and the drawings show both perspective and detail.

Some activities that require good visual perception are accounting, electronics, writing, building, repair work, computer programing and map reading. Visual perception may be a function of the left brain.

## Haptic perception

The word haptic means touch; a person using mostly haptic perception will touch the object by sight. The quality of hardness, wetness, warmth, thickness, flexibility and heaviness will be important.

A haptic artist will draw impressions or even a caricature, emphasizing whatever characteristics "touch" him. For example, the bear is seen as big, soft and even humanized, and it is the head of the person that is most important.

Some activities that require good haptic perception are touch-typing, flying, dancing, rally driving and drawing caricatures. Haptic perception may be a function of the right brain.

## Double vision

An artist's drawing of a bear (circled *above right*) records the appearance of the creature and uses detailed line work to show its surface characteristics. Comic bears by illustrators of children's books and comics depict the bear as a human with human characteristics and features, a haptic method of observation. The bears are clothed or even drawn behaving like a small child.

©DIAGRAM

65

# Chapter Three

# POWERS OF PROPHECY

Your mind can be used to "see" into the future and interpret the signs of how life will unfold. Since time out of mind "seers" have used their intuitive mind powers to unravel the secrets of time.

This chapter introduces you to the methods used. They rely upon one of three different forms of mental skills: the interpretation of nature; the interpretation of random events; and the interpretation of personal physical attributes.

The first method uses mental abilities to read the messages of time in the stars, in communication with the dead, and in observation of natural events such as flames, flight of birds, or shapes of tea leaves in a cup.

The second method, the interpretation of random events such as the fall of cards; the throwing of dice, sticks, or stones; or the observation of a sequence of events which, taken in order, indicate future events.

The third method relies upon interpreting the features of our bodies, and from these features using our brain power to see future events. Readers of physiology examine our hands (palmistry), our heads (phrenology), moles on our bodies, and our dreams.

Whichever method you favor, understanding your mind power will help you master the skills of an inner sight.

**1** Interpreting the future by nature
**a** Pyromancy
**b** Superstition
**c** Geomancy
**d** Astrology

**2** Interpreting through chance
**a** Cartomancy
**b** Tarot
**c** Sortilage
**d** I Ching

**3** Interpreting through physical features
**a** Dreams
**b** Palmistry
**c** Biorhythms
**d** Metoposcopy

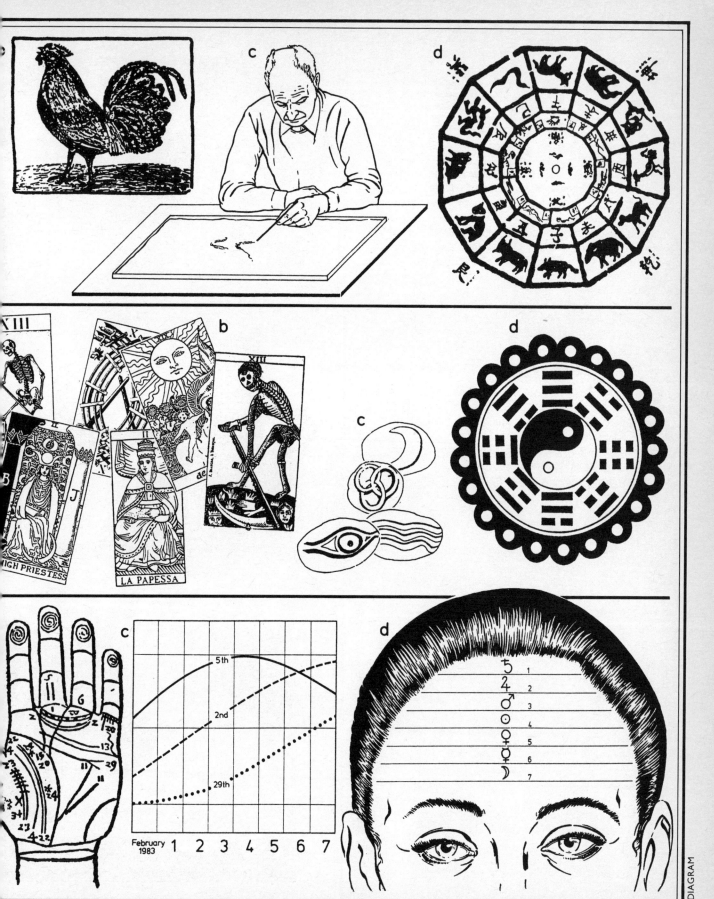

c

d

b

c

d

XIII

XIII

HIGH PRIESTESS

LA PAPESSA

c

5th

2nd

29th

February
1983    1  2  3  4  5  6  7

d

1
2
3
4
5
6
7

# Can you divine the future?

Divination is the art or science of discovering or prophesying what is going to happen in the future by studying signs or other indications and correctly interpreting their meaning.

Prophetic knowledge has always been sought; it would give us control over the unknown and the unexpected; perhaps we could even change the course of events.

A common way to be as sure as we can about the future is to plan what we want to do tomorrow, filling diaries with dates booked for this and that. Planning gives us a measure of control over uncertainty. We know that in reality anything can happen, so we try to determine our future by fixing a date for a wedding, a holiday, a conference or a visit to the zoo. Regular appointments offer even greater security and control over our destiny: a regular time to be at work; a weekly date with a friend; a monthly visit to see relatives; a six-monthly medical check-up or an annual holiday.

Another way in which we attempt to divine the future is by forecasting based on the past observation of trends such as the weather, market demands, fashion, the performance of competitors and the frequency of accidents. The discovery that some occurrences are cyclical is a useful aid to divination and commonsense tells us we can expect serious problems if, for example, we drive on bald tires.

Omens and superstitions about future events have been passed down from ancient times and many people believe in luck, fate or destiny while others are of the opinion that there is a logical explanation for everything.

## IS THE FUTURE DESIGNED?
What is the future and how is it determined? Here are some ideas that have been suggested up to the present.

### Fate

The future has been (or is continually being) determined by a totally impersonal set of circumstances, some of which may be logical but others are by sheer chance. Fate often seems purposeless.

### Evolution

We are part of a system of living things that act and react, urging onward, driven by the common desire to survive so all our futures are determined by a biological need to survive.

### The Gaia principle

The Universe is inhabited by a pervasive intelligence whose purpose is to expand, so the future is created in each moment. Human beings are not central in this intelligent world, simply one manifestation of it.

### The will of God

Very different religious orthodoxies state that the future is determined by an all-powerful deity. Believers may question why God lets certain things happen, but accept them as God's will.

### Karmic design

Each person is the vessel for a spirit that is living out a personal destiny according to the karma allotted to the spirit. Consequently, karma is regarded in Hinduism and Buddhism as a debt to be carried from one incarnation to the next.

### Human willpower

Some people believe the future is collectively in our own hands. We determine our own futures by how we willfully behave. We can use our will to power for good or evil; the responsibility is entirely ours.

## METHODS OF DIVINATION
In general, prophecies may be made from natural indications, by casting random fortunes or by seeking prophetic knowledge inside ourselves. Several of these methods are described in more detail in this chapter.

### Divination from nature

**1 Necromancy**
Or spiritualism: knowledge from those who have died.

**2 Astrology**
Reading the future from the positions of the stars.

**3 Common omens**
Observing natural events as indications of the future.

**4 Augury**
Consulting such occurrences as the flight of birds to discover the wish of the gods.

**5 Dowsing**
Locating hidden items

### Divination from random events

**1 Sortilege**
Divining the future by drawing lots.

**2 Runes**
Using the chance occurrence of symbols to prophesy.

**3 I Ching**
Throwing lots to decide which part of the I Ching (the Chinese book of wisdom) is applicable.

**4 Pyromancy**
Seeing the future in a fire or in rising smoke.

**5 Geomancy**
The future from sand trickling through the fingers.

### Divination from within yourself

**1 Palmistry**
Reading your personal future from your hands.

**2 Biorhythms**
Knowing physical, emotional and intellectual trends.

**3 Oneiromancy**
Understanding precognitive dreams.

**4 Clairvoyance**
Spontaneous prophetic visions.

**5 Scrying**
Reflected visions seen by gazing intently into crystal balls, mirrors, soap bubbles or the eyes of another.

# Using your biorhythms

The creation and discharge of energy by living things is a fundamental of biological theory. Early this century three human energy cycles were observed, lasting 23, 28 and 33 days. These were named the physical, emotional and intellectual cycles and are known collectively as biorhythms.

A biorhythm cycle can be shown graphically as a wavy line called a sine curve. Starting from the baseline on the day of birth, the wave represents the energy available for physical, emotional or intellectual activities. In the first part of the cycle, available energy rises to a peak; then it falls below the baseline to a trough. As energy is replenished it rises again to the baseline to complete the cycle.

## Positive and negative periods

A positive period occurs when the cycle is above the baseline; this is favorable for inspiration and high energy activities. The negative energy period occurs when the cycle is below the baseline; this time is favorable for slower and more pedantic activities. Biorhythms do not determine what will happen, they only indicate your probable disposition and can be useful when planning ahead.

## Critical days

These occur when a wave crosses the baseline in either direction; we are said to be at our most vulnerable on a critical day.

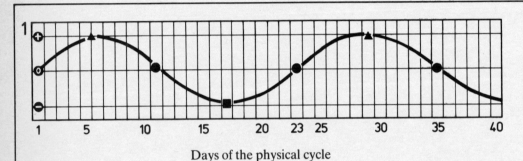

Days of the physical cycle

**1 Physical cycle**

| | |
|---|---|
| Length | 23 days |
| Peak day | 6th |
| Trough day | 17th |
| Critical days | 11th, 23rd |

Affects a broad range of physical factors such as fitness, coordination, speed, adaptability, resistance to disease, healing and all basic body functions.

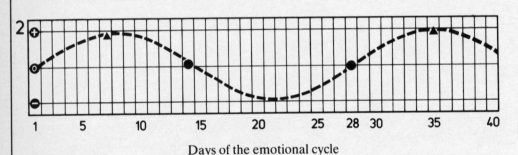

Days of the emotional cycle

**2 Emotional cycle**

| | |
|---|---|
| Length | 28 days |
| Peak day | 7th |
| Trough day | 21st |
| Critical days | 14th, 28th |

Affects emotional factors such as perceptions, attitudes, prejudices, sensitivity, moods and general mental health.

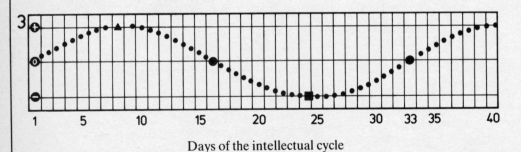

Days of the intellectual cycle

**3 Intellectual cycle**

| | |
|---|---|
| Length | 33 days |
| Peak day | 8th |
| Trough day | 24th |
| Critical days | 16th, 33rd |

Affects intellectual abilities such as memory, alertness, learning, generation of ideas and the analytical functions of the mind.

All three cycles are assumed to begin together from the same point on the baseline at the day of birth. Because they are of different lengths, it is only 58.6 years later that all three cycles rise together again from the same point on the baseline. However, once a year all three cycles cross the baseline at the same point. This is called a triple critical and is said to be a day when we should take extra care. At other times, any two of the three cycles may cross the baseline together, making that day a double critical.

## HOW TO CALCULATE YOUR BIORHYTHMS FOR TODAY

**1** Calculate how many days have elapsed since you were born. Your day of birth is counted as one day. Add one day for each leap year. (Divide your age by 4 to find how many leap years.)

**2** Divide the number of days by 23. The remainder from this division is the number of days you are into your physical cycle.

**3** Divide the number of days by 28. This remainder is the number of days you are into your emotional cycle.

**4** Divide the number of days by 33. This remainder is the number of days you are into your intellectual cycle.

NOTE if you use a calculator you will have a long decimal remainder. Multiply this remainder by the divisor and take the nearest whole number.

This method can be used for any date and can be used as a starting point for making your own biorhythm chart. To do this, trace the three cycles from this book and mark today's position on each one. Then superimpose all three cycles so that the marks you have made are all lined with today's date upon the blank chart.

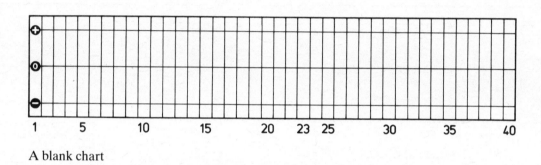

A blank chart

## BIORHYTHM CHART FOR NEIL ARMSTRONG, JULY 1969

Armstrong took off for the Moon on the 16th, landed on the 20th and made re-entry to Earth on the 24th. He would be most vulnerable on the three critical days up to blast-off but afterward his emotional and intellectual cycles were peaking, a perfect situation for the judgements and observations he had to make. His physical cycle was in a trough, advantageous for the slow movements required out in space.

**a** Take-off
**b** Landing
**c** Re-entry

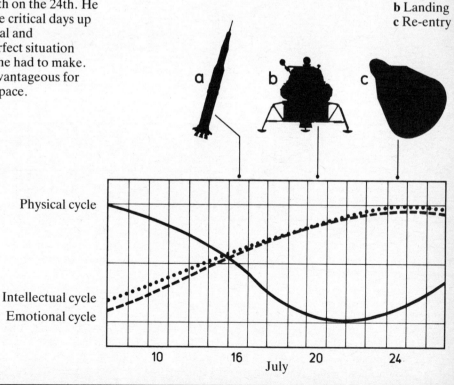

Physical cycle

Intellectual cycle
Emotional cycle

# Understanding your visions

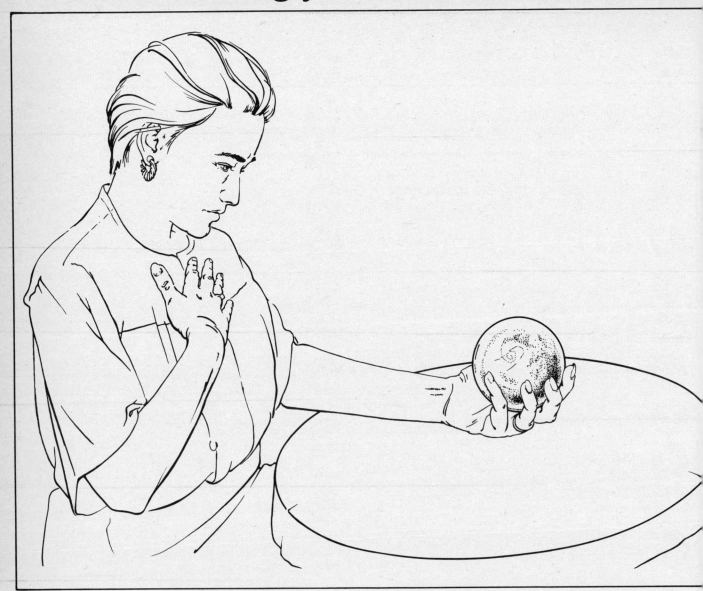

Visions can appear while gazing into a crystal or a pool of water. It is possible to see faces, events, times, places, dates and even written or printed messages. This method of divining the future is known as scrying and experts recommend a careful procedure.

### Preparing the crystal
Choose a quartz or beryl crystal sphere that is about 4in (10cm) in diameter. Wash it carefully with vinegar and water, polish it with a chamois leather or a piece of velvet and keep it wrapped up away from extreme temperatures until you want to use it. Never let anyone else touch your crystal and keep it away from direct sunlight. Moonlight is not harmful.

### Preparing the room
Choose a north-facing room when there is just enough light to read by. Place a small table in the center of the room and cover it with a black, non-shiny cloth. Place a chair by the table so that the window will be on the left and pin or hang a black cloth on the wall opposite your chair. Sit in the chair holding the crystal in your hand with the back of your hand resting on the center of the table. Some crystals are sold with a supporting plinth which can be used instead.

No more than two other people should be present and they should sit quietly away from the table.

### Using the crystal
Sit very still and quietly, emptying your mind and allowing your eyes to gaze at the crystal. You may need to spend time meditating before you try to read the crystal.

In the right conditions, the crystal should appear milky and will change through a range of colors until it becomes black. When the darkness rolls away, colors, shapes or symbols may appear which will need interpreting. Sometimes a sequence of events are shown, like a film, in which case no interpretation is needed, just say what is happening as you watch it.

## INTERPRETING THE SYMBOLS

 **White clouds** Good fortune

 **Black clouds** Misfortune

 **Rising clouds** A positive outcome

 **Clouds settled in the bottom** Hidden problems

 **Clouds on the right** Unseen help is near

 **Clouds on the left** You are on your own

 **Violet, green or blue clouds** Joy

 **Red, orange or yellow clouds** Dangers or difficulties

 **Anchor** Safety and security

 **Bird** A message

 **Crown** Responsibility

 **Eye** Take care to see the truth

 **Frog** A hidden advantage

 **Fruit** Children or creative pleasures

 **Globe** Travel

 **Heart** Love and caring

 **Lighthouse** Take care

 **Mask** Something is hidden; possible deceit

 **Scales** A judgement

 **Snake** Knowledge, health

 **Spider** Intuition will show the way

 **Star** Great success

 **Swords** A fight or a quarrel

 **Water-lily** A creative outcome

©DIAGRAM

### Vision or reflection?

In Greek mythology, Echo was a nymph who fell deeply and passionately in love with a handsome young man called Narcissus(*right*). Unfortunately, being an echo, all she could do was repeat his words so Narcissus soon grew tired of her, though in all other respects she was a perfect mate for him.

Narcissus rejected her totally and was punished for his lack of caring by one of the gods called Nemesis. The next time Narcissus gazed into a pool of water and saw his own reflection, he fell in love with himself and wasted away because he could not love another. It is said that a flower grew where he lay dying, which was called the narcissus.

This story is told as a warning to all who would try to divine the future by crystal gazing. Your visions may be of unseen futures or they may be only a reflection of your own desires. The regular practice of meditation will quiet the mind and leave it free and open to new knowledge.

# Is yours a seeing eye?

Knowing what what is going to happen, as it is in the process of happening, is called *déjà vu* (the French for "already seen"). If you experience *déjà vu*, you knew that a sequence of often trivial, ordinary events was going to happen, because it seems to have happened exactly in the same way before. If only you could have been fully aware, if only you could have grasped the reality when it first occurred, then you could have predicted events accurately. As it is, your awareness that you knew, occurs only split seconds before it happens. This experience of *déjà vu* is a very common occurence and could be regarded as instantaneous prophecy by hindsight.

## Second sight
More mysterious is when a person spontaneously sees (and sometimes hears, smells or touches) a specific event or a change of circumstances, days, weeks or months before it happens. This seeing eye that sees the future in the present is often called second sight.

Second sight is aptly named because it is a double experience. As an event is taking place in the present, the person who "sees" may have two perceptions of that event. One is the present and the other is the future. For example, a boy is walking along a beach throwing sticks for his dog. Every detail of how they appear and what they are doing is very clear. The person with second sight sees every color, every movement and each pattern of light and shade as they move along the beach.

Second sight occurs when a second, less clearly defined perception occurs of the same beach and the same person but with something else happening. For example, the boy may be seen as a very unhappy young man jogging along the edge of the sparkling sea toward a boat lying on the shingle. A person is standing in the boat smiling and waving. At this point the second sight may fade.

The prediction may be that at a time when the boy is older and very unhappy, there will be a person waiting to help, a person he will meet on the beach when he is at his lowest ebb. In the future, if it was true second sight, the scene will occur as forseen.

The most commonly reported second sight experiences are from people who have seen a major natural occurrence taking place which has not yet happened, but does happen at a later date in exactly the same place and same way. In some cases the timing is also correctly predicted.

To the seeing eye, the present and the future appear to coincide for a few moments. Second sight is a random observation of a future event or set of circumstances. Often the person with the second sight is not directly or intimately involved with the people or events forseen. However, anyone who has second sight, has also a very clear and accurate perception of the reality of the present.

## How to develop your seeing eye
It is said that at least a third of all human beings are capable of using their second sight to good effect. If you have this talent, but it is undeveloped a little practice is needed to sharpen the clarity of your random perceptions. You should remember that the seeing eye usually sees when least expected and is unable to choose what to see, so beware of your own desires getting in the way of your second sight.

## How to increase your powers of observation
There are some exercises you can do, which are a delight in themselves, even if it turns out that you do not have second sight.

## THE CAMERA WALK

You will need a friend with whom you share mutual trust to do this exercise.

To gain in confidence, you should begin where there are likely to be few people and no hazards from traffic. A garden or a museum are good places to start. You and your friend should take equal turns at being the "camera" and the "guide"; 15 minutes each is enough in the beginning.

### How to proceed

**1** Agree who is to be the camera and who the guide.
**2** The role as guide is to guide your friend around the garden or museum, selecting interesting views, close-ups and unusual angles for your friend to see. When you have positioned your friend you tap him/her on the shoulder, letting them "take a shot" of the selected view. Try to vary the distance, color and type of objects seen.
**3** The role as camera is to close your eyes and allow yourself to be led into position. When your friend taps your shoulder, you open your eyes briefly, just like the shutter on a camera, and close them again. Each "photo" that you take in this way leaves a strong impression and it is better if neither of you talk or discuss what is happening. You may wish to take a second shot of some views.
**4** When 15 minutes have passed, change roles and again in another 15 minutes, so that you gain in confidence (and imagination).

If a group of four or more friends do this exercise together, then it is very exciting to have some "shots" of each other.

Brief, limited impressions help to improve clarity of perception by cutting out the before and after and concentrating on one brief moment of exposure. Just as in a photograph a bird may be caught in a moment of flight or a fleeting expression registered on somebody's face. The angle or the flash of light on an object can be caught during this exercise and many things noticed that would otherwise be lost.

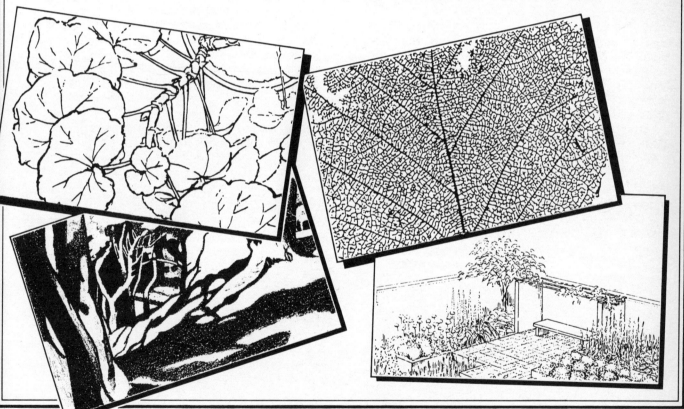

### Enjoy your perceptions

The camera walk can be extended when on your own, by closing your eyes while sitting or standing watching something happening or while viewing pictures in a gallery. In this way you can collect many pictures to recall and enjoy at a later date . . . pictures of flowers of sports in action or of a child at play.

If you have a talent for second sight, it will appear as you increase the acuity of your visual perceptions. It cannot be forced and any attempt to try and make it happen will always fail. Second sight is said to be a gift, if you have it, use it well. If it happens that you have not been endowed with this gift, use the great and wonderful gift of "first sight" to its fullest extent to unlock the power of your mind to see reality in its presence.

# Taking control of your dream worlds

Researchers have discovered that four dream periods per night is the average for most people and those who normally cannot remember dreaming are able to recall dreams when awakened from sleep during a period of rapid eye movement (REM). Dreams occur in the REM periods, approximately every two hours during a night's sleep. A regular and large intake of alcohol depresses REM sleep and consequently may deprive a person of dream periods.

**How to recall your dreams**
For dreams to be useful, they need to be remembered in some detail.
1 Keep a notebook and pen by your bed. Record anything you remember immediately on waking.
2 While relaxing in bed, just before going to sleep, repeat over and over to yourself: "When I awake, I shall remember a dream".
3 If you wake during the night aware of even a scrap from a dream, write it down immediately; don't wait until after a call to the bathroom, you will forget.

4 If, after several weeks, you have no success in recalling dreams, you may resort to asking your partner to awaken you during a REM period. This involves the partner observing when your eye-balls are moving about during sleep and waking you up to ask what you were dreaming.

If you have no partner, you can awaken yourself with an alarm clock. Set it for two hours after you go to sleep and then vary the time just more or just less than two hours until you find the best time to catch yourself during an REM period, i.e. a dream period.

**Selecting your dreams**
For the purposes of prediction or using your mind powers to best advantage, not all dreams are useful and mistakes can be made if you assume all dreams are of equal value. First you must learn to recognize important dreams by distinguishing between the different types of dreams.

---

**ELEVEN TYPES OF DREAM**

Researchers identify the following distinct types of dream, although several may be combined in one dream episode. Try to recognize your own dream patterns. Any dream accompanied by very strong feelings usually indicates a conflict in everyday life that needs to be resolved. The 11 types fall into two groups:

**Dreams that cannot be controlled**

1 **Physiological dreams** reflect the workings of your body for example, sexual dreams and pregnancy dreams; or the needs of your body, for example thirst, the need for warmth or the need to urinate.

2 **Contrary dreams** are temporary and form a balance during periods of great sadness, happiness or excitement. For example, during a period of grief, dreams may be almost comic.

3 **Residual dreams** finish off the day's affairs and sort out the trivia of everyday life.

4 **Vigilant dreams** keep you aware of the environment around you as you sleep. For example the sounds of passing traffic or the alarm clock ticking may be included in a dream.

5 **Insight dreams** may give a flash insight into your current hidden motives. These dreams are often brief and difficult to recognize, since we usually do not want to know that we may have hidden motives which could clash with our overt intentions.

**Dreams over which you can usefully exert control**

1 **Nightmares** represent your deepest and often most irrational fears, conflicts or evil desires.

2 **Recurring dreams** are often long-term or dreams of the same events or image repeated several nights in a run or over and over again at intervals across the years.

3 **Wish-fulfilling dreams** reveal your deepest hopes and yearnings.

4 **Sequential dreams** are a series of dreams in which a new instalment happens each night or each week.

5 **Transforming dreams** in which you change things or are changed represent a desire to assert yourself and may not have any connection with the subject matter of the dream.

**The problem-solving dream**
This is the 11th type of dream and reveals solutions to problems. This is likely to occur after a period of self-suggestion before sleep and would indicate that your attempts to control your dreams are working.

## CONTROLLING YOUR DREAMS

There are two ways to exert control:
1 By understanding the meaning of a dream
2 By choosing what to dream about.

### Interpreting dreams

Never tell your dream to another person until you have interpreted it yourself. Proceed as follows.
1 Write down every detail of your dream exactly as it happened.
2 Retell your dream to yourself, using the first person to describe each person, object and event, for example:
Speaking as a man in your dream: "I am a man walking along stepping stones in a storm."
Speaking as the stepping stones in your dream: "I am a set of solid stepping stones across a bog."
Speaking as the storm: "I am a storm raging. I see a man crossing the bog; I will flash my lightning at him . . ." etc. As you speak for each part of the dream, the meaning becomes clear. Allow yourself to express all the ideas that occur to you and describe each part in your own words. For example: I am a tall/short/happy/sad/angry/lost man. Use descriptive words that seem to fit and they will be the correct ones.

As you retell the dream, its meaning will become clear and less puzzling, worrying or frightening. This process is called "gestalting" or finding the whole meaning.

### Choosing dreams

By using self-suggestion as you fall asleep, you can change the ending of a recurring or sequential dream or you could change the nature of nightmares or other disturbing dreams.

For example, a very common and often frightening dream is the dream of falling. To change this dream, use self-suggestion as you relax into sleep, with words such as "when I am falling I will turn into a great bird and soar effortlessly across the sky, choosing where to land."

Alternatively you could suggest that you will turn into a feather and float down gently to the ground.

### To induce problem-solving dreams

Take a little time to examine all the facts of the situation before you go to bed. Get the facts clear in your mind and list them on paper. If you have any strong feelings that you think may interfere with the process of finding a solution, include them as facts in your list.

When you retire to bed, take the list with you. Read them aloud to yourself and then suggest to yourself that a solution will be found while you sleep. Then relax deeply, perhaps by taking a few deep breaths and allowing yourself to let go as you lie in bed. It may take some time to find a solution, but your mind will work on the problem unconsciously while you sleep and while you are awake. In a little while, a solution will occur, either in a dream or as a sudden flash of insight when you least expect it.

# How to become a dowser

Holding the forked branches of a small twig (**A**) an old man walked slowly to and fro over the bare ground of the desert. He concentrated, in a relaxed manner, on watching the twig, which he was holding quite lightly, the forked branches bent away from their parent branch. Suddenly the twig began to move up and down (**a**) and the man stopped to push a marker into the ground. Then he continued walking. He pushed markers into the ground whenever the twig reacted.

Eventually he declared that digging should start in the area surrounded by the markers. The workmen who had been watching thought it would be a waste of time. They did not believe it was possible to divine the location of water . . . but the old man's prophecy was true. A few feet below the dry surface the ground was wet and as they dug deeper a spring of water soon filled the hole.

This story occurred in a Californian desert in the 19th century but it is a story common to many places. The method the old man was using is called dowsing, which probably dates back to at least 6000 BC. Dowsers appear in many ancient Egyptian, Chinese and Peruvian carvings.

Dowsing has been used to find water, metals and some people have tried, unsuccessfully, to find oil by this method. Twigs react to the presence of water while a dowsing rod made from metal gives a more sensitive reaction, especially when searching for underground wires and cables.

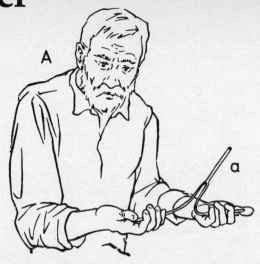

**How to use a dowsing twig**

If using a twig, hold it with palms upwards and thumbs outwards. Your thumbs should just touch the ends (**B**) and both the twig and your forearms should be horizontal. Your elbows should be kept close to your body so that you can keep your arms steady and pull the twig apart until it is slightly tense and well-balanced. As you walk slowly, using short steps, concentrate your mind on the substance for which you are searching, such as water. The twig will bend up or down or may rotate when it is above the water. Be methodical and use markers to indicate places where the twig reacts.

## MAKING A METAL DOWSING ROD

Two metal coat hangers should be cut in the places shown (**1**) and the hooks discarded. The two bent pieces of wire should be gently eased so that the angle is a right angle (**2**) and the arms remain straight. The rods can then be held in the hands as shown (**3**). A sleeve to hold the rod would be a refinement (**4**) and these can be made by removing the stopper from the empty refills from ball-point pens.

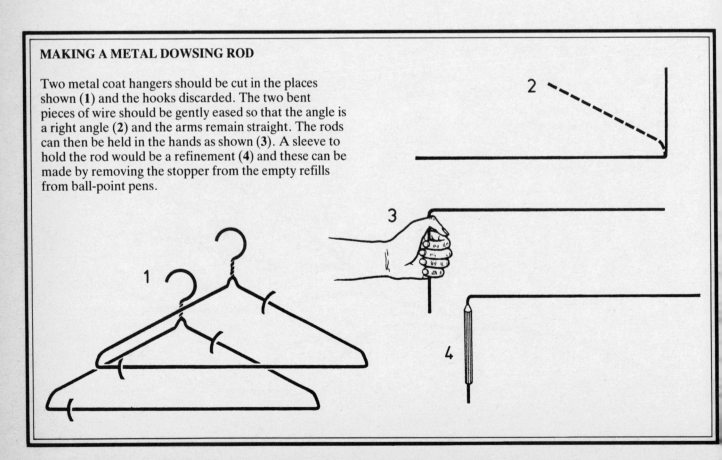

## How to use metal dowsing rods

Hold the rods in your fists with your thumb on top of your fingers. Keep your arms and the rods horizontal and parallel with each other (**C**). Tuck your elbows in and walk slowly. The rods react by swinging from side to side and may cross over each other. Metal rods can be used indoors to detect the layout of wiring under the floorboards or outside to detect the layout of underground cables. Spring water or pipes can also be found. With experience you can judge how much water and how deep down it is by the strength of reaction of your rods.

## PREPARING A DOWSING TWIG

The dowsing rod was traditionally a twig of hazel but beech, apple, birch or privet will all do the job. Choose a supple but not green branch and look for an undamaged Y-shaped twig about ⅜in (1 cm) in diameter and even throughout its length. Cut it from the branch as shown (**1**) and using a sharp knife, trim the ends but don't remove the bark (**2**).

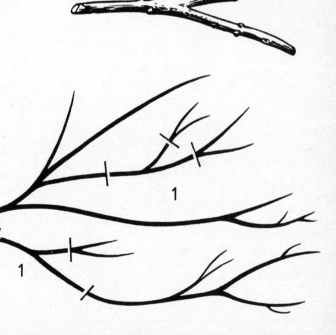

# Are you a medium?

Assuming that our consciousness is our spirit and that it leaves the body at death to begin an independent existence, the question arises: can there be any communication between the living and the spirits of those who have died? Spiritualists believe this communication can and does take place. However, because most people are unable to receive direct messages from the dead, communications are relayed via a medium.

The National Spiritualist Association of Churches define a medium as a person whose body is sensitive to vibrations from the spiritual world and is thus able to receive messages from those who have "passed over" from life into the next world. Quite often these messages may be relayed via a spirit guide. Everyone is said to have several spirit guides, each one for a different purpose, for example, healing, learning, making decisions, etc.

A few people discover they are natural mediums, while some need lengthy training and others have no mediumistic abilities at all. Similarly, some disembodied spirits can more easily communicate than others.

---

## TEST YOUR PSYCHIC POTENTIAL

Do you have the basic talent to become a medium? Psychic abilities, like all human abilities, can be developed if you already have a natural inclination. To find out if it would be worthwhile approaching a spiritualist church to be trained as a medium, first take this test; it will tell you if you have the potential to become a medium.

### How to proceed

1 Read each statement. Mark those which you think are false with a cross in the appropriate column of boxes.
2 Read all the unmarked statements again and tick in the true column the boxes that you are sure are true for you. If in any doubt, leave the box blank.

### Interpreting your final score

**Under 16 points**
You either have no natural psychic talents or are so biased against psychic phenomena that you are unreceptive. You probably have some strong analytical and researching talents which you could more usefully develop.

**16-29 points**
The higher your score the more likely it is that you have psychic talents, especially creative or intuitive abilities, although it is doubtful if they extend to mediumship unless your score is close to 29.

**More than 29 points**
You have some psychic talents and an open mind on the subject. You have the personality to develop mediumistic abilities and may already be using such talents.

Your next step might be to consult an experienced spiritualist with a view to discovering if you can usefully develop this talent, perhaps through a well-known spiritualist church or a professional spiritualist society.

| True | False | |
|---|---|---|
| ☐ | ☐ | I can communicate telepathically |
| ☐ | ☐ | Money or status are not particularly important to me |
| ☐ | ☐ | I prefer spontaneity to making plans |
| ☐ | ☐ | Psychology is a fascinating subject |
| ☐ | ☐ | Other people find my personality attractive |
| ☐ | ☐ | A positive attitude helps the healing process |
| ☐ | ☐ | I may occasionally feel guilty, but never for long |
| ☐ | ☐ | Some people make their presence felt after death |
| ☐ | ☐ | Clairvoyance can be used to locate lost property |
| ☐ | ☐ | A secure nest makes me feel trapped |
| ☐ | ☐ | There is some form of life after death |
| ☐ | ☐ | My intuition is usually correct |
| ☐ | ☐ | I have correctly predicted several events |
| ☐ | ☐ | Hypnosis interests me |
| ☐ | ☐ | I am interested in astrology |

**Seance**
A seance is a gathering of interested people during which a medium attempts to make contact with a spirit. Quite often the medium goes into a trance and speaks with a voice not his or her own.

True False

☐ ☐ Rarely am I on time for anything

☐ ☐ I have, or would like to, consult a medium

☐ ☐ Long-term planning may be necessary but it's boring

☐ ☐ I am happiest in wide open spaces

☐ ☐ Esoteric ideas are really interesting

☐ ☐ I love all imaginary worlds and legends

☐ ☐ Mental powers can cause objects to move

☐ ☐ I have had the experience of *déjà vu*

☐ ☐ My consciousness sometimes separates from my body

☐ ☐ I believe in ghosts

☐ ☐ My dreams are easy to remember

☐ ☐ I enjoy the company of other people

☐ ☐ Nobody makes me feel inferior

☐ ☐ I believe I am free to do whatever I want to do

☐ ☐ I often truanted from school

True False

☐ ☐ Some people are natural mediums

☐ ☐ I am not a superstitious person

☐ ☐ Untidiness does not upset me

☐ ☐ I think I have some psychic healing power

☐ ☐ Many people have a sixth sense

☐ ☐ I can easily lose myself in an activity

☐ ☐ I can speak in public with confidence

☐ ☐ Living alone would present no problems to me

☐ ☐ I am confident in my abilty to learn

☐ ☐ I can imagine smells, touch, sights and sounds

**Scores**

☐ True

☐ No response

☐ **FINAL SCORE**

**1** Add up the ticks in the true column and write the number in the true score box.
**2** Add up the number of unmarked boxes in the true column. Halve this number and write the result in the no response score box.
**3** Deduct the no response number from the true number and write the result in the final score box.
**4** Read the interpretation for your final score opposite.

©DIAGRAM

# How to read natural indications

The four elements of air, earth, fire and water were used in ancient times to divine future trends and many complex routines were developed. Gods or spirits became associated with each form of prophecy and many of today's popular superstitions have their roots in these ancient rituals.

In Europe, an east wind is said to blow no good for anyone. Some people say it warns of disasters to come, others say it heralds the death of a king, but are these only superstitions? Modern weather forecasters may be inclined to agree that an east wind across parts of Europe is an indicator of unpleasant things to come, such as extremely low temperatures and snow storms. As everyone knows, bad weather always brings

---

## READING NATURAL INDICATIONS

Each element is said to be associated with one of the four different aspects of thought, i.e. intellect, imagination, commonsense or emotions. Questions should therefore be addressed to the appropriate element.

### How to formulate questions
More accurate readings are given if the question is clearly unambiguous and can be answered YES or NO. For example, when enquiring about an auspicious date for an event, ask a series of questions.
**Question 1**: Would the best time for . . . be after May?
**Answer**: No. (Which means either the best time would be before May or there is no good time predictable.)
**Question 2**: Would the best time for . . . be before May?
**Answer**: Yes. (Now you can begin to eliminate periods of time to arrive at the best possible prediction.)

### The element of air (associated with intellect)
**Letting the air decide**: Take two identical pieces of paper. Color one of them black or blue with a pencil or biro. Stand by an open upstairs window holding the two pieces of paper above the ground. Ask a friend to stand beneath the window.

Concentrate hard upon your question about future trends which should be asked in such a way that can be answered as YES or NO, then let go of the papers. If the colored paper touches the ground first, the answer to your question is NO; if the uncolored paper touches first, the answer is YES.

### The element of water (associated with emotions)
**Counting ripples**: Stand by a perfectly calm pool or use a large bowl of water. Concentrate on your question and toss a small pebble into the center of the pool or bowl. Count the number of ripples that are formed from the center. An odd number, and the answer is YES; an even number, and the answer is NO.

### The element of fire (associated with imagination)
**Pictures in the fire**: Sit quietly in front of an open fire until only glowing embers remain. Throw a handful of salt onto the embers, which will burst into flames. When the flames have died down gaze carefully at any shapes you see there, interpreting them as your current concerns. After 15 minutes, if you have seen nothing, wait for at least 24 hours before trying again.
**Animal** Opportunities at work
**Bird** Waiting for a message
**Building** You are happy
**Circle** Your family or friends
**Clover** Money, prosperity
**Face** Concern about a person
**Flowers** A disappointment
**Hand** You want to make contact
**Heart** Love or your loved one
**Mountain** Plans ahead
**Ship** Travel, journeys, changes
**Steps** Sexual concerns
**Tree** You want to expand or express yourself

### The element of earth (associated with commonsense)
**Geomancy**: This method, used by the Navaho Indians, requires a flat space of ground sheltered from strong winds and some dry sand or dry earth. A sand tray could be used indoors. The method was said to be most reliable when used on the eve of the new moon.

Take a handful of dry sand and hold it about an arm's length above the ground while clearing your mind of all thoughts. Then allow the sand to slowly trickle through your fingers onto the flat surface below. The shape or shapes made by the sand should be interpreted as shown. These indications are for the person who held the sand and were generally thought only to apply to the "visible" future, which was one moon cycle of 28 days.

its own disasters.

Many people maintain that if we learnt to read the changes in the state of the natural elements more accurately, we would be able to foretell future trends. The methods listed here may or may not give accurate predictions but they will certainly increase your powers of observation.

A  Great good fortune
B  Travel, movement, relocation
C  Help available from other people
D  Gains or acquisitions
E  Successful contracts, meetings, agreements
F  Limitations and restrictions
G  Sadness, disturbance, upset
H  Happiness, pleasure, contentment
I  Surprises, the unexpected, changes
J  Difficulties, problems, bad luck
K  Stability, progress, satisfaction
L  You need to rest quietly for a while and do nothing

©DIAGRAM

# Using the speaking stones

In many ancient cultures, pieces of wood or pebbles inscribed with the symbols or seals of the spirits were used to ask questions and divine future conditions. The ancient Nordic runes have the seals of 25 different spirits carved on them; the 26th stone is left blank and represents fate.

A set of runes can be purchased from specialist suppliers or you can make a set by copying the symbols onto small rectangles of a tough cardboard. The table shows their modern names and meanings. The second interpretation is used when the runes are reversed.

## How to proceed

Turn all the runes face down and mix them while concentrating on the question you are asking. Select any three rune stones and place them face down in a pile on top of one another.

Turn the top rune face up and compare it with the drawings of runes; the interpretation applies to the past. The middle rune applies to the present and the bottom rune to your best policy in the future. If the rune is reversed when you turn it over, read the second interpretation.

## Another way to use the stones

Rune stones can be used to enquire about the year ahead by mixing the stones thoroughly then placing one stone on each of the 12 spaces, one for each month.

To interpret, begin with the stone on the current month. Turn the rune stone face upward and write its meaning in the space. The name of the stone will give a clue to the particular area of life you have selected. For example, if you happened to select 19 FAMILY, then all subsequent interpretations should be related to your family situation. When you have completed all 12, you will have a comment on the year ahead, relating to the subject indicated by the stone' for the current month.

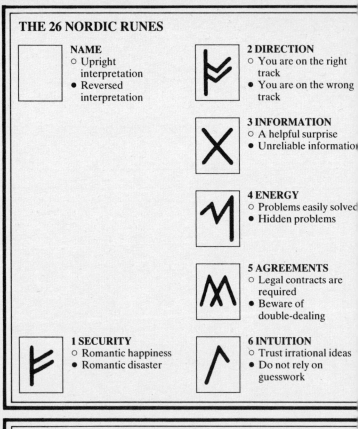

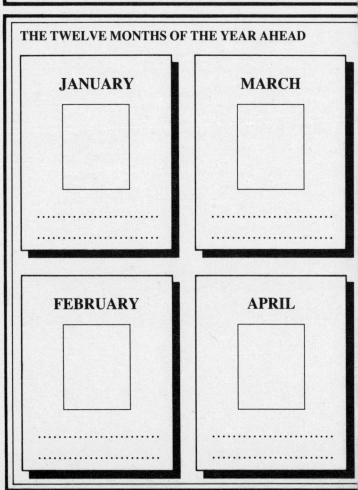

**7 STATUS**
- ○ An advantageous position
- ● A lost opportunity

**8 JOURNEYS**
- ○ Visits, travel, changes
- ● Restrictions hamper changes

**9 SUCCESS**
- ○ Just now you can't fail
- ● Delays cause frustration

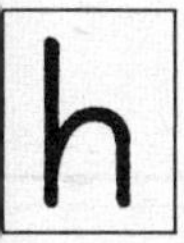

**10 CREATIVITY**
- ○ A flash of sheer genius
- ● Your view is prejudiced

**11 SELF-EXPRESSION**
- ○ Joy, love, ecstasy
- ● Sadness, grief, dejection

**12 WORDS**
- ○ Mutual understanding
- ● Communication problems

**13 TIME**
- ○ Delays increase problems
- ● Time is being wasted

**14 AGE**
- ○ Wisdom and good judgement
- ● Mistakes due to inexperience

**15 OPPORTUNITIES**
- ○ Grasp all opportunities
- ● Avoid temptations

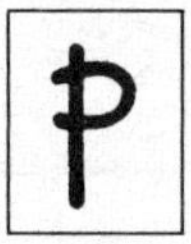

**16 JOURNEYS**
- ○ Some pleasant trips
- ● Travel is unpleasant

**17 WORRIES**
- ○ Minor problems
- ● Major problems

**18 PLANS**
- ○ Take more time and care
- ● Hasty or a waste of time

**19 FAMILY**
- ○ Closeness or cooperation
- ● Separation or disagreements

**20 SELF**
- ○ You are in good company
- ● You are on your own

**21 PROPERTY**
- ○ Money is useful
- ● Too much materialism

**22 DANGERS**
- ○ Safety if you take care
- ● Impatience causes danger

**23 UPSETS**
- ○ A change at work
- ● A dubious offer

**24 THE UNEXPECTED**
- ○ Inheritances, legacies
- ● Accidents, losses

**25 CHANGES**
- ○ New friends, work or love
- ● Losses leading to a new start

**26 CHANCE**
- ○ Random chance
- ● Inevitable fate or destiny

**MAY**

**JULY**

**SEPTEMBER**

**NOVEMBER**

**JUNE**

**AUGUST**

**OCTOBER**

**DECEMBER**

© DIAGRAM

85

# Developing your paranormal powers

People who appear to have paranormal powers may have different occupations and lifestyles but one common characteristic is contentment.

People whose psychic powers are most reliable are people who radiate a sense of inner harmony. They are often pleasant people, with a light sense of humor and are most unlikely to be morose or have any of the weird characteristics popularly associated with practitioners of the occult. Thus, in order to develop and use any psychic dimension of the body-mind you need to achieve a state in which you feel reasonably happy and undisturbed.

This state of inner calm and balance is not easy to achieve in the face of illness, personal tragedy or communal disaster. However, some people do achieve it and they communicate their inner wholeness to others. You may have met someone who is generous and calm in spirit despite chronic pain etc, and you may also know of people who are miserable or restless regardless of how good life may be to them.

So how can this inner state of harmony be acquired?

**The more you have the more you get**
Once you have tapped into this cosmic life energy and begun to achieve a state of harmonious inner well-being, the energy you have seems to go on working for you. It gives you more energy to keep up a steady and happy lifestyle, no matter what the conditions. In this state, you are more likely to be able to develop your specific paranormal activities. Whatever they are, it will become clear to you that you have a particular talent. For example, you may find telepathy easy, you may use dowsing regularly or you may become much more creative in your work, in a relationship or in a hobby. Inner well-being also reflects outward giving you confidence and attracting others.

Paranormal powers are a form of super-sensitivity, so, no matter what your occupation and interests, developing your paranormal powers will be advantageous to you. However, any attempt to force or manipulate paranormal phenomena can result in damage to yourself and sometimes harm to others.

**Negative things to imagine being washed away**

| | |
|---|---|
| Worries | Tiredness |
| Guilt | Fear |
| Failure | Anxiety |
| Hate | Mistakes |
| Nastiness | Loss |
| Aches | Hostility |
| Misery | Misunderstandings |
| Depression | |

**SIX STEPS TOWARDS A STATE OF WELL-BEING**

1 Choose a quiet place where you will not be interrupted.

4 Imagine this light is washing away all negative thoughts and worries. Say to yourself several times: "Let all negative things be washed away from me."

As you relax, do not condemn any of the negative things, just accept they are part of life but you have no need of them.

You may like to imagine actual worries or upsets falling away as the light shines around you.

**2** Lay a piece of bright blue material on the floor, or cover a bed or chair with the material. A blue sheet, blanket or towel would be suitable. Blue has the vibration of healing and its rays are said to penetrate the body and stimulate healing.

**3** Close your eyes and relax onto the blue cloth and imagine yourself surrounded by a bright light which is pouring over you.

**5** Open your eyes and focus on the blue material, imagining it is sending blue vibrations through the whole of your body. Say to yourself:"I am protected from harm and I am whole in thought and deed."

**6** Finally, relax for a few moments saying to yourself: "I happily accept my own joy."
 You can change the actual words to suit yourself, but keep the meaning clear . . . remember, it is only possible to let go of something you love, so you have to love the negatives inside you in order to let go.

# Using random insights

Do you have a truly lucky number? Have you ever picked a horse or a team, knowing it would be a winner? Were you certain that this was the right house for you from the moment you first saw it? Can you often read the intentions of another person? Do you sometimes see the solution to a problem in a flash of insight while doing something unrelated or can you guess at random what someone wants before they know it themselves? All these are examples of random insights, some of which appear to be prophetic. Cleromancy is the practice of using random insights by casting or drawing lots, to divine answers to problems or to make decisions. Cleromancy comes from the Greek word kleros, meaning lot. Greek lots were often specially marked sticks of wood that were stood in an urn, from which each person would draw his lot. The practice of cleromancy is very ancient and has appeared in many cultures. If you want to focus your ability to pick answers at random, there are several methods you can use to draw your lot.

### Cleromancy
Cleromancy is a form of gambling and the phrase "taking pot luck" means accepting what you draw out of the pot by chance. The pot may be a drum containing numbered tickets, as in a tombola, or it may be a roulette wheel as at the casino.

   The Ancient Greek oracle at Delphi gave wisdom and made prophesies. Often lots were drawn as answers to questions which supplemented the oracle. The question would be written on a lead stick and used to stir the beans in a large urn. The stick would then be withdrawn together with a single bean. If the bean was white, the answer would be YES, if the bean was black, the answer would be NO.

Cleromancy

### Bibliomancy
A collection of books by major authors should be kept together on a shelf. These might include books by a Greek, such as Homer, by the Persian poet Hafiz or by William Shakespeare. Religious books may also be used and notable works by a modern author can be included.
**1** If you have a question, concentrate upon it and let your eyes wander across the books, picking one at random.
**2** While holding the book in both hands, close your eyes, concentrate on the question, then open the book at any page and run your finger down the page until you feel inclined to stop.
**3** Open your eyes and read the line you have chosen, which is said to be an omen and will answer your question. If the line seems obscure, allow your mind to play with it and eventually its meaning will become clear.

Bibliomancy

### Fortune cookies
These are a modern version of the old practice of aleuromancy. All possible answers to a question were marked on rice paper and rolled up into balls of dough. When they had been baked, the questioner selected one, broke it open and read the answer he had chosen.

Fortune cookies

# THE TALKING STONES

Around the world, stones, sticks, carved bone or pieces of horn have been used to give fuller answers to questions than YES or NO. Colored stones are commonly used to answer questions. Nine small, flat stones should each be colored in one of the nine colors listed. The stones should be small enough for them all to fit easily into a closed hand. On one side of each stone the appropriate symbol should be marked in black or white. They can then be finished with a coat of varnish or polished and kept in a small bag made of soft material. Other people should never be allowed to handle your stones.

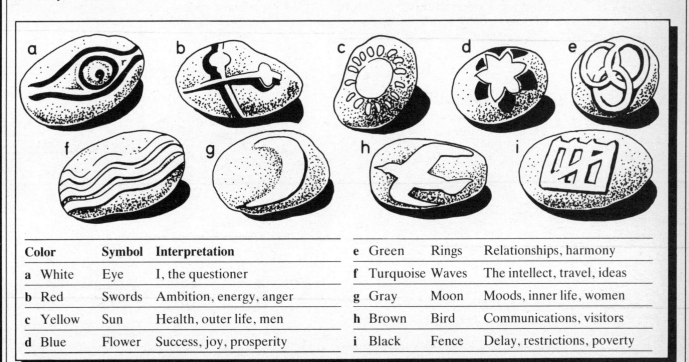

| | Color | Symbol | Interpretation |
|---|---|---|---|
| **a** | White | Eye | I, the questioner |
| **b** | Red | Swords | Ambition, energy, anger |
| **c** | Yellow | Sun | Health, outer life, men |
| **d** | Blue | Flower | Success, joy, prosperity |

| | Color | Symbol | Interpretation |
|---|---|---|---|
| **e** | Green | Rings | Relationships, harmony |
| **f** | Turquoise | Waves | The intellect, travel, ideas |
| **g** | Gray | Moon | Moods, inner life, women |
| **h** | Brown | Bird | Communications, visitors |
| **i** | Black | Fence | Delay, restrictions, poverty |

## How to use the talking stones

**1** Lay a piece of cloth approximately 10in (25cm) square on the table. Tip all the stones from the bag into the palm of your hand and cupping the other hand over them, shake them well as you concentrate upon your question.

**2** Cast all the stones on the table in front of you. Those nearest to you represent events in the immediate future or things of great importance to you; those farther away foretell more distant events or represent things of minor concern. Stones close together or touching each other should be read together. Stones upside down or not on the small cloth, should be ignored.

## A sample reading of the talking stones

**Question:** What will be the outcome if I move house now?

**Answer:** Much traveling (**f**) by the questioner (**a**) will cause strife (**b**) and this will affect relationships (**e**) and visitors (**h**). Success (**d**) is rather unlikely because (**d**) is only partly on the cloth; (**g**), (**c**) and (**i**) should be ignored because they are either upside-down or off the cloth.

All nine stones cast in reply

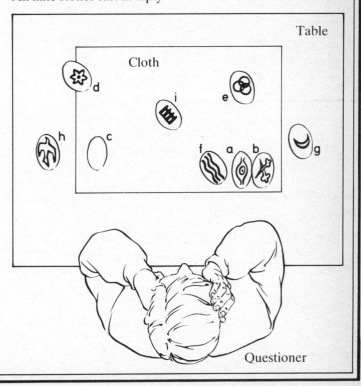

# Checking your predictions

If you intend to attempt to develop powers of prophecy, you must keep very careful records of your results. You cannot claim to be using the power of prophecy unless you have adequate proof; even then, you must always be careful not to mislead others (or yourself) as you can never have 100% success.

There are many pitfalls to be avoided. It is likely, for example, that what appear to be accurate predictions on some occasions will be coincidences. And at other times you may be so excited by what appears to be prophetic that you fail to see you have persuaded yourself into the situation. This is called a self-fulfilling prophecy.

**Beware of your perceptions**
You may feel absolutely certain about something you have seen and there may be several witnesses who agree with you. Nevertheless, there will always be others who give different interpretations of what was seen. For example, what do you think this drawing below could represent? Write down your first thought in the space provided opposite, then add any other interpretations if they occur to you.

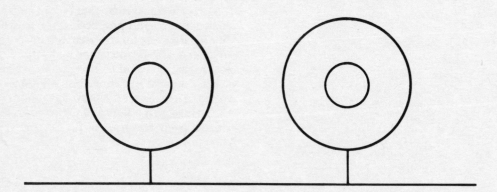

| THE PREDICTION | |
|---|---|
| **Date made** | |
| **Place** | |
| **Time** | |
| **Description of events** | |
| **Exact prediction** | |
| **Names of those present** | |
| **Comments of those present** | |
| **Signatures of those present** | |
| **Your signature and date written** | |
| **Signature of 2 witnesses to this record and date** | |

## My interpretations of the drawing

None of these will be the "right" answer, as the drawing was not intended to represent anything in particular. If you ask several friends to give you their ideas. Some may be the same as yours but it is likely that the order will be different, i.e. another person's first perception will differ from yours.

(A list of possibilities is given at the bottom of page 93 which is not exhaustive.)

This exercise was intended to demonstrate how we perceive differently and further, how any one thing can be interpreted in different ways. Try to keep this in mind as you interpret and record your attempts to predict events.

......................................................

......................................................

......................................................

......................................................

......................................................

## Making a record of predictions

Enter full details at the time of your prediction. Then ask two people to sign as witnesses to the fact that you recorded events and ask them to enter the date when they signed. Later, if and when the prediction comes true, record the details in full.

To make a complete on-going record, you will need to purchase a notebook and enter the headings as shown below. A properly stitch-bound book is desirable to avoid alterations. The pages should be used in order and any mistakes should just be crossed out and signed. Alternatively, you can simply photocopy the two charts shown below.

If, over several years, your records show a high incidence of correct prophecies, you may like to contact your local society for research into the paranormal, who would probably be interested and helpful. In no circumstances should you ever set youself up as a prophet without first consulting a reliable organization with long experience. Otherwise you may unwittingly deceive and hurt others and you will certainly lay yourself open to charges by people who are dissatisfied with your predictions.

| THE FULFILLMENT | |
| --- | --- |
| Date | |
| Place | |
| Time | |
| Description of events | |
| Extent to which the prediction was fulfilled | |
| Names of those present | |
| Comments of those present | |
| Signatures of those present | |
| Your signature and date | |
| Signature of 2 witnesses to this record and date | |

# Are you superstitious?

Modern superstitions are largely the same as omens which were handed down orally from ancient times. Omens were small nuggets of wisdom and advice gleaned from natural occurences. Many of them are common across the world as they were carried by explorers and pioneers from one culture to another but some are common to groups of people who had no contact with each other.

Dr Carl Jung (1875-1961), the Swiss psychologist, suggested that humans have some memories from earlier times during our evolution, that form our collective unconscious. For example, people from all parts of the world react to spiders. Hence the behavior of spiders is the subject of many omens or superstitions. Do you recognize any of them?

### Spider superstitions
Some are negative, for example:
Finding a spider in the morning – Sorrow
Finding a spider at midday – Anxiety
Finding a spider in the evening – Loss
Killing a spider – Bad Luck

Many are positive, for example:
A spider spinning in the morning – Good luck
A spider climbing its thread – Good news
A spider dropping on its thread – Good luck
Finding a spider on your body – Good fortune
Seeing a spider cross a wall – Good luck

Some spider superstitions are specific, for example:
Seeing a spider spinning in the afternoon – Travel
A spider's web on a doorway – A visitor
A spider on your clothes – Money

### Arachne, the spider
Arachne is said to be the missing 13th sign in the zodiac based on 13 lunar months. Arachne is associated with psychic abilities, weaving and women.

### Ladders and Salt
In legends ladders were associated with the gods who bridged the gap between earth and heaven with a ladder. Hence, walking under a ladder would anger the gods. Salt was a very precious commodity and was used sybolically when making agreements or religious sacrifices. To spill salt accidentally during a ceremony was considered to be unlucky and a sign of loss of faith. To spill it while making a contract led to financial loss. The way to regain good fortune in both instances, was to take a pinch of the fallen salt with your left hand and throw it over your right shoulder.

## HOW SUPERSTITIOUS ARE YOU?
Read the list of superstitions and check those to which you respond, whether you believe them or not?

**Things that are said to bring good luck**

☐ A robin flying into the house

☐ Sneezing three times before breakfast

☐ Meeting three sheep

☐ Looking at the new moon over your right shoulder

☐ A four-leaved clover

☐ Spilling wine while proposing a toast

☐ Putting a dress on inside out

☐ Nine peas in a pea pod

☐ Hearing crickets singing

☐ Picking up a pin

☐ A horseshoe

☐ Cutting your hair during a storm (**a**)

☐ Carrying a rabbit's foot

☐ Sleeping facing south

☐ White heather

☐ Picking up a pencil in the street

☐ Breaking clear and uncolored glass

☐ Walking in the rain (**b**)

☐ Sleeping on unironed sheets (**c**)

☐ Saying Bless you when someone sneezes

☐ Avoiding cracks in the sidewalk

☐ An itch on the top of your head

☐ Scissors hanging on a hook

☐ Two white horses

☐ A ladybird on you

☐ **Score**

### Variations
Interpretations of omens can vary from culture to culture, for example, cats. A black cat is a sign of good luck in the UK but a sign of bad luck in the USA and in other parts of Europe, although three black cats is lucky anywhere!

Colors also have significance. In some countries black is the symbol of death while in others it is a

## Things that are said to bring bad luck

☐ A bat flying into the house (**d**)

☐ An owl hooting three times

☐ Three butterflies together

☐ Looking at the new moon over your left shoulder

☐ A five-leaved clover

☐ Breaking a glass while proposing a toast

☐ Putting a shirt on inside out

☐ Red and white flowers together

☐ Hearing a rooster crow at night (**e**)

☐ Dropping a glove

☐ Peacock feathers

☐ Cutting your nails on a Friday

☐ Putting a hat on a bed

☐ Getting out of bed left foot first

☐ Violets blooming out of season

☐ A picture falling

☐ Breaking a mirror

☐ Singing before breakfast

☐ Opening an umbrella indoors

☐ Giving away a wedding present

☐ Stepping on cracks in the sidewalk

☐ An itch inside your nose

☐ Crossed knives

☐ One white horse

☐ Seeing an owl during daylight (**f**)

☐ **Score**

☐ **Total score**

### Add up your total

More than 29: You are very superstitious
21 to 29: You are fairly superstitious
10 to 20: You are lightheartedly superstitious
Under 10: You are rarely superstitious

Of course, you may have many other superstitions than those listed, if so, try listing them and putting them in place of ones on the list here that you don't know. Then try again and find your total.

### Are you optimistic or pessimistic?

It is interesting to compare your scores for "bad luck" and "good luck" superstitions. Pessimists spend a lot of time trying to avoid bad luck, so their "bad luck" score would be higher than their "good luck" score. Optimists are likely to score fairly evenly or with a bias towards "good luck" superstitions.

© DIAGRAM

symbol of luck. White, used for western wedding dresses, is traditionally the color of purity but in China a bride will be honored to wear red at her wedding and white will be used at funerals.

Many social customs are also carried out because not to do so would bring bad luck . . . which of course makes a great deal of sense in a crowded world.

### Beware of your perceptions

Some interpretations of the drawing on page 90: targets; roller skate upside-down; antennae of two spacemen hidden behind a wall; doughnuts on sticks; trees; looking down on two Mexicans relieving themselves against a wall; flowers; end views of two pipes; overhead view of two cooks frying pancakes on a verandah; two fried eggs being measured on a ruler; eyes on stalks; buttons, etc.

# Fate or free will?

If all kinds of events could be predicted accurately either they would have to be predetermined, perhaps by a natural, fatalistic force or they would have to be controlled as they occurred by the deliberate will of someone or something. This is a fairly simplistic view; but it will suffice to examine what is implied if we believe there are (and have been) people who are able to prophesy future events with certainty and accuracy.

### Fate

It may be true that simple, natural processes are clearly predictable. Heat water at the normal air pressure found in your kitchen and it will boil. Turn the ignition key of your car and current from the battery will make a spark to ignite the fuel. These processes are a logical sequence of events, each of which causes the next effect. They could be described as events which are "fated" and therefore entirely predictable.

### Accuracy of prediction

Problems of prediction only arise when either there is an unknown interference in a natural process or several processes interact; then prediction becomes much more difficult.

For example, safety officers in the nuclear industry ask the question What if . . . as they try to anticipate the course of events should a particular combination of conditions prevail.

However, despite the complexity of processes and the intervention of other factors, including the human element, many people (such as weather forecasters, medical doctors and stock market dealers) risk their reputations on their predictions or prognoses,

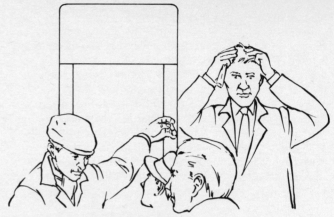

A bookmaker declares his odds

A fortune-teller reads the future

---

**WHAT DO YOU BELIEVE?**

Here are four ideas about how the universe and everything in it functions, including ourselves. Which do you believe, or do you have a different idea? Is it also possible that all four ideas are active at the same time.

Perhaps many things happen by chance, while others are fated and some are the result of willpower. You may like to ponder on these thoughts and find out your own beliefs.

**1 Fate**

Events may be predetermined according to some grand plan or pattern. The force which has predetermined events may be nature, God, some other cosmic planner or may be consequential to some action in an earlier age or incarnation.

**2 Free will**

Everything that happens can be determined by choice. People, animals, plants and all inorganic substances can choose what action to take next, which may be boundless or a choice within certain limitations according to the nature of the chooser.

**3 Chance**

Things happen at random when there are equal chances for each possibility. Perhaps fate, free will or something else can intervene and alter the balance.

**4 Purpose**

Everything in the universe acts according to its own best interests, which includes its own survival. The purpose may also include satisfying an instinct of cosmic laziness, i.e. acting in the most economical way and not doing any more than necessary.

## Free will

Many people find unacceptable the idea that everything is fated. Most of us like to think we have a choice and can create our own choices freely. If we accept that we can act wilfully, then it seems less likely that our actions could be predicted unless the apparent free choice we made, was also fated. That is a difficult question to ponder upon: even when we make a choice by free will, was it already predetermined that we should make that choice? Some religions say that whatever we do, we are fulfilling our karma the path we are destined to tread in order to reach perfect fulfillment.

## Chance

Apart from fate or free will, there is another aspect of life called chance. Snowflakes settle on the ground randomly, covering everything with a fairly even layer of snow; these chance landings become directed when a wind blows and the snow begins to drift in the same direction.

Things that happen by chance are usually part of a whole scheme of things in which a balance is maintained. For example, if you toss a coin there are two ways it can land: heads or tails. If the coin is tossed enough times it will, by chance, land heads up 50 times and tails up 50 times. Therefore, if the coin is tossed 100 times, 50 of your calls could be right by chance. Of course, this will not happen for every 100 calls you make; sometime the number of correct calls will be lower and sometime higher than 50 but on average you will get 50 right. Only if your average score is more than 60 for at least 1000 calls, could other factors be present, although even an extraordinarily high average could still be by chance, but the odds against it are very high.

## Testing your ability

If you decide to test your ability to predict the outcome of a toss correctly, ask one friend to record your calls, another to record the actual way the coin fell and a third to do the tossing. Finally, when you have made at least one run of 100 calls, you must take the scores obtainable by chance into account. The table shows scores that are of a significant level for runs of 100 calls.

| Calls | Chance score | Significant score | Average per 100 |
|---|---|---|---|
| 100 | 50 | 90 | — |
| 200 | 100 | 160 | 80 |
| 300 | 150 | 220 | 73 |
| 400 | 200 | 280 | 70 |
| 500 | 250 | 340 | 68 |
| 1000 | 500 | 630 | 63 |

## How to use the table

If the coin is tossed 100 times you will make 100 calls. If 50 or more of your calls are correct, your score is not significant unless you have 90 or more correct calls. Do remember that out of 100 calls even a high correct score, such as 67, 72 or 85 may be very exciting but is most likely to be by chance, so you must make several runs of 100.

When you have done so, add the score for each 100 together to see if you have reached a significant score. The last column of average scores, shows that even if you have a high score for every 100 run, it can still be by chance.

Bearing in mind the odds for calling the toss of a coin correctly, all apparent predictions should be viewed sceptically. Many correct predictions are made by chance and it may be impossible to prove that even a significant level of correct predictions were actually prophetic rather than by chance.

A tossed coin can fall either heads or tails, but how often one or the other occurs is a matter of complex mathematical calculations. Most players rely on chance to predict the outcome.

# Chapter four
# THE WILL TO POWER

Mind power can be interpreted and used in many different ways. Throughout history there have been people who believed that the mind is an entity that can separate from the rest of the body, becoming a visible body-spirit, an invisible observer or simply a force with powers independent of the body.

Confusion arises when beliefs such as re-incarnation and a life after death are taken into consideration. No less confusing are ideas presented by philosophers, psychologists and modern bio-physicists.

Is the mind inseparable from the body? Can the mind be used while the body is at rest or even sleeping? Is the brain home of the mind and, indeed, is it the mind?

Perhaps the mind is best defined by what we can achieve through the power of our minds. Whenever we wilfully take action we are said to be using willpower. And what is willpower? Does willpower involve determination, concentration, confidence, belief in ourselves, clarity of purpose, charisma, good timing, imagination, flexible thinking skills, direction and a knowledge of psychology?

Where is the will to be found? If willpower is a function of the mind, it can also be described as a function of the psyche, which is just another word for the mind. Having the will to apply your mind suggests that you are aware of using willpower.

This section presents some instances in which this power is used with awareness. The emphasis has been placed on the more positive uses of willpower. It should be remembered that, like all human skills, mind skills can be used for positive or negative purposes.

When considering the examples of the will to power in this section, use your wisdom to recognize your own vulnerabilities. We might want to receive healing and reject a curse, so we must have some way of opening ourselves to positive energy forces while protecting ourselves from unwelcome ones. A method for achieving this, called "Making an auric bubble", is included.

**1** Partnership skating requires both skaters to exert mind power to achieve coordination and cooperation.
**2** Courtship requires both partners to apply their mind power to achieving a mutually agreeable understanding.
**3** Games between partners exercise both of their mind powers to influence and dominate each other.
**4** Armed single combat can result in death so each participant must exert maximum mind power.
**5** Crowds generate a collective mind power which influences each participant by a mass hysteria.
**6** Society can have a master mind power as the author George Orwell suggested in his novel *1984*.

2

3

5

6

BIG BROTHER

IS WATCHING
YOU

©DIAGRAM

# The great persuaders

Persuasion is a manipulation during which one or more people are induced to believe something and act accordingly. Some persuaders are fairly gentle and, at the other extreme, some are heartless confidence tricksters but all of them appeal to the emotions.

Common emotional triggers are the desire to be sexually attractive or sexually potent; the fear of looking a fool; the desire to be fashionable; the drive to be seen as a winner; the fear of not being a good lover, wife, parent, grandparent etc., and all the emotions involved with sickness and aging.

Persuasion is an everyday example of mind over matter and, used with care, it can be a useful addition to your mind skills; some examples are given on this page.

It is wise to be aware of when you are trying to persuade others, as your own most influential persuader can be yourself. It is easy to believe your own persuasions.

**The dubious art of persuasion**
1 Gain attention and cooperation by stimulating emotional interest.
2 Use commonplace information.
3 Use flattery.
4 Exploit reactions.
5 Pretend to know more than you do.
   These five points are also a key to recognizing when you are being subjected to persuasion.

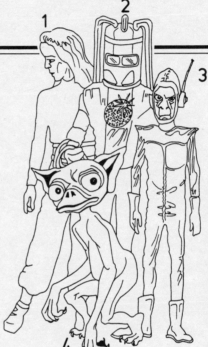

**Some well-documented extra-terrestrial visitors**
1 Man sighted near Desert Center, California, 1952.
2 UFO crewman seen near Francisco de Sales, Brazil, 1957.
3 UFO crew member encountered by Police Officer Herbert Schirmer at Ashland, Nebraska, 1967.
4 Creature from a spaceship that landed at Hopkinsville, Kentucky, 1955.

## UNIDENTIFIED FLYING OBJECTS (UFOs)

One of the most interesting examples of persuasion, affecting many people across different cultures, began in the late 1940s and early 1950s when numerous sightings of flying saucers or UFOs were reported.

### US panel of investigation
In July 1952 several radar detections coincided with visual sightings of unidentified objects in the air over the National Airport in Washington DC. A panel of physicists, engineers, meteorologists and an astronomer was set up to investigate.

In its early days this panel was organized by the Central Intelligence Agency (CIA) and kept secret. Later, when the observations were declassified, it was revealed that 90% of the investigated UFO sightings were explainable. They were bright planets, meteorites, auroras, ion clouds, other aircraft, balloons, birds and searchlights, or due to unusual weather conditions. It is common during the night for town lights to be reflected high up on the warm air and, during hot weather, refracted light can give rise to illusions, such as mirages.

### The extra-terrestrial hypothesis
Another panel in 1966 came to similar conclusions, and they also left about 10% of sightings of UFOs unexplained. A few scientists and engineers hypothesized that a small percentage of the most reliable unexplained gave definite indications of extra-terrestrial visitors.

This extra-terrestrial hypothesis persuades some people to believe UFOs come from outer space. Others dismiss the idea completely, presumably persuaded by their commonsense that visits from extra-terrestrials are impossible. It is extremely difficult to prove either way. Some people leave the question open, awaiting more evidence on which to base a decision; they are the sceptics who are not easily persuaded either way.

### Are you persuaded?
One of the most puzzling and best documented of all the unexplained sightings of UFOs occured between 2300 on 13 August 1956 and 0330 the next day at Lakenheath, England.

It was a clear, moonlit night. Two RAF ground radar stations detected some objects. One was at 4000ft moving westward at about 3000 miles per hour. At the same time, flight control tower operators reported a bright light moving westward overhead and a pilot in a plane, 4000ft up, also reported seeing a streak of light moving westward beneath him.

Other similar sightings were made, both visually from fighter planes that went up to investigate and by radar in the planes and on the ground.

While simultaneous visual sighting and radar detection is the most reliable evidence of the presence of an object, it is not proof.

## Persuaders

Advertisers are clearly persuaders yet their adverts can be deceptively honest. Washing fluids may indeed make your wash appear whiter, since such products contain substances that reflect ultra-violet light to add a sparkle.

Popular newspaper advertisements (*right*) attract the reader's eye with punchy, suggestive headlines which often make extravagent claims about the product or service that are are, sadly, often not matched in reality.

---

| YES | NO |
|-----|-----|
| ☐ | ☐ |

**1** Do you think there is enough evidence to reach a conclusion?

| YES | NO |
|-----|-----|
| ☐ | ☐ |

**2** Do you believe that unidentified objects were seen?

| YES | NO |
|-----|-----|
| ☐ | ☐ |

**3** Do you believe the objects could have been extra-terrestrial?

| YES | NO |
|-----|-----|
| ☐ | ☐ |

**4** Do you believe that the sightings were illusions?

| YES | NO |
|-----|-----|
| ☐ | ☐ |

**5** Do you believe that there is a simple explanation that wasn't found at the time?

If you answered YES to **1**, **2**, **3** or **4** you have been persuaded. If you answered YES only to number **5** you are an open-minded sceptic and are using your mind-powers to think.

## Psychological persuasion

By 1970 there were 12,000 reported sightings of UFOs. Psychologists were able to sort them into categories: those explainable as other phenomena; those probably due to psychological causes; those as yet unexplained.

These studies gave much information about mass hysteria, hysterical contagion and hallucination, including the Isakower syndrome, which occurs when a drowsy person spontaneously visualizes events from the past.

The amount of interest in UFOs is difficult to understand. There are books, articles, movies and clubs still thriving around the world. The amount of emotion stimulated, both in the people who have had sightings and in the scientists who have investigated them, is apparently out of all proportion. Perhaps there are reasons for this in the history of the human race; after all, it must have seemed to our ancestors that our lives were controlled by "beings" in the sky.

## Hangar 18

Released in 1980, *Hangar 18* was a movie about a UFO encountered during a space maneuver. The result was a collision destroying a one-man capsule. The incident was witnessed by two astronauts who, on return to earth, discover all evidence of the encounter has been eradicated. Meanwhile, the damaged UFO makes a forced landing in the Arizona desert and is promptly removed to Hangar 18 for inspection.

The secrets of an alien, and probably superior, culture are beginning to be revealed when the hieroglyphics in the spaceship are seen to be similar to those found on ancient sites on earth. At this point the politicians, fearful of losing votes, decide to blow up the hangar.

If stories like this are an indication of what might happen should visitors from other planets ever arrive on earth, it seems highly probable that we shall never know where extra-terrestrial UFOs come from. . . if they exist.

# Can you keep a cool head?

Remaining sufficiently cool-headed to negotiate, even under the most difficult circumstances, is an application of mind power that can bring outstanding results in daily life. To understand the art of negotiation, it is useful to contrast it with the process of persuasion or manipulation.

We are all persuaders sometimes and subject to persuasive images such as TV advertisements, political propaganda and newspaper headlines. A sense of humor can help us to keep a balanced view. Learning to use negotiating skills gives us a powerful tool and helps us to recognize the subtle persuaders.

## Negotiation
This is a process of coming to an agreement that satisfies as far as possible the interests of both parties. It is a creative act during which each person feels the presence and reality of the other's situation and negotiates accordingly.

### Characteristics of negotiators
1 Honest and authentic in dealings with others.
2 Aware and takes an interest in the other party.
3 Accepts responsibility for outcome of own actions.
4 Trusts self and prepared to trust others.
5 Values self and has regard for the other person.
6 A negotiator is aiming to get the best deal for himself by recognizing that the other person is likely to respond helpfully by getting something he wants.
7 If opposed, a negotiator retains self-control and a cool head, reviews the situation and may use another of the negotiator's alternative approaches.

## Persuasion
This is a strategy to induce others to believe something and act accordingly. It is a process that destroys relationships because the persuader regards the other party as an object to be manipulated into taking a predetermined line of action.

### Characteristics of persuaders
1 Pretentious and dishonest in dealings with others.
2 Unaware and has no interest in the other party.
3 Blames others for the outcome of own actions.
4 Is cynical and mistrusts others.
5 Does not value self and disregards others.
6 A persuader is aiming to get the best deal for himself by attempting to control other people.
7 If opposed or frustrated, a persuader will lose self-control, become hot-headed, use even more underhand methods than before and threaten severe reprisals.

Negotiating to strike a bargain takes time. Haggling over a bazaar price may take a couple of hours but eventually the price satisfies both parties and the equally important social need for a chat-game is fulfilled.

Persuading the customer to buy a super-car involves inferring claims for its performance that are beyond its actual capabilities, such as leaping over chasms or guaranteeing the driver's sexual potency. All good fun, but not worth the extra cash on the price.

## Negotiating skills

1 Avoid underselling yourself, especially to a persuader. Agreeing to demands or first offers gives the impression that you are a pushover and leaves you no room for further negotiation.

2 Create an impact on the other party by asking them for information, trying to discover what they really want. This is information you need to create a negotiating balance.

3 Regard everything, even terrorist demands, as negotiable. Accepting terms without any discussion will make another negotiator think you haven't really thought out your position and may want to change your mind later. A persuader will not regard the terms as binding and make more demands. This happens in blackmail situations.

4 Never give discounts, it is a sign of weakness. Ask what the other finds attractive in your offer. There are many variables in any negotiation.

5 Encourage the other party to negotiate by helping them to think and tell you what they are thinking. You can even teach a hardened persuader to negotiate and, when they do, they get a stronger sense of power and are less likely to do something rash. Conceding or threatening always leads to future difficulties.

6 Never accept the first offer or the first demand. Haggling makes both parties feel they have got a bargain.

7 Always leave room for further negotiation by creating a space for it, such as leaving time open-ended.

**US embassy hit again by Beirut bombers**

**massacre 25 at Tel Aviv airport**

**Terrorists stage new wave of attacks**

**Beirut: TWA hostages freed after 16 days**

## NEGOTIATION AND TERRORISM

Terrorists are forceful persuaders, threatening to murder and bomb and frequently doing so. Hostage-taking is a typical terrorist act, designed to be very persuasive.

Those who have to respond to terrorist demands in these situations have a choice: persuade the terrorists to surrender or negotiate for the return of hostages. Persuasion leads inevitably to the use of more and more force and might be a last resort but would not be to the hostages' advantage.

### The Spaghetti House siege

At 0145 on 28 September 1975 several managers of restaurants from the Spaghetti House chain in London, were gathered at their Knightsbridge restaurant, as they did every Saturday to bank the night's takings.

This routine was probably their mistake; they were held up by three heavily armed men. As the gunmen were grabbing the money, a member of the restaurant staff escaped and alerted the police who quickly surrounded the building. The gunmen took the restauranteurs and held six of them hostage in a 14ft by 10ft basement room for five days.

Throughout the negotiations, small requests were granted and demands were printed in newspapers as requested but few other concessions were made. The state of the gunmen was monitored by listening at a ground-level grille to their conversations and responding accordingly, calming the situation when they became tired.

The end of the siege came when the gunmen agreed to give up their demands after the ring-leaders of the gang had been caught and questioned. The only injury was to one of the gunmen . . . they had argued among themselves.

This situation was relatively easy to resolve because taking hostages had not been part of the gunmen's plan and they were vague about their demands. They had not set out to take hostages. When taking hostages is a deliberate plan, the situation is more difficult to handle.

### The London Iranian Embassy siege

At 1130 on Wednesday 30 April 1980, 21 people were deliberately taken hostage at the Iranian Embassy in London by Iranian gunmen.

The hostages included Iranian diplomats, a London policeman, a Lebanese journalist and two British visitors. The gunmen demanded the release of 91 political prisoners from detention in Iran and an aircraft for their own escape. Their threat was to blow up the embassy if their demands were not met.

Thus the scene was set for a lengthy and complex set of negotiations. In this situation, the gunmen had planned the taking of the hostages and were evidently prepared to hold out to the death, not only of the hostages, but also of themselves.

Special training undertaken by the police was valuable in this situation. Eventually, negotiations broke down and two hostages were shot dead. In this situation, action has to be taken quickly as further negotiation is usually impossible. In this case, the Special Air Service Regiment stormed the building, rescuing the remaining 19 hostages safely. In the process, three of the gunmen were killed and one was injured.

Every incident increases the understanding of such situations for the people who undertake the difficult task of negotiating with kidnappers and terrorists.

# Using imagination

Imagination is the mind-tool with which we create poetic images. Our images can be in lasting things like words, paint, inventions, music, song, dance, design or architecture. We can also create poetry in everyday activities, in cooking, love-making or the way we arrange our home or garden; with imagination, we can be poetic in the way we live our lives.

René Magritte, the great Belgian surrealist painter who died in 1967, used to paint what appeared to be very precise, realistic images. For example he painted a man looking into a mirror, staring at the reflection of the back of his own head . . . an ordinary image suddenly made powerful because of how the picture is arranged. What appears to be ordinary is a mystery.

Magritte himself defined the art of painting as: "the science of juxtaposing colors in such a way that their actual appearance disappears and lets a poetic image appear . . . There are no subjects and no themes in my painting. It is a matter of imagining images whose poetry restores to what is known, that which is absolutely unknown and unknowable."

Fantasy can take many forms, drawing from other cultures, transformations of animals or objects, or simple distortions of reality.

## POWERFUL MINDS CAN TELL STORIES

Are you a story-teller? Most people can relate an incident that was personally exciting such as a wedding, a sports event, an accident or a meeting with a new friend; and many parents have found they can tell their children bedtime stories with ease.

There are two very useful ways of setting about practicing the art of story-telling.

**1** Imagine the characters and tell stories about their lives. Teams of television, radio and comic writers, and cartoonists produce thousands of such episodes weekly.

Sometimes the storyline is a serial in which there is a continuation of the story each week and you are always left wanting to see what happens next. In a series, each episode consists of the same characters appearing in a complete story.

Television series and serials, whether classical or modern have a wide appeal. The 'soaps' such as the American 'Dallas', the British 'Eastenders' and the Australian 'Neighbours' capture international audiences.

**2** Imagine a reason for a set of stories to be told. In this method, the stories can be quite unrelated. Some of our greatest collections of stories were built in this way.

### The Seven Sages of Rome

These seven medieval stories by seven advocates on behalf of a prince condemned to death, delay his execution until enough evidence had been collected to clear his name.

### The Canterbury Tales

These were written in the Middle Ages by Geoffrey Chaucer, as told by a group of ordinary people on a pilgrimage to Canterbury in southern England.

### The Decameron

Written by Boccaccio at Florence in 14th century Italy at the time of the Black Death. Each of ten people reveal themselves by telling stories as they face death from the plague.

### The Thousand and One Arabian Nights

King Shahryar kills his unfaithful wife and all her lovers. Consequently hating all women, he remarries each day and kills each new wife in the marriage bed.

Shahrasad (Scheherazade), daughter of the King's adviser, believes she can stop the carnage, so she marries the King.

On their first night, she tells the King a story so exciting that he is eager to know how it ends but she says she is tired and will complete the story the following night, which she does. Each night for 1001 nights she begins a new story, leaving its ending until the following night. The king is so entertained he gives up the idea of executing her, preferring to hear stories, such as Sinbad the Sailor, Aladdin, The Thief of Baghdad and Ali Baba. Some of these tales may date as far back as 8th century Baghdad, then a new Arab capital.

©DIAGRAM

### Using your imagination

Many people assume they don't have a very active imagination, probably because they aren't using it. To become imaginative, you have only to let your awareness roam freely around your world.

Imagination is not something to be learnt but a natural activity to be released. One very effective way to stir imagination is to work within limitations.

The boundaries that you impose on yourself tend to concentrate your eye or your ear and make you more aware of the world around you.

Another method to stimulate imaginative awareness is to tighten the boundaries you set yourself and do repetitive work, for example, photograph or draw only one object for a week. This will make you see the object from many different angles and in different conditions. Musicians can do the same thing with one note, making the sound in different ways and with different rhythms.

### Music

If you are musical, compose tunes from only eight notes, choosing, for example, every third note. If you prefer to sing, choose one word, phrase or sentence and set it to whatever type of music you prefer, repeating the same word, phrase or sentence over and over, but each time in a different way.

### Writing

To write stories, tell about the life of only one character, perhaps beginning with the life of a dollar, or some other everyday object, letting the dollar tell the story. Later try telling the story of one person starting with a name, for example: "I am Sandy and this is my story . . ."

### Drawing and painting

Using only a pencil or a pen, choose either curves or straight lines and fill a sheet of paper with only curves or straight lines. If you prefer painting, use any colors you like but paint them only as squares, touching, separate, overlapping or superimposed but only squares.

### Photography

Spend a day taking pictures within limitations, for example, choose only to photograph things that are yellow on one day and on the second day only things that are no larger than your hand . . . and so on.

# The power of submission

In this highly competitive world of ours, much attention is given to means by which a person, a company, or a nation can win, dominate or get to the top of the tree. Dominance is a position of power and authority; power is also available to those who lose, submit or are placed lower in the pecking order.

There are several ways in which members of a group or of a society are organized. Two of the most common hierarchical organizations are the linear and the pyramidal.

**Linear hierarchy or pecking order**

**Pyramidal hierarchy**

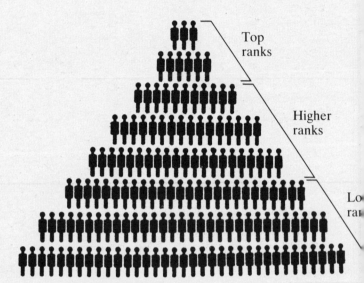

Top ranks

Higher ranks

Lo
ra

### The linear hierachy
Each member of the group has a position in relation to all the others. Each member is superior to the one below and inferior to the one above. The member in last position is inferior to all.

This kind of hierarchy is often called the pecking order, a name which comes from the behavior of chickens. In any group of chickens, social order is established as two chickens peck each other until one submits, leaving the other dominant over all. The loser then pecks at another chicken; the loser of that battle is then temporarily in third place and has to challenge another chicken, and so on.

Once the positions are decided, they remain stable. There is reduced aggression and peace reigns. Every chicken knows its place. However, in times of food shortages, those in higher positions eat and those lower down starve.

It would appear there is little advantage to the losers with very low positions but a position somewhere between second and about halfway down must be quite comfortable. With nobody challenging them for first place and little likelihood of being left out during shortages, those accepting a moderately inferior position can usually enjoy life in comfort.

### The pyramidal hierarchy
Each member of the organization belongs to a sub-group of peers and it is the sub-groups that are placed in rank order. The lowest in rank contains the largest number of members and the highest the least.

In pyramid organizations the top ranks depend on the lower ranks to keep them in their high position. If all the members of the lowest ranks rebelled and reorganized themselves, they could cause the downfall of those at the top. Presidents and Prime Ministers are particularly vulnerable to the lower ranks in their own parties and to the great mass of the public who are at the bottom of the pyramid. This is an example of the power of the submissive. The person elected to be at the top depends on those who put him or her there.

### Them and us
In many situations whole groups of people pay allegiance to dominant or submissive groups in order to play the power game. Workers versus management, people versus government, students versus teachers, children versus parents and so on. The dominant group is determined to stay in control, perhaps because they fear losing it and becoming dominated themselves. The submissive group is determined to get the dominant ones to do things for them, perhaps because they fear taking the responsibility of doing it themselves and thus becoming dominant.

## APPEASEMENT

Many animals use appeasement behaviour when faced with aggressors from the same species. They demonstrate their submission by sounds and gestures which inhibit aggression and save them from injury. Such behavior is very important to those other members of the group who are dependent on their leader for protection against attacks from outside their own group. Combating wolves turn their tails in when defeated, cats roll on their backs to deter attack, and female baboons groom and stroke aggressive males.

Human beings show submission in body gestures such as curtsying, bowing, kneeling, crouching and raising their hands.

**Disarmament** (*right*) A satirical cartoon by the French 19th century artist Daumier, shows two opposing officers each gesturing submission to the other.

©DIAGRAM

### Relationships

The power balance in the relationship between two people, such as husband and wife, often clearly illustrates how the power of the dominant partner is no greater in the long run than the power of the submissive partner. Any couple attempting to relate on equal terms has to dispense with the advantages of both positions.

### The power of the doormat

The doormat or rug is a wonderful metaphor for the power of submission. While doormats remain passive, people can wipe their feet on them but those who stand on mats are only secure as long as the rug is not pulled from under their feet.
- He remains master only as long as she will serve him.
- She dominates only as long as he submits.

In the relationship between husband and wife, each must take responsibility for certain roles and submit to the other in his or her partner's roles. Should this not be mutually agreed then conflict will occur as illustrated by this 18th century print of a couple fighting about who should wear the pants.

105

# Dying to live

A bioenergetic therapist might speak of growing yourself as a way of forming yourself. We, as bodies with minds of their own, vibrate with the energy of life and form ourselves. In this process of growing we have to give up each little past and step into each little future, over and over again.

This letting go is like a little death; part of us dies as a new part is formed. Each time we relax into sleep, we allow ourselves to slip into a dreaming oblivion, giving up the day we have just lived and waking again the next morning to welcome a new day. We can gladly enjoy this daily rhythm of life and when it is time for us to die and leave this earthly body, we can relax into our dying with the same pleasure.

Knowing how to die is to know how to live. If we cannot let go of each past and renew ourselves with each little future, then we fail to live our lives to the fullest.

**A life rhythm loop**

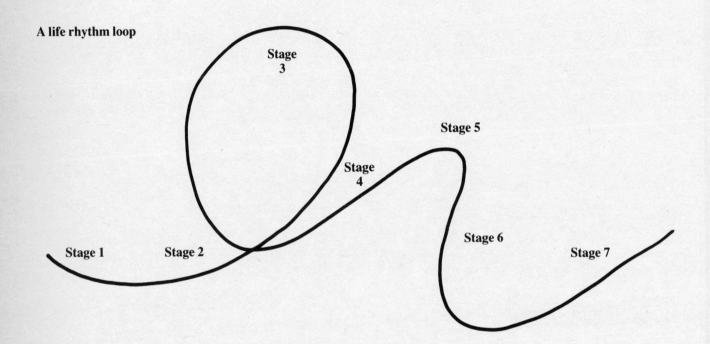

Stage 3

Stage 5

Stage 4

Stage 6

Stage 1   Stage 2

Stage 7

### The growing process
Steps in our formative process are sometimes major changes, for example when menstruation begins, a woman must leave behind the girl she was and take on her new form. Similarly, a man has to leave his boy self when he changes into a man and takes on a new, adult life.

In terms of life energy, we become stimulated, build our energy to a peak and release it as we express ourselves. During this growing process we form ourselves by expressing our uniqueness in every sphere of life: physically, mentally, emotionally, socially and spiritually.

We all have limitations and unseen potentials. These are due to our genetic patterns and to some extent are caused by outside factors beyond our control, such as geography, politics and community cultures. Within these external boundaries we have enormous scope to grow and, in the process, know ourselves very intimately.

### A formative loop in the rhythm of life
**Stage 1** Our energy builds, stimulating our interest.
**Stage 2** We decide to get involved.
**Stage 3** We contain ourselves as we prepare for action.
**Stage 4** We take action and express ourselves.
**Stage 5** Our expression reaches a peak.
**Stage 6** We relax and let go, enjoying satisfaction.
**Stage 7** Our energy begins to build again . . . and so on.
The loop can represent any life activity over a short or a long period of time. For example, making love; playing a round of golf; baking a cake; meeting a new friend; creating a baby; buying a house, etc.

Problems can occur at any point. Sometimes we back out at stage 2 by losing interest. Often we get stuck at stage 3 because we fail to make the decision at stage 4 to let go and express ourselves . . . we fail to "live our dying". Anxiety, stage fright, fear of failure and all manner of excuses can stop us. Our formative loops can become distorted by these problems but as they are solved and we learn to relax and let go, our life rhythms become easier and smoother.

## THE RHYTHMS OF LIFE

Our life rhythm is the pattern made by a succession of our individual, formative loops. The way we form our bodies as we use them, our changing voices, our increasing experience, our attitudes, hopes, fears, loves, hates, joys and achievements. With all this stuff of life, we each form an individual pattern which itself changes over the years. This rhythm of life will show what kind of person we are, regardless of age.

### Some individual life rhythms

The comments apply equally to women as to men. What shape would your life rhythm be? Perhaps you might like to draw it.

**a** This person has high energy and builds to a peak but somehow can't contain himself long enough to express himself, so the energy suddenly deflates, as in premature ejaculation. The larger loops towards the right show he has been learning how to contain himself long enough to give shape to his actions.

**b** This person is so busy and so active he is always on the move, working and performing he makes no time to stop and think. At the righthand end the rhythm line becomes fainter as he begins to burn himself out. This is the life rhythm of a typical workaholic who often feels he has never yet achieved anything.

**c** This person has very little rhythm to his life; full of fixed ideas and daily routines his life rhythm becomes a prison and he gets stuck in a rut, going round and round in circles and finally feels trapped and frustrated with no way out.

**d** This person gets easily excited and has become more disorientated over a period of time, as shown by the disorganized scribble his life rhythm has become on the righthand end. He is brimming with ideas but begins to live in an imaginary world unconnected with reality because he can never get anything together.

**e** The regular loops show this person makes regular formative decisions and learns from experience. He is a creative person, whatever his occupation and his life rhythm flows along fairly easily with a few uneven patches. He feels very satisfied with life.

**f** This person uses very little of his energy. Perhaps he is depressed or very nervous and just about manages to get along in life. However, sometimes he gets himself moving and takes a step forward in his self-development, as shown by the occasional loops. On the whole, life to him is dull and he expects little.

© DIAGRAM

### Live today

At the age of 31, an attractive, vivacious Englishwoman was happily married and had three young children. She was full of life, ambitious for her family and a very determined and busy young woman, involved in her local community.

One day, with little warning, she had to accept a new life . . . that of a person fighting leukaemia. She described her reaction as "quite wild". There was a lot of anger and crying and then she made a decision so typical of her. She found out all she could about the disease and both she and her family changed their life accordingly. They also worked tirelessly for a charity connected with leukaemia, in addition to their normal work and social interests.

Two years later, in September 1988, she was too frail to take any more chemotherapy treatment. Her doctors said she would not be able to celebrate Christmas . . . so the whole family celebrated Christmas on 29 October instead. She had already learnt how to die by letting go of her old life and giving all she had got to her new life.

"Time is precious," she had said, "I want to make the very best of whatever is left. Every day is crammed full of things to do . . . everyday I survive is a bonus."

Denise Morse, the young mother described above, died in hospital in Stoke-on-Trent, England on 7 February 1989 with her husband at her side. During the last nine months of her illness, she raised half a million pounds for a bone marrow donor register, to help save others suffering from leukaemia.

There are many similar stories that can be told, of people who used the power of their minds to live their dying.

# Are you using your charisma?

Derived from a Greek word meaning grace, your charisma is your personal power or talent to inspire others with enthusiasm. Because very charismatic people have an attractive aura, they often have many devoted followers. Charisma is a presence, a subtle energy which is felt by others at a subliminal level. Presence is a most potent personal expression.

Great leaders invariably have a sustained output of charismatic power, which attracts others to them and to their cause. Charisma is neither good nor bad; it is an amoral talent and everyone has some of it.

### Charismatic religious leaders
These people had outstanding charisma; when in their presence, others felt deeply touched by them and often became their devoted followers: Moses inspired the Israelites to leave Egypt; Jesus Christ inspired people to love one another; Muhammed inspired submission to the will of Allah; Gautama Siddhartha, the Buddha, inspired people to work towards enlightenment.

### Charisma, the art of theater
Live music and live theater, like any other live performance, is sheer magic; the performer can touch you deeply.

The setting, the lights and the build up to an entrance all enhance the charisma of a performer yet the most lavish presentation will be of no avail to someone without charisma.

### Charismatic people
You may never have considered that some of your friends have charisma. Just like major public figures they can emulate a power. Using the chart opposite try to evaluate what qualities you think contribute to your friends' charisma. Rank their power on a scale of 1 to 10 and list their qualities.

## CHARISMATIC TRAINING

It is possible to cultivate your presence so that others feel trusting and trusted. You can help to liberate the way people think by using your charisma. If you decide to try these exercises, do them with a spirit of enquiry. Try to find out how much energy you can direct towards others and how you can best use this energy.

If you misuse this energy, you will attract devotees who are not prepared to learn, who only want to lean on you. In the end they will be disappointed and turn upon you. The most positive use of charisma is to inspire enthusiasm in others. Once you have stirred your own charisma into life, you will be able to choose when to use it to best advantage.

### Finding your vertical energy
Between the soles of your feet and the top of your head a powerful energy force flows back and forth. This is your vertical charismatic energy that both keeps you firmly grounded on the earth and lifts you upward from the earth.

Any imbalance will leave you either held down by too much gravity or floating detached from reality. To keep a regular flow of energy up and down your body, the following exercises are useful. They should be done for fun rather than as a strict discipline. They need only take about 20 minutes a day and afterward you should feel looser and more naturally balanced.

### Exercise 1 Stimulating your vertical energy
Stand with your feet parallel about shoulder width apart. Keep your spine, neck and head in as straight a line as you possibly can while letting your knees bend slightly. Pull upward and feel the vertical flow of energy.

Now stretch your arms and hands upward as high as you can reach, still keeping your spine straight. Hold your stretch for a few seconds, then relax, repeating the stretching several times.

This exercise can be usefully repeated while sitting in an upright chair and while lying flat on the floor. Any help to stretch is useful, such as pulling on a door jamb, while standing, or on bed rails when lying down.

In everyday life, be aware from time to time of how well grounded you are. Are you pulled down by too much gravity or are you out of touch with the earth reality beneath your feet? Increasing your awareness will help you to keep a balance.

### Exercise 2 Vocal charisma
Choose a poem or a short piece of prose that you particularly like. Learn the lines by heart. Then, while alone, speak the poem aloud, using as much voice power as you can muster. Keep reciting your poem, trying variation of speed, using pauses and varying the tone of your voice.

Do your reciting with all your heart and soul. When you feel the need for a change, learn another verse or another poem. You might also find it helpful to read

| Name of friend | Charismatic power (rated 1-10) | Qualities that you think produce their charisma |
| --- | --- | --- |
|  |  |  |
|  |  |  |
|  |  |  |
|  |  |  |
|  |  |  |
|  |  |  |
|  |  |  |

aloud sometimes, but always take deep breaths and give it everything you've got.

People who are fearful of using their charismatic voice often gabble away quickly without pauses and use no variation of tone. Charismatic speakers can tolerate the pause that is full of meaning and can let their soul come right through their words.

### Exercise 3 Charismatic contact
There are two ways of improving your ability to make contact with other people with your energy, without actually touching them physically.

Eye contact is a most powerful way of touching others and allowing your charisma to flow to them. Do be careful not to pass too much of your energy to those who are so bound up that their own charisma is frozen or negative. You can practice eye contact by looking at your own eyes in a mirror, just staring and allowing all the feelings you have to flow outward. This method can also be used between two people and is a most powerful method, so be prepared for an outpouring of emotion.

The second way to make contact with your charisma is to listen intently to another person, giving them your total, undivided attention and imagining that at the same time your energy is flowing out and touching them. When your charisma touches another person, they will respond and feel that you understand. This kind of touching is what occurs when you feel empathy for the other.

### Exercise 4 Performance charisma
If you have a sport or hobby that involves some physical activity, then practice it without trying to make yourself do it. Let your body make its own response.

This technique is used to achieve an "inner" control of your sporting skills. Your mind transcends its instructional abilities and develops intuitive skills. For example, when practicing tennis, have dozens of balls and keep serving them, letting your body-mind give its own feedback to itself. Simply say aloud exactly where the ball landed each time and your adjustments will be natural. This is an example of your performance charisma at work.

When dancing, skating, running, jogging, walking, swimming and so on, keep on the move; give it everything you've got and try to find your own natural rhythm. Avoid being negatively self-critical and ignore mistakes, your body-mind will make any adjustments necessary. Soon you will find yourself aware of two dimensions, your normal physical self and your charismatic self.

Performance charisma can be stimulated anywhere at any time. All you have to do is give your performance your heart and soul and do not hold back for fear of failure. You will make mistakes, but your charisma will carry you through.

# Taking transactional advantage

The intellect is a small part of the mind, the power of which can be used coldly to out-think an opponent, in any tactical activity such as playing chess. It is the mental tool most parents use when teaching their children how to behave in the world to get the best out of it.

The intellect is parent-like; we use it to make logical sense of the world, but if you have observed a lively young baby trying to communicate, you will have realized that we are born with another kind of mentality called emotion.

While using our intellect, we can ignore any emotional signals from the body and while using emotions, we can ignore any mental signals from the intellect. Western education has tended to teach us to ignore emotions and some people, attempting to compensate, have swung in the opposite direction and concentrated on feelings at the expense of intellect.

In addition to our childlike emotion and our parent-like intellect, we have a very sensible, adult ability called intuition which, used properly, is a balance between hot emotions and cold intellect.

## Transactional analysis

The psychological theory of the process of transactional analysis is based on observations of how we actually behave when we communicate with each other. A transaction is a way in which two people communicate.

During a transaction between two people, each person can choose how to behave. They can behave as "parent" (**P**), as "adult" (**A**) or as "child" (**C**), i.e. they can use:

**P** = parent-like intellect, reasoning authoritatively;
**A** = adult-like intuition, linking feeling and logic;
**C** = childlike emotion, responding spontaneously.

Thus there are nine possible combinations in any communication between any two people, for example, a married couple.

## Possible transactions between a couple

The couple are beginning to discuss where to go on holiday. Each numbered transaction shows the first comment each might make if they were behaving as Parent (**P**), Adult (**A**) or Child (**C**) as defined above. In these examples either the husband or the wife is speaking first. You can choose which.

| One partner | | | The other partner |
|---|---|---|---|
| **P** | We should go camping again; we have the equipment. | ⟷ **P** | Yes we spent a lot last year; it would be a waste not to use it again. |
| **A** | I'd like to do a tour, seeing a variety of places. What would you like? | ⟷ **A** | I'd like to take things easy. Perhaps a cruise with two or three days in each port. |
| **C** | Oh, let's go to that dreamy hotel we found on our honeymoon. | ⟷ **C** | We could take the car this time and have some fun in the woods as well. |
| **P** | We shall have to take mother with us, we shouldn't leave her on her own. | ⟷ **A** | Perhaps we could ask her what she would like to do and then arrange something to suit us all. |
| **A** | I wonder if John and Mary might like to come with us? What do you think? Would you like them along? | ⟷ **P** | We can't ask them, unless we also ask Mark and Rebecca; it wouldn't be right. |
| **C** | I have a super idea; let's go to that naturist island. We could bask naked in the sun and . . . so on! | ⟷ **P** | How could we ever go naked; it wouldn't be decent. Anyway, we are too old for it now. |
| **P** | We can only afford to take a week this year. | ⟷ **C** | Oh, you old stick-in-the-mud, you never want to do anything exciting. |
| **A** | I've brought a variety of brochures. Would you like to look at them? | ⟷ **C** | Look at that beach and the swimming pool . . . oh, doesn't it just make you feel warm all over? |
| **C** | I want sun, sea and lots of fun. I just want to leave it all behind . . . and have no responsibilities. | ⟷ **A** | This looks a likely place. I'll check it really is close to the sea. |

## Taking transactional advantage

As you can see from the examples, once a person begins a transaction in one mode, they are likely to stay in that mode. The parent-like part of us is wary, on guard and concerned with what should or should not be done. The childlike part of us is relaxed, playful and innocent. The adult-like part of us is aware of alternatives and intuitive. At any point in a transaction, you can change the mode you are in and affect the outcome. In arguments, often one person becomes parent-like and the other becomes childlike. This produces deadlock. To alter the situation you can use the same mode as the other person or change to the mode neither of you is using.

Such a changes can be very helpful in intimate relations. In the example, the mode being used is in parenthesis at the end of each comment.

**Husband**: "You haven't got my dinner ready." (**C**)

**Wife**: "It will be ready in five minutes. Why don't you go and put your feet up and I'll bring you the newspaper and a drink? You know you should relax." (**P**)

**Husband**: "It's every day I have to put up with this. I slave away all day and the drivers are getting worse, like that stupid man over the road." (**C**)

**Wife**: "Well, you shouldn't let it upset you. Try to keep a tighter control on your feelings, dear." (**A**)

**Husband**: "Oh, for god's sake stop nagging me." (**C**)

**Wife**: "If you are going to start swearing, I will have to go out until you have calmed down." (**P**)

This kind of argument may have a familiar ring. One partner tries to reason with the other, who responds emotionally. To change the situation, both partners could benefit from a good, hot emotional catharsis and then make-up afterward.

Later, reason can take over, or better still, adult-like intuition, during which the problems underlying the emotional outbursts can be given an airing and perhaps some adjustments made.

---

## TYPES OF TRANSACTION

### P – P

Two people speaking with authority. This works very well when both parties are using the same rules and belong to the same belief system.

International discussions in the parent mode can be frustrating and become hostile, since the parties make very different assumptions.

### C – C

Two people relaxed and playful together. This is the best mode to be in for a party and for making love. Each person responds with a natural innocence, i.e. openly, without trying to take control of the other.

Things can become difficult when the parent mode intervenes, e.g. one person lays down a condition or makes a negative criticism. Then the transaction can become very volatile, or one partner will drop into parent mode.

### A – A

Two people respect each other enough to take the time and trouble to discuss all aspects of a situation, taking each other's feelings and intellect into consideration, and to negotiate fully should there be a dispute. Refer to **Chapter Four: Can you keep a cool head?** (pp. 100-101).

### P – C

Two people at loggerheads. At the most basic level, one person speaking from an authoritative base and the other is speaking from the heart. Invariably they clash.

At its worst, this combination is a re-enactment of unfinished business in the original child-parent relationship. Hence, the one in parent mode still thinks they "know best".

The Parent-Child combination can be either delightful or disastrous in a love relationship. At a mild level it is one partner occasionally playing parent to the other and vice versa. With plenty of A mode behavior in a relationship, the P – C combination can be a pleasure.

At the extremes, a P – C relationship becomes sadomasochistic, one person dominating and the other submitting. As with real children, our C mode can become quite helpless and the result can be beatings, rape and psychological castration.

### A – C

A situation in which the person in A mode understands and accepts the feelings being expressed by the other person. In this relationship, the one in A mode feels empathy with the one in C mode and is also aware of the implications of those feelings. For example, this relationship can occur between friends, when one is grieving the loss of a loved one (C mode) and the other is being there for that person, without criticism, but ready to respond as necessary.

### P – A

This is a relationship in which the person in A mode can hold their ground against claims of logic, authority or belief.

It is a very powerful position for the A mode person and difficult to maintain without slipping into P mode or C mode, as we all have a tendency to slip one way or the other.

This relationship is a good example of mind over matter. The whole being, intellect and heart, of the one in A mode can take advantage over the one who only has the P mode to draw upon.

# Psychic focusing

If psychic powers exist at all, they can certainly be used both positively and negatively. Here are some examples of attempts to focus psychic energy on objects, for entertainment, and to focus psychic energy on people, either to control them or to heal them.

## Disposing of negative energy

Believing in yourself is very important. A change of company and a touch of humor is always good for you. If you are being influenced negatively, you should get counselling or therapeutic help, so that you can see the pattern clearly and deal with it effectively.

Almost any kind of physical activity will loosen and

---

### PSYCHIC FOCUSING BY INDIVIDUALS

#### Psychic focusing on objects

Uri Geller hit the headlines in 1973 when he claimed to be bending cutlery and mending watches by psychic influence. Many people, especially children, have since claimed to be able to do the same and there are hundreds of bent keys and forks as evidence. Many were clearly cheating but the mystery remains. Uri Geller and many others are still performing.

During the 1960s Ted Serios became known for his "thoughtographs". He was a happy American from Illinois with no job and a taste for beer. He used a polaroid camera for his performances. He would peer at the camera and take his own photograph without touching the camera. He also took photographs of distant places and there are some polaroid prints of the Chicago water tower and a Canadian aircraft hanger. His sessions would be frenzied and, although he was studied by several scientists, it was hard to come to a clear conclusion, since his results were erratic.

#### Pure magic

Those amazing people who perform as professional magicians can do things that appear impossible. James Randi, one of America's most famous and accomplished magicians, has demonstrated how to bend spoons. He did this to prove that Uri Geller was using the same magic-psychology as he did.

Randi also did other things to discredit claims of psychic phenomena. He once put his assistant on a radio show, claiming to be a psychic, who asked people to phone in if anything remarkable happened during the program. The switchboard was jammed with calls: light bulbs exploded, mirrors cracked, refrigerators broke down, cats went wild and a host of other things happened. Randi now has a very hard job convincing people he is NOT psychic but a clever magician.

#### Testing psychic focusing

Tests to evaluate the powers of psychic focusing were carried out by Dr. Robert Morris at the Psychical Research Foundation of North Carolina. A person outside the room tries to influence the cat in its choice of squares to walk on. An observer compares the actual steps with the psychic wishes.

release negative energy that often blocks up your body. As you loosen up, so your attitude changes. The important point to remember is that the physical activity should be done for fun and not to win or break a record.

A brisk walk or a session of free dancing to your favourite tunes will often be sufficient. If your are unable, for example, to walk, then exercises can be done just as well in a chair. Nor is expensive equipment essential. Running or walking upstairs and down again several times, without holding the wall or the balustrade, is just as good as time spent on a cycling machine.

### Psychic focusing on people

### Witchcraft, voodoo and hexing
In all these activities, a person is said to influence another by spells, potions and curses. An outstanding example of a person apparently influenced by a curse occurred in 1960 at a well-equipped hospital in Oklahoma City, USA.

In January of that year, Finis P. Ernest, a successful businessman of 53, was admitted to the hospital with an acute attack of asthma. Soon he was well again and discharged.

Within 48 hours he was re-admitted, having a worse attack than ever. This occurred several times and as the months passed, he began to have fits and convulsions, yet several highly qualified doctors could find no organic cause for his condition.

Every time he was in hospital he said he felt depressed and hopeless. It became evident that whenever he had been in contact with his mother, his condition worsened. Doctors kept them separated, and Mr. Ernest improved. On 23 August he was cheerful and well, ready to go home to his wife, Josephine. He phoned his mother from the ward at around 6pm and was found gasping for breath at 6.35pm. He died twenty minutes later.

His doctor was so distressed, he investigated Finis Ernest's background, with the help of his wife, Josephine Ernest. It transpired that Finis was very influenced by his mother. He'd married twice but when his mother showed her disapproval, there had been sudden divorces.

Finally he'd married Josephine, whom his mother accepted. After 15 years of marriage, Finis and his wife had decided to sell the family business. When his mother was told, she became angry and said that something dire and bad would happen to him. When he had gone ahead with the sale he became ill. He believed that his mother was right; all the evidence pointed that way.

While in hospital, he had begun to see the connection between his illness and his mother's will, yet still felt she might be right. On the night of his death, he had plucked up the courage to tell his mother he was buying a new business, in which his mother would have no part. She apparently made no comment except to repeat her earlier warning. Within minutes he was dying.

### A miracle of healing
Many are the reports of people being miraculously healed by the psychic influence of a person who gave them attention, touched them and told them to be well.

Such an occurence took place during an acupuncture training session in London attended by ordinary medical doctors in 1972.

One doctor, Paul Henry, was a young man, qualified only five years earlier and interested in all forms of medicine that might be used to help his patients. In his own childhood, he had suffered polio and had been left with a very thin weak right leg and a tendency to lose his balance.

One day in June of that year, he was a little late for the training session and ran up the steps two at a time. He tripped, fell and rolled down to the bottom again. Fortunately he had no broken bones but some nasty bruises, including one on his cheekbone that would turn a spectacular purple color in a few days. He also had a cut over his right eye and looked a sorry mess when he finally stumbled into the training session.

The acupuncture doctor who was giving the training suggested that Paul be the "patient" for this session. Paul agreed and lay on the inspection couch. The doctor slowly and gently massaged Paul's bruises and strained muscles, sometimes pressing at certain points with his finger tips.

Paul said he felt better and could something be done about his face? The doctor worked on his face, talking to him all the while, telling Paul his bruise and his cut would soon be healed. Paul described the experience as being like shots of electricity passing through his skin.

Paul then left the inspection couch and the training session then continued for a further two hours. As he was getting ready to leave, he asked a friend how his faced looked. All the 12 people present were amazed to see that Paul's face was clear. There was a slight scar where the small cut had been and a pinkness where the bruise had been.

# Pain control

Our reaction to pain is to prevent serious injury and to warn us of dangers in the world around us. Without it we would be a danger to ourselves yet we have the power to control pain.

**How pain messages are sent to the brain**

There are two types of nerve fiber that carry pain impulses. One set responds to surface touch such as a bang or a prick and the other, more numerous set of fibers, conducts their impulses to the brain very slowly from both the surface and from every organ inside the body.

These two sets of fibers account for why we often have two sensations of pain, for example when you bang a toe. The first sensation is immediate and sharp as the nerve fibers from the surface announce the pain. The second sensation, a little later, is a throbbing, spreading pain that even shoots up your foot and lasts much longer. These impulses are transmitted from both surface and internal parts of your toe and foot; they may take as long as a second to reach your brain.

In the brain, surface impulses reach the parietal lobe, which maps all kinds of body sensations but the others are registered in the part of the brain's frontal lobe that is closely connected with emotional reactions.

**The perception of pain**

Apart from people who have deficiencies of nerve or brain cells, researchers have found that awareness of pain varies from person to person and in different circumstances.

A study of World War II soldiers showed that only one in three of those severely wounded asked for morphine to control their pain after the initial shock period was over.

A study of civilians undergoing voluntary surgery involving similar wounds showed only one in five asked for morphine. From these studies it was concluded that the amount of pain perceived is due to many factors, one of which is the significance of the wound.

In daily life many people appear able to control pain.

Ballet dancers know that certain steps are extremely painful, yet when they are performing there is no sensation of pain. All sports have some kind of pain barrier to be crossed and many ordinary people have undertaken immense acts of courage while somehow holding pain at bay.

Similarly, there are people who apparently feel no pain while undertaking various religious rituals, such as stabbing themselves, passing needles through the skin or walking on hot coals.

So how is the sensation of pain regulated? Does active courage or the action of performance turn a tap controlling pain messages? Certainly it has recently been discovered that people who are mobile feel less pain that those who are forced into immobility.

**Pain control is an activity**

To control pain there has to be an active belief in one's own ablity to heal and to survive.

Pain control is not a matter of "grin and bear it". Crying because of physical or psychological pain has a calming effect and stimulates the release of pain-killers in the body. A good, deep sobbing from the bottom of the belly is extremely relieving and can easily turn into a more positive feeling of power . . . and even into a healing belly laugh.

The stimulation of the whole body through sobbing and laughing are two of the activities encouraged in pain clinics, where people go for relief from all kinds of pains.

Some pain becomes chronic because of damage to the body but sometimes pain remains when everything is healed. This seems to occur to people who tend to believe they have to suffer or who expect to suffer. Some people may overprotect the previously injured area and even become frightened of the pain getting worse.

Once this attitude of mind is changed, usually through exercises that release the tensions, the pain disappears. In these circumstances, putting the painful areas to work

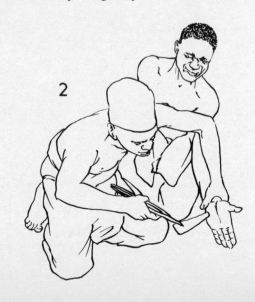

again helps to release pain.

It would appear there is a strong case for "mind over matter" in the area of self-regulated pain control.

## Pain regulation

In 1969 it was discovered that specific stimulation of the brain stem produced analgesia as effective as that produced by morphine and other opiates. The stimulation of the brain stem activates certain nerves which use peptide substances called enkephalins. These natural enkephalins act on the pain messages in a way similar to the effect of morphine. Enkephalins are our natural opiates.

Eighteen analgesic peptides have been identified in the brain. One of these can be 50 times more effective than morphine and is called β-endorphin. This natural painkiller is released directly into the bloodstream from the pituitary gland in times of physiological stress. Thus, under creative stress, we are capable of releasing our own natural painkiller.

Chinese acupuncture, which has been used for over 4500 years, is now recognized as a method of pain control. Its effect can be so analgesic that major surgery can be performed while the patient remains awake. It is thought that the acupuncture needles also stimulate the production of our natural opiates.

It is important to realize that non-creative stress is a chronic condition that can interfere with the easy flow of natural body regulation. Quite often we are unaware of chronic stress, for example in our muscles, until we begin to exercise them. This is why any exercise routine should be developed slowly.

Some drugs, such as naloxone can block the action of morphine in the body; the same drug can also block the production of natural opiates, such as β-endorphin, and can negate the effect of acupuncture.

## Power of the mind to control pain

Your expectations can affect your actual situation. This kind of statement is made in many situations. Its validity can be confirmed in a medical context.

## The placebo effect

In 1988 John Levine of the University of California in San Francisco was experimenting to discover how belief can alleviate pain. Healthy volunteers who had had wisdom teeth extracted were told they would be given a pain-killer intravenously. In fact they all received injections of harmless saline placebo.

Half the volunteers were given the placebo injection by Dr. Levine himself who was wearing a white coat with a stethoscope hanging from the pocket. He went through a ritual of giving great attention to each person and making it obvious as he was injecting them.

The other half of the volunteers were given their placebo injections by computer-controlled equipment, without a doctor or nurse in sight.

All the volunteers were asked to judge their pain levels at intervals on a numerical scale. Those given the injection by machine suffered a great deal of pain while those given the personal attention of the doctor suffered very little.

It would appear that belief in the power of the person giving the injection ascribed power to the injection itself. Thousands of people participated in these experiments with the same results. Why was the perception of pain by the two groups so significantly different? Belief that they would feel no pain apparently stimulated the release of natural endorphins. It is interesting that when volunteers in the same experiments were given naloxone, which inhibits the effect of pain-killers, the placebo effect was also inhibited, i.e. naloxone had inhibited the release of natural endorphins.

Expectation, emotion and arousal all influence our perception of pain. Movement, including rubbing of surface injuries, stimulates the release of natural pain-inhibitors but belief in one's ability to get better, survive and be free from pain is also a powerful means of stimulation.

**1** The Indian mystic Kuda Bux demonstrated his powers of overcoming pain by walking over hot ashes for the University of London Council of Psychical Investigation in 1935.

**2** Kenya's Digo tribe use trial by fire to test a suspect's guilt or innocence. If he or she is burned after the application of a hot iron guilt is considered proved.

**3** North American Indians, as well as many other primitive societies, used pain as an initiation test. In this endurance test youths are strung up on hooks inserted just inside their skin.

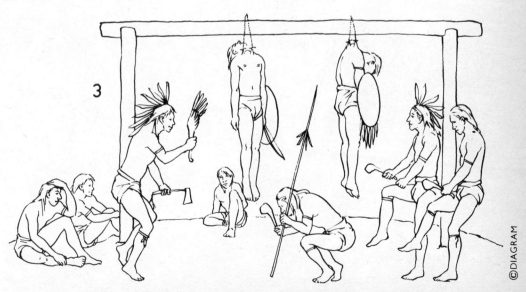

# Holding your ground

Stating a case against opposition involves remaining stable and holding a strong position. This includes a sound mental argument, a strong emotional thrust and a grounded physical position. If any one of these three elements are weakened or missing, the opponent is likely to gain from it.

In personal assertion training, the development of each of these three elements stimulates the growth of the weakest of the three.

Time is needed to think through an argument before launching into it. This in itself gives a sense of physical strength and clears the mind of irrelevant emotions.

Time spent talking through any strong emotions and allowing them to flow, will sort out feelings and add fuel to the mental argument. Emotional output in a debate needs to be felt but it should not be overpowering.

### Fear versus charisma

A little anxiety can be stimulating, making you ready for action. Too much anxiety turns into frozen fear when movement becomes essential to survival. If your charisma, presence or sense of self is easily available, then fear can be motivating.

If a person is pessimistic and believes only the worst will happen, the brain sends messages to the heart and to the immune system. Little, by little the body will lose its vitality, although no organic change will happen. Extreme fear can precipitate inexplicable death. Personal charisma will guard against such losses.

To understand more about your charisma, refer to **Chapter Four: Are you using your charisma?** (pp. 108-109):

### The importance of physical attitude

Physical position is a strong element in any debate, clash of opinion or battle. There are three aspects that need to be given attention.

**1** Physical bearing has its own message: a person standing upright and looking directly at an opponent is already asserting himself. The position of the feet is very important when holding that position: feet slightly apart and knees slightly bent gives flexibility.

**2** Physical position in space adds a powerful dimension. Being locked in a corner is generally a weak position. The direction of the light in a room can be used to advantage. Having it behind you and falling directly on an opponent can be useful in situations where you wish to dominate. People who wish to appear as authority figures have a habit of doing this. However, you can lose control if an opponent moves to avoid the light, so it is wise to chose a more satisfactory position for both.

**3** The positive physical presence of several other people. An entertainer in a movie studio has a much harder job projecting himself than an entertainer on stage. In the presence of many people who are involved, the energy field pulsates to and fro among them. The combined effort becomes greater than the sum of the individual efforts.

This applies to a performer whose performance is greater with an audience than ever it could be when he is alone. It also applies to any group of people performing together: a troupe of dancers, a gang of hooligans, an army unit, a pressure group or a party at a fiesta.

Humans, when confronted with a threat, are stimulated by a physiochemical reaction which produces a flight or fight response.

Humans, when in combat or under serious threat, use their heightened emotional reactions to vitalize their actions.

## The power of the circle

The best effect can be achieved when a group of people combine their energies in a circular form. The energy then passes from one member to the next and creates a strength that is hard to penetrate.

When people "close ranks" they also close their combined energy field and erect an invisible wall of power. This is probably the most effective way there is for a group of people to hold their ground against an aggressor. And if the aggressors dash round and round outside that circle, the power of the circle is enhanced.

Anyone at the center of such a circle will receive stimulation. This central position can be used positively, to enhance sexuality or healing, if occupied by a member of the group or negatively, to engender fear or despair, if occupied by a prisoner of the group.

Such arrangements occur in many situations daily. The power of the circle helps each member to hold their position in it. Thus, members of teams perform beyond their individual capacities by helping, healing or winning. In negative situations, many individuals will do acts of cruelty which they would never do when alone.

Throughout history and in all cultures, circle dancing around sacred objects had the aim of evoking extra powers within the group. This example is an Apache fire dance.

## THE BATTLE OF MIRBAT

There are many stories of small groups of people holding what appear to be impossible positions under extreme conditions. The strength of collective energies may have made the difference in what was a delicately balanced situation. The Battle of Mirbat in Oman, South Arabia, is a modern example of just such a situation.

A group of ten SAS soldiers, from the British Army Training Team, had been training the Sultan's counter-guerrilla groups, known as "firqas" to resist attacks from the Marxist guerrillas of the Dhofar Liberation Front. They were expecting to leave on Wednesday, 19 July 1972, in the middle of the monsoon season.

On the previous night, all seemed quiet enough but the guerrillas were amassing 250 of their best men for an outright frontal assault on the tiny coastal town of Mirbat. Before dawn broke on that Wednesday, this small garrison town was surrounded by 25 units each of ten guerrillas, armed to the teeth with mortars, machine guns, Kalashnikov assault rifles, grenades and a Carl Gustav rocket launcher.

Mirbat was isolated, protected only by its surrounding barbed wire. Inside the wire were the ten SAS men in their team house and 30 Askaris from northern Oman with slow firing rifles who occupied Wali's Fort; inside the town itself were 40 of the local firqa, asleep just before dawn; finally there were about 25 men of the Dhofar Province Gendarmerie just inside the fence at the DG Fort, in front of which was an old 25-pounder gun.

The first attack was on eight Gendarmerie just outside the hill, four of whom survived and escaped to the town. The ensuing battle was heavily weighted in favor of the attacking guerrillas but coordination between the very different defending groups within the wire was outstanding.

The SAS Captain M.J.A. Kealy, aged 23, was responsible for making many difficult and impeccable decisions and the response of all the men involved was courageous in the face of what appeared to be impossible odds. Under the leadership of Captain Kealy, the very mixed army of 113 men who held their ground at Mirbat, evidently believed in their combined ability to keep the better-armed and initially more organized guerrillas at bay.

The rebels were defeated and when the war ended four years later, it was revealed that so shaken were they by the resistance met from Mirbat, that they never managed to deploy as many troops again. The total Mirbat casualties were 8 dead and 3 seriously wounded. The 250 guerrillas left 30 bodies and 10 wounded behind but the total was thought to be much higher.

117

# Using your natural genius

Are you a genius? Do you have any of those qualities generally associated with being a genius? In common usage, the word genius is applied to someone who does something extraordinarily well. Also, it can be used affectionately to describe someone close who has done something particularly clever or kind.

Historically, the word has a wider meaning. In the English Oxford Dictionary, definitions of genius include:

- the guardian spirit of a person
- the spirit that influences a person for good
- a prevalent feeling, drift or inspiration
- natural ability
- instinctive and extraordinary imaginative, creative or inventive capacity

These definitions indicate that everyone has genius. It may take the form of a personal guardian spirit or an openness to influences for good. Your genius may also appear when you become involved in the prevalent mood among many people. Certainly your natural abilities are a part of your genius and, since you have instincts, you will have some imaginative, creative or inventive capacity, which may not yet have been revealed.

Genius can be recognized in all walks of life, as in these examples:

**1** In the arts: Shakespeare; Rembrandt; Mozart; and Anna Pavlova.

**2** In science and technology: Galileo; Pasteur; Bell; and Einstein.

**3** In war and politics: Alexander the Great; Napoleon; Bismarck; and Churchill.

## IMPROVING YOUR PHYSICAL GENIUS

### Your genius at work
Most people associate the orgasm with sexual intercourse. Orgasm is a manifestation of your power for genius. When you put your heart and soul into your love-making, your genius is revealed as an instinctive, creative pleasure response. Orgasm has the touch of genius when all goes well.

Mature lovers, who put their heart and soul into their love-making, know how to extend the pleasure sensation for a period of time, like half an hour or more, before they climax and collapse; they also know how to spend all day making love by using their genii for touch, massage, relaxation and play.

### What turns you on?
Do you confine yourself to sex or have you a rich life full of things and experiences that can turn you on? Does your sport turn you on? Can your genius respond to a sunset, a glorious view, a fragrant flower, the memory of wood-smoke, a picture, a photograph or a favorite tune?

Can you enjoy life? Do you love watching your children play, seeing your grandparents happy or stroking the cat? Is a sunny day enough to make you happy? Are you constantly amazed at the wonder of the world around you? The technology, the noises, the voices and the many ways of living?

Sexual orgasm is a very special expression of genius, but any form of excitement and interest can turn into a little energy orgasm of sheer physical pleasure. If more people in this world could enjoy the pleasure to be had from the expression of their genius, then molestation, rape and other violences associated with fear of sex, would disappear.

### Genius demands your heart and soul
Your creative genius is not confined to sexual intercourse. Your genius can be released orgasmically in many activities providing you do it with all your heart and soul, such as dancing, painting, inventing, acting, sport, building, designing, creating things and so on.

Some of these activities need specific skills. Expression through the voice is probably one route to the expression of genius that is available to all who can open their mouths and make sounds.

## Protecting your genius

We find it difficult to get on with some people and others are directly antagonistic. Being in crowds of people can also be most disturbing. These unwanted influences from outside may interfere with the aura and impinge on your internal genius.

To protect yourself from these unwelcome intrusions you can create a balloon-like structure around yourself that will prevent interference.

Begin by imagining a large, heavy balloon on the ground in front of you. It is big enough for you to walk into through a door in its side.

Go into the balloon, close the door and layer the inside with cushions until you have enough to be able to sit or lie down on the cushions, close your eyes and relax.

Now imagine in your mind that the walls of the balloon are becoming tougher and harder, completely protecting you from everything outside. Never try too hard when visualizing. Just let it happen.

When you are satisfied that nothing harmful can penetrate the hardened skin of the balloon, relax for a few minutes. Then get on with whatever you have to do. You will be able to handle unwelcome influences quite easily, without any disturbance to your genius.

## The genius in your voice

If you think you can't sing, the bathroom is a traditional place for making whatever noises come from your larynx. While taking a shower, make noises and enjoy it. The louder, the better.

Begin by taking a few deep breaths and then, while breathing steadily outward, make a single sound at a pitch that is most comfortable. Try using vowel sounds aaaaa, eeeeeee, oooooooo, iiiiiii, uuuuuuu. Then add consonants for example: beeeebeeeebeeee, daaadaaadaaa, loooloooolooo and so on until you find some you like.

As you become more confident, make familiar phrases, such as yo ho! yo ho! yo ho! and yippee-i-ay! If you have children in the house, they are wonderfully inventive and usually have a wealth of tunes and noises for you to repeat. They too will enjoy having an adult around who will join in and make a noise too.

If you can pick up tunes, try imitating favorites you hear. You don't have to join a choir, unless you have a good voice, but do join in wherever there is some happy, hearty singing. Gospel singers and barbershop groups are usually in great voice.

If singing is just not your line, then try chants or fast rapping. Rhythmic chants are very powerful and if you prefer just talking, try doing it as fast as you can, then slowing down and varying the pitch of your words.

If you practice with all your heart and soul, you will soon find yourself expressing your genius as a voice-orgasm! The sheer delight of bursting free from deep inside your lungs can open a whole new world for you. You will feel alive and more able to express yourself in many ways.

Men will perhaps find the use of the voice during love-making a less familiar experience than women, but using your voice will extend orgasmic pleasure throughout the body. Some sex therapists recommend that men cultivate this form of the energy orgasm. As the flow of excitement rises during love-making, transfer some of that energy into sound.

Just before physical ejaculation, let your voice make the most uninhibited, free, sustained sound from the bottom of your heart. This should be done immediately before the peak where a man can hover with a crescendo of pure, vocal release that will suffuse throughout his body. In this way he can enjoy repeated orgasms in harmony with his partner, while retaining a high level of arousal. The voice can be an erotic ejaculation as powerful as any seminal ejaculation.

# Capturing an audience

An audience is entranced, captured or held enthralled by performances in which the performer can only communicate to them through their five senses: sight, hearing, touch, smell, taste but adds an additional response which they experience as a sixth sense – their reaction to the performer's charisma.

Entertainers down the years have tried to explain what is this energy. If you haven't got IT no amount of technique will bring the audience to its feet. If you have plenty of IT you can leave your mark in the world of entertainment for a while even without much skill. If you have the skill plus that exciting IT, then you will be a truly great performer.

IT captures your audience. and it has to be genuine. Most performers will tell you IT is a projection of your truest self and the hardest thing to achieve. Modern

## POLITICAL ORATION

Here are some memorable words which were the expressions of powerful leaders in democracies.

### Abraham Lincoln
His Gettysburg Address was unprepared and not scheduled when part of the battlefield of Gettysburg was consecrated as a permanent cemetery on 19 November 1863. This is how his entirely inpromptu speech began:

"Four score and seven years ago our fathers brought forth on this continent a new nation, conceived in Liberty and dedicated to the proposition that all men are created equal.

Now we are engaged in a great civil war, testing whether that nation, or any nation so conceived and so dedicated can long endure. We are met on a great battlefield of that war. We have come to dedicate a portion of that field as a final resting place for those who here gave their lives that the nation might live. It is altogether fitting and proper that we should do this.

But in a larger sense, we cannot dedicate – we cannot consecrate – we cannot hallow – this ground. The brave men, living and dead, who struggled here, have consecrated it, far above our poor power to add or detract."

In Lincoln's second inaugural address, made on 4 March 1865 six weeks before his murder and the Civil War's end, he included this powerful statement:

". . . on the occasion corresponding to this four years ago all thoughts were anxiously directed to an impending civil war. All dreaded it, all sought to avert it. While the inaugural address was being delivered from this place, devoted altogether to *saving* the Union without war, insurgent agents were in the city seeking to *destroy* it without war – seeking to dissolve the Union and divide effects by negotiation.

Both parties deprecated war but one of them would *make* war rather than let the nation survive, and the other would *accept* war rather than let it perish, and the war came."

### Sir Winston Churchill
Political leader of a World War II coalition government in Britain, Churchill roused people with his speeches. He made them believe they would win. He stirred pride, national feeling, a sense of purpose and the will to do impossible things.

A short speech, given to the boys of his old Harrow School in England on 14 October 1941 when Hitler's armies were closing in on Moscow,included this passage:

"Do not let us speak of darker days; let us speak rather of sterner days. These are not dark days. These are great days, the greatest days our country has ever lived; and we must thank God that we have been allowed, each according to our stations, to play a part in making these days memorable in the history of our race."

Controlling the audience may take the form of conducting their actions, instructing them, enthusing them, influencing them, or inspiring them by example.

**Expressing your fantasies**
Fantasies that never see the light of day are liable to distort reality and turn life into a nightmare. When they are enjoyed, owned as our own and given some space for their expression, fantasies can be powerful tools of the mind and can stimulate a sense of humor and help us to bring about changes that we hardly believe possible.

There are several ways of giving expression to your fantasies, such as: writing a story; drawing a picture; building a theme park; performing a play, movie or video; singing and dancing; creating fantasies in fashion, costume or fancy dress; playing fantasy games with an intimate partner; using special occasions to dress as you fantasize.

find out much about yourself that you didn't know before. You may even want to create the room for yourself in reality.

**2 Creating a new appearance**
Dressing-up is an activity as old as the human race. Ever since people walked this earth, they have daubed themselves with colors, arrayed themselves in an amazing range of clothing and added jewelry and symbols of their identity.

Dressing for our many occupational and cultural roles is part of normal daily life. We respond to uniforms, career-wear and the fashions of social groups. Dressing-up can be enjoyed in private or with a few chosen family or friends. If you venture outside in your new fantasy dress, you must expect different reactions. You can learn much about how to present yourself by trying out different styles of clothing.

You might like to select an already designed mode of dress or you might prefer to invent your own. Ideas can be collected from magazines, other people in the streets, museums, waxworks, plays, movies, videos and television.

Changing your appearance can boost confidence and stimulate new ideas about self-presentation and the effect you have on other people. Most of all, enjoy yourself.

# How to blow your mind

Mind-blowing experiences are not a new phenomenon, although the terminology might give the impression that they began only in the 1950s and 60s.

Mind-blowing means putting yourself into a state in which your perceptions are altered. This can vary in intensity from attaining enlightenment to having free-rolling halucinations; in some instances the body does something that defies mental logic, such as walking on hot coals.

The realization of an entirely new point of view is often called mind-blowing and may be linked with the old saying: "Take a breath of fresh air and blow the

## BLOWING YOUR MIND

You may already use some of these methods. Some are temporary, others produce a more permanent shift in outlook. Whatever you decide to do, be aware that you are doing things that will alter the bio-chemical balance in your brain, which affects your behavior. Some of these methods lead to habit-forming dangers and disturbances in your health and well-being.

### 1 Cultural adjustment

Anyone who spends some time living in cultures or groups different from their own will find the experience affects their views and is mildly mind-blowing when making adjustments. Known as culture shock, the effect of being in a group of people who live according to rules that are different from your own can change your perceptions and be an exciting experience.

One way to begin to adapt to a different culture is to dress as the people do. Imagine the changes of behavior and outlook that would have to take place if these pairs of people changed their clothes and their roles with each other.

- A rock star exchanged with a Sikh business person.
- An Indian princess exchanged with an American cheer leader.
- A white executive exchanged with an unemployed colored person.
- An army officer exchanged with a Hell's Angel.

### 2 Physical routines

To achieve a mind-blowing state a regular program of physical exercise should be followed, building from simple to more complex activities. Instructions are normally available in classes and at meditation centers.

Also we are capable of producing our own soothing pain-killers, called endorphins, that are released in the brain during physical exercise and massage.

- Bio-energetics to cathart tensions.
- Pre-natal excercise to prepare for overcoming birth pains.
- Hatha Yoga to open the chakras (energy centers).
- Aerobics to increase oxygen supply to the blood.

### 3 Therapies

Many therapeutic processes are mind-blowing. Indeed, if your perceptions are not altered, the therapy has been of little use. There are many available: all should be undertaken only with qualified therapists.

**a** Freudian psycho-analysts examine your relationships and your views of authority figures.

**b** Encounter therapists clear emotional hang-ups in peer relationships.

**c** Gestalt therapists identify and unite your top-dog and your under-dog.

**d** Counselling helpers act impartially, listening to your thoughts and expressions of your feelings with the intention of helping you release your own anxieties.

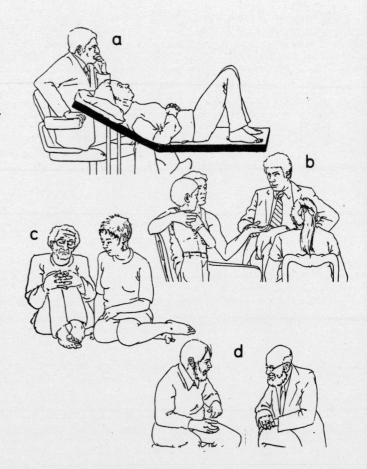

cobwebs away". To most people, mild inebriation, a brisk walk or a good night's love-making will suffice.

Cobwebs are metaphors for the clutter we carry around in our minds. Fixed attitudes, precious beliefs, stale assumptions and outdated information can all be given a shake-up when we partake in a mind-blowing activity.

The mind-blown state in which we find ourselves can be idyllic or quite terrifying. The change in our perceptions may be good or bad and because we change our viewing point does not mean we see any more of the whole picture than we did before.

## 4 Alcoholic liquors

Ethyl alcohol, a colorless liquid, is the basis of all the common intoxicating drinks such as wines, sherries, beers and spirits. In small amounts liquor releases inhibitions and can cause loss of control. Some people get happy, others become violent. It is addictive and can cause damage to the oesophagus, stomach and liver. Taken in moderation it can lighten the mind and the head. Large quantities in the blood will cause death. Because of its effects on the brain and people's actions in the community after drinking, some religions and societies consider taking alcohol an evil. Most have laws fixing a minimum to age for alcohol consumption.

## 5 Drugs

A drug is any chemical compound which can affect the body's functioning. The use of drugs should be confined to medical purposes. Drug abuse is the use of any drug for a purpose other than a medical one. One of the major damages of drug taking is its addictive ability to control the body's physical needs.

**Increased stimulation from various types of drugs**

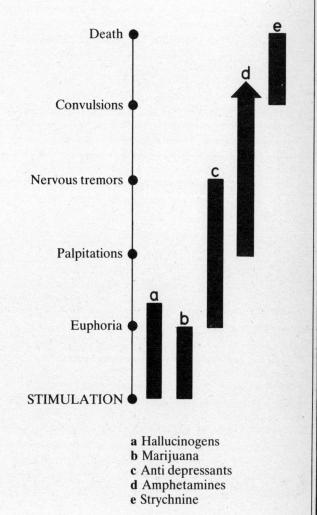

a Hallucinogens
b Marijuana
c Anti depressants
d Amphetamines
e Strychnine

**Concentration of alcohol in the blood**

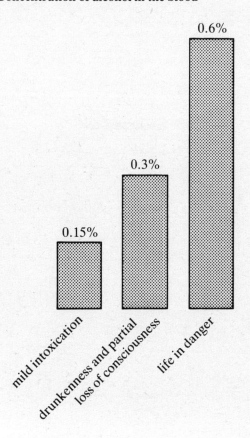

# Flying high

There are many human activities that can make you feel "high", i.e. feel as if you were flying. Some people get high on drugs or coffee, others on sex and dancing. Vast mountain ranges, glorious sunsets or profound music lift the spirits of many and some get high on collectables, sailing ships, cats or the latest in avant garde fashion.

Feeling high, however, is not the same as actually being able to lift yourself high off the ground by apparently supernatural powers. Levitation is the ability to suspend your body above the ground with no means of

## LEVITATION

### Levitation: one of the Great Siddhis

In the yogic tradition there are eight Great Siddhis or accomplishments. These are powers which form a step-by-step progression towards the ultimate state of consciousness called enlightenment.

According to the Maharishi, there are eight channels in the human body through which each of the Siddhis can manifest, making 64 channels of enlightenment in all. Of the eight Great Siddhis, the Maharishi considers Strength, Friendliness, Omniscience, Invisibility and Levitation to be the most beneficial.

### The powers of meditation

In the early days of TM training, many devoted practitioners of the techniques reported strange experiences such as seeing visions, feeling invisible and being able to see through other people.

Some reported they felt as if they had become floaters and almost like air itself as they seemed to expand and fill the universe. In this way they lost their sense of identity. Were these experiences real or imagined?

### Hallucinations

Among the strangest experiences the human mind can create for us are illusions known as hallucinations. These are known to occur in specific conditions, including during periods of sensory deprivation. When the brain is deprived of stimulation it appears to create its own diversions, in the form of hallucinations.

The most common are visual hallucinations but others occur quite frequently, i.e. auditory, tactile and gustatory hallucinations. Perhaps the most alarming is the hallucination of being touched, for example by insects crawling over the skin.

Meditation effectively cuts off messages to the brain from outside and diminishes the number of messages being received by the brain from inside the body. It has been suggested by scientists, that people who meditate regularly for lengthy periods are creating their own hallucinatory "siddhis" through sensory deprivation.

### The Maharishi European Research University

The Maharishi wanted to determine the truth. Were experienced meditators experiencing the siddhis or were they only hallucinating? The Maharishi opened his university of meditation at Seelisberg, a small Swiss town near Lake Lucerne, in 1975.

Programs of transcendental meditation were run for people who were already experienced meditators. In 1976 research into the siddhis began. Objective siddhis such as Levitation were chosen for investigation as they could be observed; there was no way in which a meditator could, for example, hallucinate levitation.

Initially people who had been regular meditators for 15 to 20 years were chosen to undertake a program of simple exercises designed to release the siddhis. This program was built upon the Yoga Sutras of Patanjali and the participants were not told what to expect.

Many of those people reported having experiences beyond their wildest imagination and some spoke of breaking the boundaries of normal existence.

In December 1976 there was a gathering at Seelisberg of about 900 TM instructors from all over the world. They all participated in six months intensive instruction and, according to the reports from that conference, 40% of the meditators achieved levitation and a few were able to become invisible.

In the ancient Vedas (Hindu Scriptures) there are stories of people levitating who had attained the necessary coordinated harmony of mind and body. After the completion of his research program, the Maharishi claimed that those who practiced TM could achieve the mind-body coordination to release the Siddhi of Levitation.

### A challenge from Swami Vishnu Devanada

Founder of the International Sivanada Yoga Vedanta Centres, whose headquarters are in Quebec, Canada, Swami Vishnu is author of several books on meditation and an advanced yogi himself. He expressed doubt about the Maharishi's claims and suggested that the appearance of levitation could be achieved by hopping movements which he claims can be achieved while in the lotus position.

Members of the Vedanta Centre demonstrated the hopping techniques while in the lotus position. Photographs of them showed the strain involved to make the hop. In photographs of levitators issued over the years by the Maharishi, the meditators are relaxed and their hands lie easily in their laps.

Swami Vishnu does not discount levitation; he claims that it can be achieved but takes years of practice of breathing exercises and careful diet and cannot be taught in a short course.

support. In 1977 the Maharishi Mahesh Yogi declared that he could levitate his body from the ground and that he could teach others to do the same using his technique of Transcendental Meditation (TM).

## HOW LEVITATION IS POSSIBLE

It is part of yogic tradition that the body can take different forms according to the state of consciousness that a person is in. Levitation can therefore occur only when in a particular state of consciousness.

| States of consciousness | Body manifestation |
|---|---|
| Ordinary waking state | Normal physical body |
| Dreaming sleep | Subtle or astral body. In Sanskrit (ancient Indian language) this is known as the linga sharira and consists of three sheaths: jiva, the vital force; the manas, the mind; the buddhi, the understanding. |
| Dreamless sleep | The jivatman: the volitional or causal body. |
| Cataleptic state | The invisible body |
| Undifferentiated consciousness of Bliss | The universal body |

### Yogic states of consciousness
These different states are achieved by breathing exercises known as pranayama and should never be undertaken by anyone without guidance. Yogic tradition claims that everyone spends some time of each day in all these states but is not conscious of them.

Each state of consciousness is also characterized by a different type of breathing known as pranic states. In the *Sivagama*, an ancient yogic book, the human aura is said to demonstrate the state of breathing or prana. Normally the aura surrounds the body by a distance of about 12 fingers. This changes according to the type of activity and the type of breathing.

When a person is at rest, the size of the aura is said to indicate the type of person. According to the ancient book of *Sivagama*, types of aura are measured again in finger widths.

As length diminishes the results become more extraordinary. You can see from the table below where you stand. If you are a true poet, for example, you have a better chance of levitating than an ordinary person.

### The relationship between mind and breath
Breath is known as prana in yogic traditions and in the practice of aikido (the Japanese martial art), prana is directed by visualization. There are many aikido exercises which use the mind to direct the breath. The practice of aikido involves harnessing an aggressor's energy and turning it back upon him.

All serious sportspeople, dancers and other performers know that correct breathing is essential to success: many also know that visualizing the pranic energy shooting through the body makes the activity appear so effortless.

| Type of person | Size of aura | | |
|---|---|---|---|
| An ordinary person | 12 | A great orator | 8 |
| Person free from all desires | 11 | A person with second sight | 7 |
| A pleasant person with a sense of humor | 10 | A levitator | 6 |
| A poet | 9 | A person with supernatural speed | 5 |
| | | A person who manifests all 8 Siddhis | 4 |

© DIAGRAM

# The power of emotion

The capacity to be open and experience inexplicably deep and moving emotions means that you are available to life; you are capable of expressing and living life to the full. The word emotion. . . E-MOTION means outward movement. With it you will have stamina, strength and suppleness of heart, mind and body. We give names to our feelings, but they all come from the same source within us.

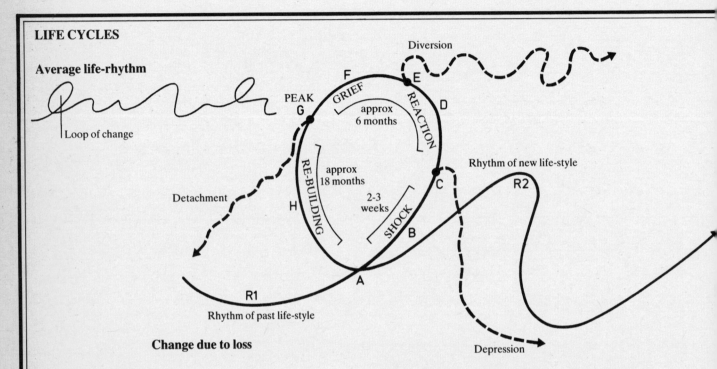

**LIFE CYCLES**

**Average life-rhythm**

Loop of change

PEAK G

F GRIEF

approx 6 months

RE-BUILDING

approx 18 months

2-3 weeks

Detachment

H

SHOCK

B

A

R1

Rhythm of past life-style

**Change due to loss**

Diversion

E REACTION D

Rhythm of new life-style

C

R2

Depression

**The natural stages of grieving**
**R1 Past life-style**: The pattern of life continues until a sudden or expected loss.
**A The loss**, due to: Death of close person; illness; miscarriage; theft; attack; separation; divorce; disappearance; accident; failure; retirement; redundancy, etc.
**B Shock**: A natural temporary numbness or blankness during which the shocked person appears to carry on as normal. Most people's immediate response to a great shock is utter disbelief. Some people become more efficient and organized and others more dreamy and relaxed. During the shock period, there may be sudden outbursts of emotion. Occasionally, a person will be in shock longer than the average two or three weeks, will cut themselves off from the event and refuse to talk about the deceased person or allow anyone else to use their name. Depression may take over and prevent the grieving period even beginning properly. Shock can occur twice: once when, for example, getting news of a terminal illness or a serious accident and then when the person dies.
**C Onset of reaction**: React to the loss or opt out of the grief cycle by depressing all emotion. Sometimes a physical illness may release the unexpressed grief or

there may even be abnormal behavior or loss of memory.
**D REACTION**: Anger at life, at God, at self, at the dead person; helplessness, sense of relief, guilt, asking "why?", dreaming, disappointment when deceased does not come through the door as usual, yearning and a heartfelt "NO" to what has happened. Reaction often overlaps with grieving.
**E Onset of grieving**: Here the most powerful emotions emerge and the deepest reality of the loss is being felt. The choice is to plunge into the grieving period or opt out of the cycle. The latter get busy with a hundred and one diversions, such as compulsive sex, work, sports, having affairs, moving house, eating, drinking, smoking or drug-taking, which use up the emotional energy but leave the grieving unfinished. . . and can go on for years. Some people suddenly lose all interest in these compulsions.
**F GRIEVING**: Wholesome grieving involves deep sobbing from the belly and is physically painful until released when there is great relief and pleasure. Like the belly-laugh, belly-sobbing hurts until afterward when it is as pleasantly rewarding. Friends simply holding give strength and helps the person stay grounded. Never ever tell a grieving person to control themselves. Give them

**Some named emotions**
- Laughter expresses humor and pleasure. Sarcasm denies them.
- Love expresses compassion and sexuality. Hate denies them.
- Anger expresses aggression and outrage. Hostility denies them.

- Grief expresses loss and regret. Indifference denies them.
- Fear expresses vulnerability and uncertainty. Bravado denies them.

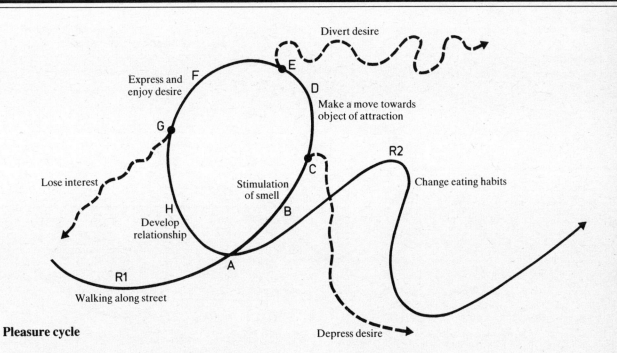

**Pleasure cycle**

protection from harm and space to grieve.
**G PEAK of change**: People often remember exactly when this moment comes, when the loss is realized and the possibility of a future also becomes a reality. About six months after the loss, the person either moves toward re-building and making a new life or becomes detached and start wandering back into memories. Detachment can lead to chaos and deterioration in health.
**H RE-BUILDING**: May begin during the grieving period, but leave major, irreversible decisions until about six months after a profound change in life.
**A Leave the loss behind**: During re-building the loss is fully realized and allowed to remain in the past. Mention of the lost person will little by little bring happy and positive memories to enjoy without the yearning. As a new life-style is built, the natural rhythm of life is regained.
**R2 New life-style**: Generally fully formed two years after the loss. New people do not replace the lost person; they each have their own place in the order of things.
   This grieving cycle applies to all kinds of losses. It may have a double loop for people who are supporting, for example, a spouse, parent or friend who is also going through changes brought about by a terminal illness.

**Pleasure cycles**
This cycle has similar stages and when big changes are taking places. Even two weeks' holiday has all the stages of a pleasure cycle.

**A simple pleasure**
**R1** Walking along the street.
**A** Smell of fresh baked bread.
**B** The smell sets my mouth watering.
**C** Choice between finding baker's shop or depressing interest in the delicious smell.
**D** Find the bakery.
**E** Choice to fully enjoy the experience or divert my interest elsewhere.
**F** I enjoy the smell at the door of bakery.
**G** Choice of making decisions or, for example, arguing myself out of proceeding for one reason or another.
**H** Decide to buy some fresh baked bread to try at home. (All kinds of possibilities, such as buying later, tasting, eating, rejecting flavor, deciding not to buy any of this bread, just enjoying smelling and watching for a while and then going on my way, etc.)
**A** Commit self to new experience.
**R2** Have changed eating habits and enjoy this new bread

# The pleasure principle

During the 19th century there was little that we would call a pleasure for most people. Work was hard, pay was low and conditions in mines and factories were inhuman. Even among the wealthy classes, children were "seen but not heard," men were expected to adhere (at least publicly) to strict codes of behavior and women had to conduct themselves with corsetted decorum. Anyone who laughed, frolicked or danced with sheer joyful abandon was frowned upon. On the whole, pleasure was regarded, along with sex, as quite immoral.

Work, learning and social conduct were very serious activities. Even today, many people fail to understand the great value of pleasure, especially during a serious and important undertaking. Throughout the 20th century there have been several individuals who have recognized that laughter, spontaneity of expression and heartfelt joy are very productive attitudes. One such person was Dr. Georgi Losanov.

## IF MUSIC BE THE FOOD OF LOVE . . .

In 1988 the London Symphony Orchestra (LSO) voted to invite Michael Tilson Thomas to become its principal conductor. Tilson Thomas accepted the post with great pleasure. He sees the orchestra as a versatile, exciting collective talent that constantly astonishes him. But why did this outstanding orchestra of international standing pick Michael Tilson Thomas?

While he has all the tools of technique, Tilson Thomas believes that the main purpose of a performer is to find the part of him or herself that identifies with the work that is being performed. To do this himself, he trusts his basic instincts and responds to the music.

He has said that you must let your heart tell you how it should be played and the rest will fall into place. He believes that a virtuoso orchestra must develop a characteristic sound of its own and that it should be able to make the appropriate sound for each composer and each period of music.

Tilson Thomas seems to inspire the LSO to these remarkable achievements through sheer pleasure. He enjoys hard work, he enjoys the individual members of the orchestra and he enjoys the music. He is no less enthusiastic about his work as artistic adviser to the American New World Symphony, which is a youth orchestra similar to the European Community Youth Orchestra.

How Tilson Thomas manages to integrate technical exactitude with spontaneous, expressive interpretation may seem a mystery. Perhaps his theatrical background, his flair for composition and song-writing and his avid interest in arts, crafts and exotic clothing can account for his amazing vitality.

## THE LOSANOV METHOD OF LEARNING

A Bulgarian physician and psychotherapist, Losanov was interested in making learning easy and effective.

His basic premise was simple: doing something for fun is advantageous because there is nothing to lose; doing something for a purpose has a disadvantage because there is much to lose.

Losanov said that the fear of failure reduces the effectiveness of anything we undertake. So he designed courses in foreign language learning into which he structured FUN.

He called his method Suggestopaedia. The courses were structured on four-hour Suggestopaedic Cycles during which the unconscious and stimulating influence of pleasure decreases fears and anxieties, and facilitates free flowing speech.

### Losanov language learning

This is an outline of methods first developed by Losanov in Bulgaria during the 1950s and 1960s to teach second languages such as English, French, German and Spanish.

The room would be pleasant and cheerful with soft lighting. The floor would have carpet and the seats were comfortable, reclining chairs arranged in an open circle.

The teachers were not only fluent in the language to be taught, they were also trained in psychology and in acting so that they could suggest meaning through gesture and intonation.

The students were taught in classes of six women and six men for four hours per day on six days of the week.

### The four-hour Suggestopaedic Cycle

**1 THE REVIEW** of the previous day's work by the direct method. For example, there would be conversation, sketches, games, etc. Each student would also play a role in the foreign language with a name, address, occupation, family etc.

**2 THE NEW MATERIAL** would be introduced in real life dialogues about situations familiar to the students and with emotionally relevant content, and therefore motivating. A printed manual matched the spoken dialogues.

**3 THE SEANCE** (or session) would provide reinforcement of the learning of the new material at an unconscious level. This session would last one hour.

For this session, the students would relax, probably in a yoga savana posture, on the reclining chairs. The students were taught to breath in a regular pattern during the whole of the session.

The breathing pattern:
    2 seconds inhale
    4 seconds hold breath
    2 seconds exhale

This breathing rhythm would match two other rhythms used during the session:

- the rhythm of the teacher reading during the active and the passive parts of the session,
- the slow moving beat of baroque music in the background.

**The active period of the seance** (20-25 minutes)
The students follow the language program on a page of
the manual while the teacher reads phrase or sentence in
a rhythm of 2:4:2 seconds as follows:

    2: Native translation of the phrase read quickly in a
       low monotone.

    4: Foreign language phrase read aloud. Students
       each repeat it internally.

    2: Pause.

The material is arranged in groups of three, A, B and
C so the rhythm would run as follows:

    A  2:4:2
    B  2:4:2
    C  2:4:2 and so on through the text.

The three phrases or sentences, A, B and C are not
related to each other and at this stage the teacher uses no
emotion, just varies the loudness of voice for each one,
for example, A: whisper, B:normal and C:loud.

**The passive period of the seance** (20-25 minutes)
During this period the attention given to the language is
passive so that interiorization can take place.

- Introduction, 2 minutes. Music is played while all
  listen, for example the saraband from Bach's
  Goldberg variations.
- Internalization, approximately 20 minutes.
  Music in 2/4 or 4/4 time with 60 beats to the
  minute and a sustained melody on the strings is
  played softly, for example, 18th century concerti
  grossi. Work by Handel, Bach, Vivaldi, Corelli or
  Telemann would be appropriate.

During internalization, the teacher acts out the
dialogue of all the new material, using pleasant emotions
and lots of artistic intonation. The students listen with
their eyes closed and are also encouraged to meditate, in
imagination, on the text at the same time.

- Awakening, 2 minutes. An excerpt of cheerful,
  lively music, such as the flute, is played to bring
  the students out of the relaxation.

It is thought that this passive period induces a type of
self-hypnosis; certainly it does increase the alpha-state
on an electroencephalogram of the brain waves, which is
conducive to learning with pleasure.

The Losanov method has been adapted in many
countries and is used effectively for the accelerated
learning of different subjects. The method has been
enjoyed by adults and children, and has been popular
with those who previously had learning difficulties.

The FIRST FLUSH

Mind power can be applied to the learning process by a
variety of methods:
**1** By observing a demonstration (hygienic toilet
disposal)
**2** By acting as a receptacle for knowledge (French
cartoon of pupils absorbing knowledge like medicine)
**3** By personal study and endeavor (19th century
encyclopedia illustration of geometric principles)
**4** By practice (learning to throw a lassoo)

# Brain training

The millions of neurons in your brain can each make up to 10,000 connections in the network of activity called brain power. This includes all the automatic work done to keep your body alive, your intelligence, your memory, your capacity for love and dozens of other activities.

There are many ways to train your brain in learning, remembering, recalling and so on. Most of the popular methods involve thinking and many people have begun to recognize that teaching people how to think is an important part of their education.

Brain training can be done by means other than thinking. The use of sound and music is one approach that has been used since ancient times and is still being developed.

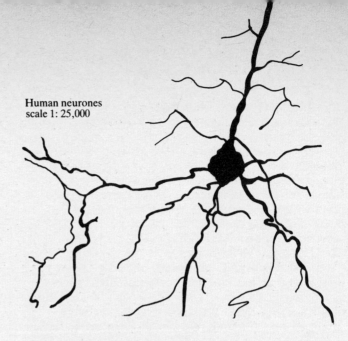

Human neurones
scale 1: 25,000

### Tuning-in
If you can liberate your voice you can liberate yourself. Speech, voice, sound and breathing are intertwined. With sound you can bring a state of clarity to your mind and transform your outlook.

By tuning into appropriate sounds your brain will respond bio-chemically, altering the rhythm of brain waves and clearing away arhythmic patterns which are disturbing. Inappropriate sounds will have the opposite effect.

Rhythmic chanting, rhythmic movements of the body and rhythmic breathing together can lead to a state of mental bliss and remove worries, resentments, passions and things that block your choice of mental viewpoints.

Mantra are sacred sounds preserved in ancient languages. Each mantra has a different purpose; some are for illnesses, some clear the thoughts, others help you to tune into learning or the way others do their thinking.

Mantra are used throughout the world, especially in India and Tibet. The Sufis are the mystics of Islam. They combine breathing, sound and movement. The whirling dervishes pray while rotating on the spot to the sound of the flute, which is very akin to the human voice.

Most liturgies are chanted or sung and in Christian churches psalms and hymns are sung. As we chant, sing, hum or dance together we tune in together. When breathing patterns match these rhythms we can transcend ordinary experiences and partake in what are universally called spiritual experiences.

Harmonic and overtone chanting are approaches she uses to bring out the internal core of the sound that has a magical effect. The use of the tongue and the lungs in unusual ways to achieve this effect, exercises little used neural pathways and stimulates the brain.

To gain some sense of the power of sound, a simple way is to join a choir or any sing-along. From opera to jazz, from hymns to pop, any kind of singing will help to tune you into the world about you. Let your breathing deepen and your body move in the rhythm and your whole life can become a revelation. Music can have a healing and therapeutic effect.

To be healthy is to be sound in mind and body. When we sing together we unite and resound together. Each person has their own sound. It is possible to find this sound by learning deep breathing and making sustained sounds. Listening inwardly to these sounds, it is possible to bring your whole being into resonance when the pitch of your voice will become lower and richer and your whole body vibrates when speaking. This kind of development needs expert guidance to prevent strain.

### Sound ranges
The logarithmic hertz scale (*below*) shows the wide frequency of a man's hearing (white bar) and the still considerable range of voice power (black bar) as compared with a dog's great hearing but very limited vocal range.

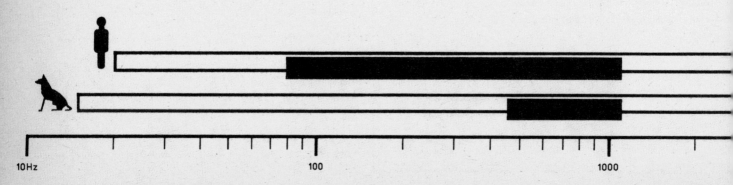

10Hz          100          1000

## CAN SOUND AFFECT MATTER?

Hans Jenny, a Swiss engineer and doctor who was influenced by the work of Rudolph Steiner, made a life-long study of how sound affected matter. He vibrated substances, such as liquids, powders and finely ground metals, with different wavelengths of sound. The sounds caused the substances to make the patterns that occur naturally in nature. When the sound was intensified, so the patterns became clearer. If the substance or the sound was changed, so the pattern would change.

Lawrence Ball, an English musician and mathematician, has experimented with high frequency sounds fed into computers to make acoustic images. He and Isobel McGilvray, an experienced healer, have produced a set of sounds recorded on tapes that induce different shapes. These tones are claimed gently to restore a person's internal resonances, creating a powerful sense of well-being. It is said that their harmonies are not only musical but also psychological.

There are seven of these Shapetapes which Ball and McGilvray link with the seven chakras of the body. Chakras are the ancient name given to positions on the subtle or auric body through which the vital life force, or kundalini energy, flows.

### The mystic spiral (*below*)

It is interesting to note that the logarithmic spiral does not (yet) appear in this work as one of the sound-shapes, yet this shape is found in the natural world over and over again, as Jill Purce has shown in her book.

### The chakras and the sound-shapes

Correspondences according to the work of Lawrence Ball and Isobel McGilvray in London.

| Chakra | Purpose | Sound-shape | Effect of sound-shape | Computer shape |
|---|---|---|---|---|
| Crown | Enlightenment | Lines | Clears and focuses the mind |  |
| Third eye | Powers of mind | Helix | Stimulates arousal and excitement |  |
| Throat | Communication | Rose | Soothing and sensitizing |  |
| Heart | Love and affection | Four-leafed clover | Expanding and centering |  |
| Navel/solar plexus | Raw emotion | Triangles | Stimulates creativity |  |
| Splenic/sacral | Sexual drives | Circles | Relaxing and nourishing |  |
| Root | Primitive survival | Squares | Reassuring and grounding | 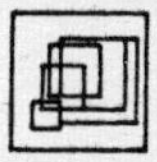 |

©DIAGRAM

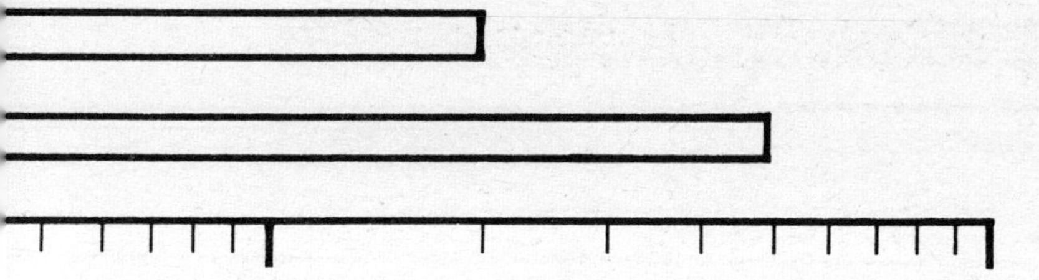

10.000          100.000 Hz

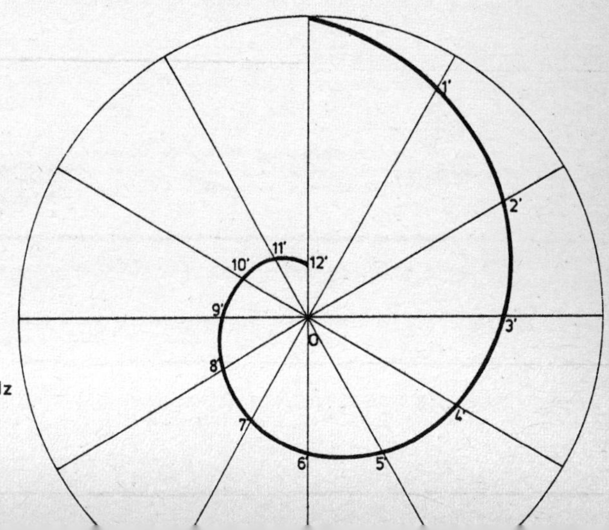

# Powerful beliefs

Belief is a most powerful driving force. People have died for their beliefs. Some have given up everything while others have grabbed everything, all because of a belief. Behind all kinds of behaviour there are all kinds of beliefs.

What do you believe in? Where do you place your faith, trust and confidence? In which direction are you driven by your beliefs?

Are you sure which beliefs are determining your behavior? On the righthand page is a selection of beliefs. You may find it interesting to check yours and add more personal details. Then you may like to consider your behavior and discover if you have omitted any beliefs or mistakenly checked any.

## Personal beliefs

Some of the people we see on television or read about in history or meet on the street express strong personal beliefs:

- Victor Kiam chose to believe he could make his newly purchased Remington company into a winner so he appeared in the adverts himself.
- The Duke of Windsor believed in love and gave up the British throne to marry Mrs. Simpson.
- Bob Geldof believed in compassion and used his resources to bring help to Ethiopians.
- Margaret Thatcher believed in her policies and won a third term as Prime Minister of Britain.
- The actress, Cher, believes in self-glorification and uses her glamor to advantage.
- The driver of an American customized truck quite obviously believes in himself.

Holding a personal deep belief in your own ideas either taken from others or created yourself can take many forms:
1 Religion
2 Commercial
3 Love
4 Compassion
5 Political
6 Artistic
7 Personal

---

## CHARIOTS OF FIRE

This 1981 British movie has been an outstanding success. Set in the 1920s it is the true story of two winners whose beliefs in their countries, in their religions and in themselves are put to the test at the 1924 Paris Olympic Games.

Harold Abrahams was a Lithuanian Jew and the star runner at Cambridge University. Eric Liddell was a Christian Scotsman who was studying to become a missionary in China like his father. He was the star performer at Highland Games events.

Both men train hard for the 100 yds 1924 Olympic Games. When Liddell hears the heat is to be on a Sunday he withdraws on religious grounds. Lord Lindsey offers him his place in the 400 yds event.

Abrahams wins the 100 yd gold medal, believing himself to be a winner against the prejudice he has experienced for being a Jew and for having an unorthodox coach, Sam Mussabini.

Liddell wins the 400 yd gold medal because, inspired by his religion, he believes he is running for God.

The ethos of the 1920s is captured in the movie. National pride and standards of fairplay reign supreme; in particular the traditional British spirit.

Liddell died in 1945 in a Japanese internment camp and Abrahams in 1978.

## WHAT I BELIEVE IN

| Some beliefs | My belief | Consequence of belief |
|---|---|---|
| Belief | | |
| My country | | |
| My religion | | |
| My community | | |
| My family | | |
| My occupation | | |
| My political outlook | | |
| Equality of opportunity | | |
| Striving for personal gain | | |
| Charitable contributions | | |
| Being paid for work I do | | |
| Free speech | | |
| Human rights | | |
| Making money | | |
| Survival of the fittest | | |
| My freedom of choice | | |
| Other's freedom of choice | | |
| Honesty | | |
| Monogamy | | |
| Polygamy | | |
| Life | | |
| Sexual faithfulness | | |
| Several sexual partners | | |
| Homosexuality | | |
| Woman as the prime parent | | |
| Man as the prime breadwinner | | |
| Abortion by choice | | |
| Euthanasia by choice | | |
| Ecological responsibility | | |
| Responsibility as a citizen | | |
| Me as a winner | | |
| Me as a failure | | |
| Me as an achiever | | |
| Me as a lover | | |
| Me as a worker | | |
| Me as a partner/spouse | | |
| Me as a parent | | |
| Me as a friend | | |
| My personal attractiveness | | |
| My talents | | |
| My personality | | |
| My determination | | |
| My self-confidence | | |
| Ability to survive | | |

# Mystical places

The power of mind over matter is the capacity of the brain to organize, order and monitor the attitudes and behaviors of the person who is the brain.

There is no doubt that a person can use his/her mind to influence another living person, animal or plant. Can mind-power also be used to influence objects, time and the elements or leave its mark in certain locations? Furthermore, can mind leave the matter of the body and move independently about in the world, carrying messages or visiting old haunts?

These questions have been explored throughout this book, yet there are no exact and clear answers. As evidence mounts, suggesting that there is more mystery in this life than we ever dreamt possible, these old mysteries continue to capture our imagination.

## Mind over place?

There are many mystical places on this earth that inspire the spirit and can bring to us an indefinable sense of peace, contentment and security. Such places have been used and visited by thousands of people since time began.

Do these places retain something of each person who goes there? Are these mystical places, which people revere, a sanctuary for the collective mind of humanity?

Mystical places seem to have a power of their own, a power that can affect those who visit; even those who don't know it is mystical ground upon which they stand, are affected by it. Are we, and our ancestors, responsible for the mystery, or is there "something else"? You must make up your own mind. Here are some places that many people regard as mystical.

- The grotto at Lourdes, France
- Stonehenge, England
- An ancient Greek theater
- The Wailing Wall in Jerusalem
- The Ziggurat at Ur

You will know of other places both public and private, some of them might be ordinary places that excite or relax you for no apparent reason. Here are a few of them suggested by different individuals.

- A corner of a city park
- In a theater
- In a church
- Among mountains

## By the sea-shore

Do you have a mystical place of your own? They may be mystical only to you because of personal associations.

## The features of mystical places?

Similarities between mystical places have been investigated and three sets of conditions seem to be common. Could these conditions be the reason why such places feel mystical?

**1** Association with religious beliefs, such as the grotto at Lourdes.

**2** A place where the proportion of negatively charged ions in the atmosphere shows a regular increase above the normal, such as at Tiburon, where the Pacific Ocean currents first sweep ashore under the Golden Gate Bridge into the bay of San Francisco. Tiburon is an old Indian name meaning shark, because sharks were washed onto its shore after storms. Tiburon is the site of a spiritual community who claim that being there calms all fears.

**3** When the shape of a place converges to a central point, as with a cathedral, parts of mountains and the pyramids.

The church on the tiny island of Iona, off the west coast of Scotand has all three characteristics: religious association, a converging shape and high negative ionization due to the proximity of the sea. A thriving Christian community exists on the island which attracts young people from all over the world.

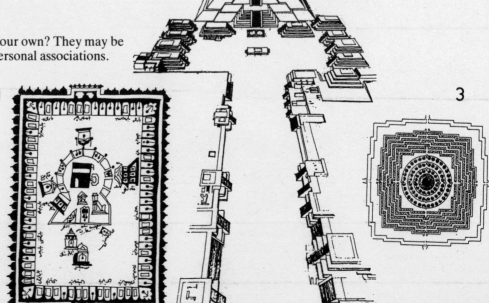

**Mystical places**
1 Mecca, Arabia
2 Teotihuacan, Mexico
3 Barabadur, Java
4 Ziggurat at Tchoga Zanbil, Elam (Iran)
5 St Peter's Square, Rome
6 Stonehenge, England

## The effect of changes in atmospheric ionization

In normal clean air over land there are from 1500 to 4000 ions per cubic centimetre. The ratio of positive to negative charges is 1.2 to 1. Many modern conditions alter the concentration of ions and changes the proportion of positive to negative, causing negative ion depletion.

Research has shown that offices, shops, streets and houses with air conditioning and central heating become ion-depleted and the result is tiredness, loss of mental and physical efficiency. There is much evidence to show that an increase in ions can have beneficial effects.

Ion-depletion also takes place in thundery weather and when warm winds are blowing such as the Bavarian Föhn, Alpine south wind and the Sharav in Israel. The effect of drowsiness, fatigue, irritation, nausea and proneness to accidents is similar to the effects that can be felt if you spend any length of time in a crowded, airless room. Pollutants also deplete the ions.

Some areas, such as in moutains, near waterfalls and some coastal areas have a natural abundance of ions. When ion therapy is used for medical purposes, the effect is calming, pain is reduced, burns heal quickly and resistance to infection is increased.

It may be that mystical places have a high ion count.

## The Egyptian pyramids

Pyramids built in Egypt were tombs for Kings of the Old and Middle Kingdoms, 2700 to 1786 BC. They formed part of a larger complex which included embalming areas, corridors and cult temples. They were expensive economicallly and thousands died during their construction, but they promoted political and religious unity.

The largest pyramid contains about 2,300,000 blocks of stone and measures 755ft on each side and rises to a height of 481ft. The sides are perfectly orientated to the four main points of the compass, the entrance to the pyramid's complex of tunnels and rooms was usually on the north side.

The oldest is the Step Pyramid at Saqqara designed by Imhotep, just to the south of modern Cairo and consists of six tombs on top of each other, forming a stairway.

The design of pyramids became more refined later and the two very large pyramids at Dahshur are quite outstanding. Both were built by Sneferu. The Great Pyramid at Giza by his son, Cheops, was finished in about 2600 BC.

The Pyramid Texts, painted and carved on the walls make it clear that Egyptian Kings were regarded as gods who ascended to heaven either by a staircase or by the sun's rays.

Pyramidology is the study of the proportions of the Great Pyramid; it is believed by some people that from the study of this pyramid will emerge a new world order. Small pyramids are often seen on sale for cleaning silver coins and some people have erected their own pyramid shape in their homes because it is said that at the center of a pyramid there is good, strong healing energy. These ideas have emerged since the embalmed bodies of ancient kings were discovered so well preserved.

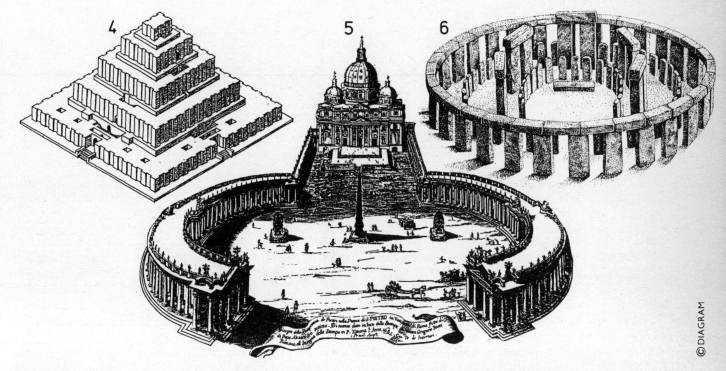

# New minds for old?

There are two areas of medical research which are already challenging our concepts of individuality and normality. One is genetic engineering, the other is brain transplantation. Both areas of investigation open up the possibility of being able to bring about a radical change in the very being of a person.

Can the mind of mankind control and change the very matter of which we are composed? To begin to answer this question, we must first understand the nature of what we call our individuality and how the the two areas of research might change it.

### What is individuality?

A human karyotype, found in every cell of the body, consists of 23 pairs of chromosomes, one of each pair is inherited from each parent. This karyotype is of a male because the 23rd pair is Xy. All females have XX in this position.

Each chromosome is a double helix chain of DNA molecules. The two parts of the chain are held together by four base substances, known as ATGC, which always appear in the same pairs, AT (Adenine/Thymine) and GC (Guanine/cytosine).

The sequence in which these letters (substances) are arranged is called the human genome. There are some 3 billion letters in a human genome and it has been said by many researchers that the major job of biology in the 21st century will be to discover the genetic sequence of every chromosome.

The DNA profile of every person is different and it is possible to extract small quantities from blood or tissue samples to examine the genetic fingerprint. From these paternity can be established.

### Genetic engineering

Diseases and disabilities are due to "spelling mistakes" in the chains of molecules. For example, a spelling mistake can be seen in the three letters at the end of the sequence.

G A T A G C T T A T C G A   correct sequence
G A T A G C T T A T G C T   incorrect sequence

The genome is the recipe for life. Once the sequences or spelling has been found and recorded, then changes could be made by replacing faulty parts of chromosomes. The difficulty lies in being able to read the genetic sequence.

Already it is known that spelling mistakes in the tip of chromosome 4 causes Huntingdon's disease and cystic fibrosis occurs when there are spelling mistakes on chromosome 7.

Genetic engineering consists of correcting the spelling mistakes to prevent diseases in the developing fetus. It would be wonderful if all these crippling diseases could be prevented.

Once it becomes possible to use genetic engineering to correct the spelling mistakes, it would be an easy step towards altering the spelling to encourage talents or to ensure perfect mating. Further, it is possible to replicate gene sequences and this process is called cloning. The ultimate implication would be to make a perfect repeat. How would you feel at the propect of meeting two, three or more of you, i.e. your clones?

The whole question of eugenics would then be raised yet again. Eugenics is the science of improving the race. Genetic engineering could become a prime example of "mind over matter" in the next 20 years.

A human karyotype has 23 pairs of chromosomes. The final, 23rd pair determine the sex of the person, in this case male.

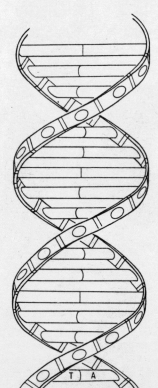

The chromosomes consist of long layers of complex chains of DNA (Deoxyribonucleic acids).

## Brain transplants

Heart, lung and kidney transplants are now fairly commonplace, though there is still a long way to go to make the operation a 100% success in all cases. Skilled work is also done frequently to re-connect limbs that have been torn from the body.

The transplantation of brain tissue is already being tried. Surgeons in Mexico have been working toward the transplanting of adrenal tissue since 1986 and in Sweden work is progressing to use aborted fetal tissue to replace degenerated brain tissue. In particular, it is the cordate nucleus in the center of the brain that may prove to be the most useful.

It is the degeneration of fibers in the brain that is the result of many diseases. People suffering from Parkinson's disease have to will the brain to work. The boxing champion Muhammad Ali suffered from this disease.

Another degenerative condition, called Alzheimer's disease, caused the death of movie star Rita Hayworth in 1987. Other diseases that could be helped by new brain tissue are muscular dystrophy and multiple sclerosis, which brought the career of cellest Jacqueline du Pré to an early end.

## Would the next step be a head transplant?

The idea of a whole head transplant is very new. An American Dr Robert Smith has already attempted to transfer the head of one monkey onto the body of another. The transplant was not successful.

If a whole head could be transplanted, which would you opt for if any, a new head or a new body? For a brain and mind to adapt to a new body would be a massive job. Can you imagine having to teach your new body to do things the way your brain has become accustomed.

The immense problems facing the head/body transplant surgeons are not only technical. There are religious, moral and humanistic issues to be considered long before we attempt to put mind over matter in this way.

## Find yourself and be yourself

Perhaps it is a good idea, after all this startling speculation, to bring ourselves back to one of the most fundamental questions that has been asked throughout history: WHO ARE YOU? Did you know that you are a one in 300,000 billion chance creation. You are unique. There is no one just like you. Also, yours is a unique mind. Learning to find yourself and be yourself is perhaps the hardest of life's challenges, but it is also the most exciting. There is no greater misery than trying to be someone you aren't. You have a body and a mind of your own . . . enjoy it.

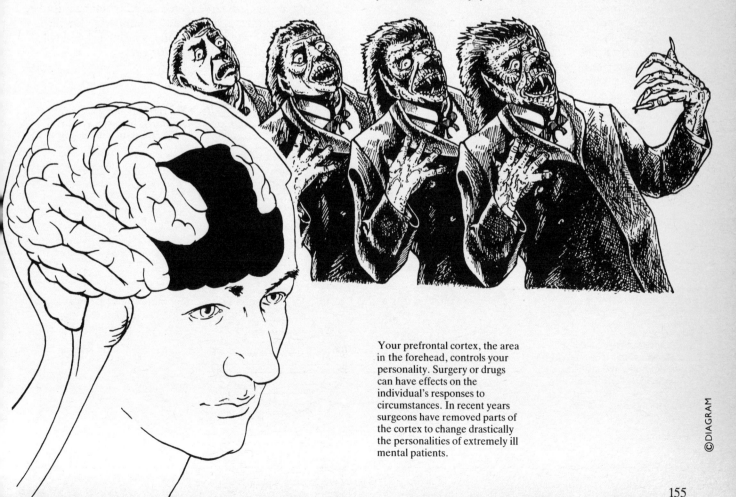

Your prefrontal cortex, the area in the forehead, controls your personality. Surgery or drugs can have effects on the individual's responses to circumstances. In recent years surgeons have removed parts of the cortex to change drastically the personalities of extremely ill mental patients.

©DIAGRAM

# Astrological tables

These tables are for use with the instructions in the text in parts of **Chapter Four.**

## TABLES OF THE HEAVY PLANETS
The heavy planets moved into the zodiac signs on the dates given and stayed in that·sign until the next date and sign shown.

### Table for Jupiter

| 1989 | | *Cancer* | 1997 | 21 Jan | *Aquarius* |
|------|--------|-------------|------|--------|-------------|
| 1990 | 18 Aug | *Leo* | 1998 | 4 Feb | *Pisces* |
| 1991 | 12 Sept | *Virgo* | 1999 | 13 Feb | *Aries* |
| 1992 | 10 Oct | *Libra* | | 28 Jun | *Taurus* |
| 1993 | 10 Nov | *Scorpio* | | 23 Oct | *Aries* |
| 1994 | 9 Dec | *Sagittarius* | 2000 | 14 Feb | *Taurus* |
| 1996 | 3 Jan | *Capricorn* | | 30 Jun | *Gemini* |

### Table for Saturn

| 1989 | | *Capricorn* |
|------|--------|-------------|
| 1991 | 6 Feb | *Aquarius* |
| 1993 | 21 May | *Pisces* |
| | 30 Jun | *Aquarius* |
| 1994 | 29 Jan | *Pisces* |
| 1996 | 7 Apr | *Aries* |
| 1998 | 9 Jun | *Taurus* |
| | 25 Oct | *Aries* |
| 1999 | 1 Mar | *Taurus* |
| 2000 | 10 Aug | *Gemini* |
| | 16 Oct | *Taurus* |

## SUN-SIGN TABLES
**1** Find the year of your birth.
**2** Look along the line until you come to the column headed by the correct month.
**3** Note the number where the line and the column meet.
**4** If your birthdate was earlier than the number, your sun-sign is at the top of the previous column.

**5** If your birthdate was the same as or later than the number, then your sun-sign is at the head of that column.
**Examples**
1931, 19 May: sun-sign Taurus.
1931, 29 May: sun-sign Gemini.

### Sun-Sign Table for 1916 to 1935

| | JA | FE | MR | AP | MY | JN | JL | AU | SE | OC | NO | DE |
|------|----|----|----|----|----|----|----|----|----|----|----|----|
| | *Aq* | *Pi* | *Ar* | *Ta* | *Ge* | *Cn* | *Le* | *Vi* | *Li* | *Sc* | *Sg* | *Cp* |
| **1916** | 21 | 19 | 20 | 20 | 21 | 21 | 23 | 23 | 23 | 23 | 21 | 22 |
| **1917** | 20 | 19 | 21 | 20 | 21 | 22 | 23 | 23 | 23 | 23 | 22 | 21 |
| **1918** | 20 | 19 | 21 | 20 | 21 | 22 | 23 | 23 | 23 | 24 | 23 | 22 |
| **1919** | 21 | 19 | 21 | 21 | 22 | 22 | 23 | 24 | 24 | 24 | 23 | 22 |
| **1920** | 21 | 19 | 20 | 20 | 21 | 23 | 23 | 23 | 23 | 23 | 22 | 22 |
| **1921** | 20 | 19 | 21 | 20 | 21 | 22 | 23 | 23 | 23 | 23 | 22 | 22 |
| **1922** | 20 | 19 | 21 | 20 | 21 | 22 | 23 | 23 | 23 | 24 | 22 | 22 |
| **1923** | 21 | 19 | 21 | 21 | 22 | 22 | 23 | 24 | 24 | 24 | 23 | 22 |
| **1924** | 21 | 19 | 20 | 20 | 21 | 21 | 23 | 23 | 23 | 23 | 22 | 22 |
| **1925** | 20 | 19 | 21 | 20 | 21 | 21 | 23 | 23 | 23 | 23 | 22 | 22 |
| **1926** | 20 | 19 | 21 | 20 | 21 | 22 | 23 | 23 | 23 | 24 | 22 | 22 |
| **1927** | 21 | 19 | 21 | 21 | 22 | 22 | 23 | 24 | 24 | 24 | 23 | 22 |
| **1928** | 21 | 19 | 20 | 20 | 21 | 21 | 23 | 23 | 23 | 23 | 22 | 22 |
| **1929** | 20 | 19 | 21 | 20 | 21 | 21 | 23 | 23 | 23 | 23 | 22 | 22 |
| **1930** | 20 | 19 | 21 | 20 | 21 | 22 | 23 | 23 | 23 | 24 | 22 | 22 |
| **1931** | 21 | 19 | 21 | 21 | 22 | 22 | 23 | 24 | 24 | 24 | 23 | 22 |
| **1932** | 21 | 19 | 20 | 20 | 21 | 21 | 23 | 23 | 23 | 23 | 22 | 22 |
| **1933** | 20 | 19 | 21 | 20 | 21 | 21 | 23 | 23 | 23 | 23 | 22 | 22 |
| **1934** | 20 | 19 | 21 | 20 | 21 | 22 | 23 | 23 | 23 | 24 | 22 | 22 |
| **1935** | 20 | 19 | 21 | 21 | 22 | 22 | 23 | 24 | 23 | 24 | 23 | 22 |

### Sun-Sign Table for 1936 to 1955

| | JA | FE | MR | AP | MY | JN | JL | AU | SE | OC | NO | DE |
|------|----|----|----|----|----|----|----|----|----|----|----|----|
| | *Aq* | *Pi* | *Ar* | *Ta* | *Ge* | *Cn* | *Le* | *Vi* | *Li* | *Sc* | *Sg* | *Cp* |
| **1936** | 21 | 19 | 20 | 20 | 21 | 21 | 23 | 23 | 23 | 23 | 22 | 22 |
| **1937** | 20 | 19 | 21 | 20 | 21 | 21 | 23 | 23 | 23 | 23 | 22 | 22 |
| **1938** | 20 | 19 | 21 | 20 | 21 | 22 | 23 | 23 | 23 | 24 | 22 | 22 |
| **1939** | 20 | 19 | 21 | 20 | 21 | 22 | 23 | 24 | 23 | 24 | 23 | 22 |
| **1940** | 21 | 19 | 20 | 20 | 21 | 21 | 23 | 23 | 23 | 23 | 22 | 21 |
| **1941** | 20 | 19 | 21 | 20 | 21 | 21 | 23 | 23 | 23 | 23 | 22 | 22 |
| **1942** | 20 | 19 | 21 | 20 | 21 | 22 | 23 | 23 | 23 | 23 | 22 | 22 |
| **1943** | 20 | 19 | 21 | 20 | 21 | 22 | 23 | 23 | 23 | 24 | 22 | 22 |
| **1944** | 21 | 19 | 21 | 20 | 21 | 22 | 23 | 23 | 23 | 23 | 22 | 21 |
| **1945** | 20 | 19 | 20 | 20 | 22 | 21 | 23 | 23 | 23 | 23 | 22 | 22 |
| **1946** | 20 | 19 | 21 | 20 | 21 | 22 | 23 | 23 | 23 | 24 | 22 | 22 |
| **1947** | 20 | 19 | 21 | 20 | 21 | 22 | 23 | 24 | 23 | 24 | 23 | 22 |
| **1948** | 21 | 19 | 20 | 20 | 21 | 21 | 23 | 23 | 23 | 23 | 22 | 21 |
| **1949** | 20 | 18 | 20 | 20 | 21 | 21 | 23 | 23 | 23 | 23 | 22 | 22 |
| **1950** | 20 | 19 | 21 | 20 | 21 | 21 | 23 | 23 | 23 | 23 | 22 | 22 |
| **1951** | 20 | 19 | 21 | 20 | 21 | 22 | 23 | 23 | 23 | 23 | 23 | 22 |
| **1952** | 21 | 19 | 20 | 20 | 21 | 21 | 22 | 23 | 23 | 23 | 22 | 21 |
| **1953** | 20 | 18 | 20 | 20 | 21 | 21 | 23 | 23 | 23 | 23 | 22 | 22 |
| **1954** | 20 | 19 | 21 | 20 | 21 | 21 | 23 | 23 | 23 | 23 | 22 | 22 |
| **1955** | 20 | 19 | 21 | 20 | 21 | 22 | 23 | 23 | 23 | 23 | 23 | 22 |

| Table for Uranus | | | Table for Neptune | | | Table for Pluto | | |
|---|---|---|---|---|---|---|---|---|
| 1989 | | *Capricorn* | 1989 | | *Capricorn* | 1989 | | *Scorpio* |
| 1995 | 1 Apr | *Aquarius* | 1998 | 29 Jan | *Aquarius* | 1995 | 21 Apr | *Sagittarius* |
| | 9 Jun | *Capricorn* | | 23 Aug | *Capricorn* | | 21 Apr | *Scorpio* |
| 1996 | 12 Jan | *Aquarius* | | 27 Nov | *Aquarius* | | 10 Nov | *Sagittarius* |
| up to year 2000 | | | | | | up to year 2000 | | |

## Key to abbreviations for months

| JA | January | MY | May | SE | September |
|---|---|---|---|---|---|
| FE | February | JN | June | OC | October |
| MR | March | JL | July | NO | November |
| AP | April | AU | August | DE | December |

## Key to abbreviations for signs

| Aq | Aquarius | Ge | Gemini | Li | Libra |
|---|---|---|---|---|---|
| Pi | Pisces | Cn | Cancer | Sc | Scorpio |
| Ar | Aries | Le | Leo | Sg | Sagittarius |
| Ta | Taurus | Vi | Virgo | Cp | Capricorn |

**Sun-Sign Table for 1956 to 1975**

JA FE MR AP MY JN JL AU SE OC NO DE

| | Aq | Pi | Ar | Ta | Ge | Cn | Le | Vi | Li | Sc | Sg | Cp |
|---|---|---|---|---|---|---|---|---|---|---|---|---|
| **1956** | 21 | 19 | 20 | 20 | 21 | 21 | 22 | 23 | 23 | 23 | 22 | 21 |
| **1957** | 20 | 18 | 20 | 20 | 21 | 21 | 23 | 23 | 23 | 23 | 22 | 22 |
| **1958** | 20 | 19 | 21 | 20 | 21 | 21 | 23 | 23 | 23 | 23 | 22 | 22 |
| **1959** | 20 | 19 | 21 | 20 | 21 | 22 | 23 | 23 | 23 | 24 | 23 | 22 |
| **1960** | 21 | 19 | 20 | 20 | 21 | 21 | 22 | 23 | 23 | 23 | 22 | 21 |
| **1961** | 20 | 18 | 20 | 20 | 21 | 21 | 23 | 23 | 23 | 23 | 22 | 22 |
| **1962** | 20 | 19 | 21 | 20 | 21 | 21 | 23 | 23 | 23 | 23 | 22 | 22 |
| **1963** | 20 | 19 | 21 | 20 | 21 | 22 | 23 | 23 | 23 | 24 | 23 | 22 |
| **1964** | 20 | 19 | 20 | 20 | 21 | 21 | 22 | 23 | 23 | 23 | 22 | 21 |
| **1965** | 20 | 18 | 20 | 20 | 21 | 21 | 23 | 23 | 23 | 23 | 22 | 22 |
| **1966** | 20 | 19 | 21 | 20 | 21 | 21 | 23 | 23 | 23 | 23 | 22 | 22 |
| **1967** | 20 | 19 | 21 | 20 | 21 | 22 | 23 | 23 | 23 | 24 | 23 | 22 |
| **1968** | 20 | 19 | 20 | 20 | 21 | 21 | 22 | 23 | 22 | 23 | 22 | 21 |
| **1969** | 20 | 18 | 20 | 20 | 21 | 21 | 23 | 23 | 23 | 23 | 22 | 22 |
| **1970** | 20 | 19 | 21 | 20 | 21 | 21 | 23 | 23 | 23 | 23 | 22 | 22 |
| **1971** | 20 | 19 | 21 | 20 | 21 | 22 | 23 | 23 | 23 | 23 | 22 | 22 |
| **1972** | 20 | 19 | 20 | 19 | 20 | 21 | 22 | 23 | 22 | 23 | 22 | 21 |
| **1973** | 20 | 18 | 20 | 20 | 21 | 21 | 22 | 23 | 23 | 23 | 22 | 22 |
| **1974** | 20 | 19 | 21 | 20 | 21 | 21 | 23 | 23 | 23 | 23 | 22 | 22 |
| **1975** | 20 | 19 | 21 | 20 | 21 | 22 | 23 | 23 | 23 | 24 | 22 | 22 |

**Sun-Sign Table for 1976 to 1995**

JA FE MR AP MY JN JL AU SE OC NO DE

| | Aq | Pi | Ar | Ta | Ge | Cn | Le | Vi | Li | Sc | Sg | Cp |
|---|---|---|---|---|---|---|---|---|---|---|---|---|
| **1976** | 20 | 19 | 20 | 19 | 20 | 21 | 22 | 23 | 22 | 23 | 22 | 21 |
| **1977** | 20 | 18 | 20 | 20 | 21 | 21 | 22 | 23 | 23 | 23 | 22 | 21 |
| **1978** | 20 | 19 | 20 | 20 | 21 | 21 | 23 | 23 | 23 | 23 | 22 | 22 |
| **1979** | 20 | 19 | 21 | 20 | 21 | 21 | 23 | 23 | 23 | 24 | 22 | 22 |
| **1980** | 20 | 19 | 20 | 19 | 20 | 21 | 22 | 22 | 22 | 23 | 22 | 21 |
| **1981** | 20 | 18 | 20 | 20 | 21 | 21 | 22 | 23 | 23 | 23 | 22 | 21 |
| **1982** | 20 | 18 | 20 | 20 | 21 | 21 | 23 | 23 | 23 | 23 | 22 | 22 |
| **1983** | 20 | 19 | 21 | 20 | 21 | 21 | 23 | 23 | 23 | 23 | 22 | 22 |
| **1984** | 20 | 19 | 20 | 19 | 20 | 21 | 22 | 22 | 22 | 23 | 22 | 21 |
| **1985** | 20 | 18 | 20 | 20 | 21 | 21 | 22 | 23 | 23 | 23 | 22 | 21 |
| **1986** | 20 | 18 | 20 | 20 | 21 | 21 | 23 | 23 | 23 | 23 | 22 | 22 |
| **1987** | 20 | 19 | 21 | 20 | 21 | 21 | 23 | 23 | 23 | 23 | 22 | 22 |
| **1988** | 20 | 19 | 20 | 19 | 20 | 21 | 22 | 22 | 22 | 23 | 22 | 21 |
| **1989** | 20 | 18 | 20 | 20 | 21 | 21 | 22 | 23 | 23 | 23 | 22 | 21 |
| **1990** | 20 | 18 | 20 | 20 | 21 | 21 | 23 | 23 | 23 | 23 | 22 | 22 |
| **1991** | 20 | 19 | 21 | 20 | 21 | 21 | 23 | 23 | 23 | 23 | 22 | 22 |
| **1992** | 20 | 19 | 20 | 19 | 20 | 21 | 22 | 22 | 22 | 23 | 22 | 21 |
| **1993** | 20 | 18 | 20 | 20 | 21 | 21 | 22 | 23 | 23 | 23 | 22 | 21 |
| **1994** | 20 | 18 | 20 | 20 | 21 | 21 | 23 | 23 | 23 | 23 | 22 | 22 |
| **1995** | 20 | 19 | 21 | 20 | 21 | 21 | 23 | 23 | 23 | 23 | 22 | 22 |

©DIAGRAM

# Index